Georgia Capitol Building

TREASURES OF
Georgia

by Damon Neal

a part of the Morgan & Chase Treasure Series
www.treasuresof.com

THE
TREASURE
SERIES

Morgan & Chase Publishing, Inc.
531 Parsons Drive, Medford, Oregon 97501
(888) 557-9328
www.treasuresof.com

Printed and bound by Taylor Specialty Books—Dallas TX
First edition 2007
ISBN: 978-1-933989-14-3

I gratefully acknowledge the contributions
of the many people involved in the writing and production of this book.
Their tireless dedication to this endeavour has been inspirational.
—William Faubion, *Publisher*

The Morgan & Chase Publishing Home Team

Operations Department:
 V.P. of Operations—Cindy Tilley Faubion
 Travel Writer Liaison—Anne Boydston
 Shipping & Receiving—Virginia Arias
 Human Resources Coordinator—Heather Allen
 Customer Service Relations— Sue Buda, Marie Manson, Eric Molinsky
 IT Engineer—Ray Ackerman
 Receptionist—Samara Sharp

Production Department:
 Proof Editor—Clarice Rodriguez
 Editor/Writers—Gregory Scott, Robyn Sutherland
 House Writers—Megan Glomb, Prairie Smallwood
 Photo Coordinator—Wendy L. Gay
 Photo Editor—Mary Murdock
 Graphic Design Team—C.S. Rowan, Jesse Gifford, Tamara Cornett, Jacob Kristof

Administrative Department:
 CFO—Emily Wilke
 Accounting Assistants—David Grundvig, Tiffany Myers
 Website Designer—Molly Bermea
 Website Software Developer—Ben Ford

Contributing Writers:
 Mary Beth Lee, Lynda Kusick, Mark Allen Deruiter, Katheryne Kyle Wilcox,
 Denise Deneweth, Dave Fox, Earl Osborne, Sharon Spencer, Andrea Washington,
 Freida St. Germain, Margie Rhodes, Paul Hadella, Mary Knepp, Chris McCrellis-Mitchell,
 Laura Young, Todd Wels, Karuna Glomb, Kevin Monk, Marek Alday

Special Recognition to:
 Casey Faubion, Terrie West, Danielle Barkley, Pam Hamilton, Gene Mitts

We dedicate this book to the most influential humanitarian of our time. Former president Jimmy Carter has lived his life as an honest, hardworking role model for peace and understanding. He is surely an inspiration to those who have met him, and many more who will never have the privilege of thanking him in person.

Blue Hole Falls, Chattahoochee National Forest

GEORGIA FACTS:

Admitted to the Union: 1788, the 4th state

Population (2006): 9,363,941

Largest City: Atlanta, 483,108

Largest Metro Area: Atlanta, 5,138,223

Highest Elevation: Brasstown Bald, 4,784 feet

Bird: Brown Thrasher (*Toxostoma rufum*)

Fish: Largemouth Bass (*Micropterus salmoides*)

Flower: Cherokee Rose (*Rosa laevigata*)

Insect: Honey Bee (*Apis mellifera*)

Motto: Wisdom, Justice and Moderation

Nicknames: Empire State of the South, Peach State

Song: Georgia on My Mind

Tree: Southern Live Oak (*Quercus virginiana*)

Foreword

Welcome to *Treasures of Georgia*. This book is a resource that can guide
you to some of the best places in Georgia, one of the most vibrant and
exciting parts of America. From the bustle of downtown Atlanta, to
the quiet beauty of the Blue Ridge Mountains, to the rich estuaries
of the Atlantic shore, Georgia is a state of great contrasts.

In many ways, Georgia's history is the history of America. The last of the
13 original colonies to be founded, Georgia was the fourth state to ratify the
Constitution. By the 19th century, plantations dominated the economy and
cotton was king. Large numbers of Georgians fought for the Confederacy under
Robert E. Lee, but the state itself became a battlefield only at the very end, when
William Tecumseh Sherman burned Atlanta and marched to the sea. The march is
perhaps the most retold event in Georgia history. After the war, Georgia became
a key center of the industrial New South, and later of the Civil Rights movement.
Today, Georgia is one of the fastest-growing of the United States, and metro
Atlanta has become one of the most important urban centers on the entire planet.

Countless attractions await visitors to Georgia. You can visit the birthplace
of Rev. Dr. Martin Luther King, Jr. or shop in Underground Atlanta.
You can ride horseback in the North Georgia Mountains or take tea in
Alphretta. See Atlanta from a helicopter or while riding a Segway. View
ancient Indian mounds at Cartersville. See the headquarters of Coca-Cola
and CNN. You can take in the Atlanta Ballet—or root for the Braves.

As everyone knows, Georgia is home to the nicest people you'll ever meet. In
preparing this book, we talked to literally thousands of business people about their
products, their services and their vision. We visited boutiques in Newnan and
a cigar shop in Savannah. We looked at antiques in Chamblee and art galleries
in Norcross. We stayed in a bed-and-breakfast on the Chattahoochee River
and visited a dairy farm near Canton. We dined on ribs in Marietta and sushi
in Athens. We munched on pecans in College Park and fried green tomatoes
in Juliette. You are holding the result of our efforts in your hands. *Treasures of
Georgia* is a 361-page compilation of the best places in Georgia to eat, shop, play,
explore, learn and relax. We did the legwork. All you have to do now is enjoy.

—Cindy Tilley Faubion

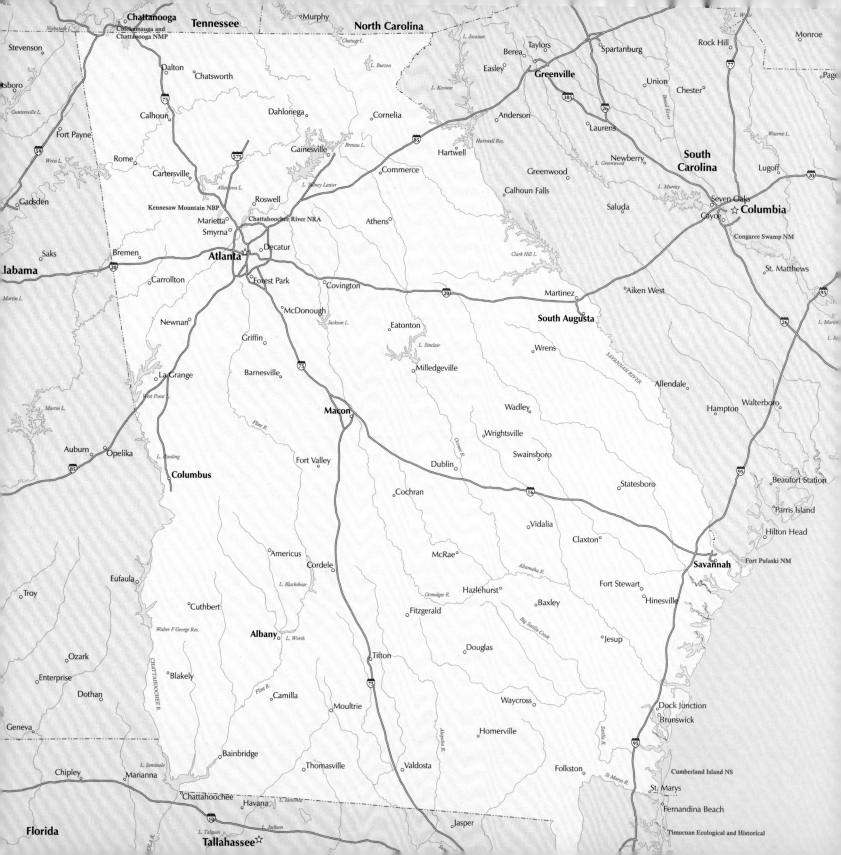

Accommodations & Resorts.................. 2

Attractions & Culture........................ 42

Bakeries, Treats, Coffee & Tea 94

Fashion & Accessories 110

Galleries & Fine Art......................... 122

Health & Beauty 142

Home & Garden.............................. 150

Lifestyle Destinations 190

Markets & Delis 194

Recreation & Fitness........................ 204

Restaurants & Cafés..........................218

Shopping & Antiques.........................278

Weddings & Events........................... 324

Wineries & Breweries 344

Indices 350
   Index by Treasure 350
   Index by City 354

How to use this book

Treasures of Georgia is divided alphabetically into 14 categories, starting with Accommodations & Resorts and ending with Wineries & Breweries. If you want more specific information, such as where to get dinner in Atlanta, just check under Atlanta in the Index by City, and scan down the page until you find Restaurants & Cafés.

We have provided contact information for each Treasure in the book, because these are places and businesses which we encourage you to visit on your travels through Georgia.

We hope you find this book to be both beautiful and useful.

Accommodations & Resorts

Lakehouses on the shore of Lake Burton

All photos by Gregory Daniel

Above the Rest Luxury Cabins

Set among 1,500 acres of private mountain forest with magnificent panoramic views of the Blue Ridge Mountains of North Georgia, Above the Rest Luxury Cabins provides exquisite accommodations for a singular experience. Each of the cabins is a fully furnished and equipped log home with one to four bedrooms. Exceptional seclusion is afforded by the large lot sizes of one to eight acres. All homes have central heat and air, a hot tub, satellite television, barbeque grill, fireplaces and full laundry facilities. Many offer high-speed wireless Internet and game rooms with pool tables, foosball and darts. All have extensive decks that offer breathtaking views and fresh mountain air. Every budget can be accommodated, from a cost-effective getaway to supreme indulgence in one of the resort's Ultimate Log Cabins. Owners David and Jeanette Jenkins take pride in matching guests with the perfect vacation home and offer full concierge services, such as in-cabin massage, flowers and personal chef services.

Above the Rest is also centrally located, with Atlanta and Chattanooga 90 minutes away, and the Tennessee and North Carolina borders a short 10 to 12 mile drive. Nearby Lake Blue Ridge and Lake Nottely have pristine beaches perfect for swimming and picnicking. The marina rents fishing and pontoon boats, and jet skis. The surrounding U.S. Forest Service land is criss-crossed with hiking paths, including the Benton MacKaye and Appalachian Trails. Majestic waterfalls are the reward for many of the hikes and the perfect spot to cool off on a summer day. Rivers in the area support tubing, whitewater rafting, kayaking, canoeing and fishing. Three excellent golf courses are within easy access, as are horse stables that provide guided trail rides through the lush mountains. The charming town of Blue Ridge, only 15 minutes away from the cabins, is host to antique stores, galleries and upscale shops. For a vacation experience that combines superior service and the comforts of home, book a stay at Above the Rest Luxury Cabins.

1662 My Mountain Road, Morganton GA
(877) 374-2057
www.abovetherestcabins.com

Hilton Garden Inn Atlanta Perimeter Center

Just minutes from the heart of Atlanta, the Hilton Garden Inn Atlanta Perimeter Center offers a full array of services for the business and casual traveler. The Garden Inn is adjacent to a variety of high-tech businesses such as Hewlett Packard, and terrific shopping is available at the nearby Perimeter Mall. The inn features 107 rooms with king-size beds and 72 double queen rooms. Eight rooms are handicap-accessible. All rooms offer amenities such as dual-line phones with voice mail and data ports, free Internet access, plus a full array of entertainment equipment. You can order from room service or dine at the Great American Grill, which offers a variety of breakfast, lunch and dinner options. The Pavilion Lounge is a full-service bar and a comfortable place to relax. If you'd like some exercise, you'll delight in the hotel's fitness room and indoor pool. For a workspace with security features, visit the 24-hour business center. The Garden Inn supports corporate and social events with eight meeting rooms that can be configured in a variety of ways. Audio/visual equipment, a photocopying service and videoconferencing technology are available. Come to the Hilton Garden Inn Atlanta Perimeter Center for the lodging and amenities that will make your business or pleasure trip a comfortable success.

1501 Lake Hearn Drive, Atlanta GA
(404) 459-0500
www.atlantaperimeter.gardeninn.com

Sugar Magnolia Bed & Breakfast

Enjoy your next Atlanta visit to the fullest with a stay at Sugar Magnolia Bed & Breakfast, where you can relax and savor genteel hospitality and Old World charm while reveling in modern amenities. Colonel T.W. Latham, a prominent area businessman, constructed the stunning Queen Anne Victorian home as a private residence in 1892, complete with a three-story turret, grand staircase and six cozy fireplaces. Today's owners, Debi Starnes and Jim Emshoff, met in Atlanta after each moving to the area independently to take jobs in psychology. They opened Sugar Magnolia together in 1993. Located in Atlanta's first suburb, the Inman Park area, Sugar Magnolia Bed & Breakfast features two elegantly appointed rooms and two equally lovely suites with Jacuzzi tubs, private balconies and a myriad of comfortable amenities that will have you feeling right at home. With convenient meeting rooms, an in-house business center and complimentary wireless Internet access, this is the ideal place for those traveling on business or pleasure. Centrally located just minutes from the train station, Sugar Magnolia is also the perfect launching point for a sightseeing tour of this amazing city or as a home away from home for the parents of nearby college students. Experience gracious hospitality, delicious morning meals and all the famous charm of the South with a visit to Sugar Magnolia Bed & Breakfast.

804 Edgewood Avenue NE, Atlanta GA
(404) 222-0226
www.sugarmagnoliabb.com

Misty Mountain Inn & Cottages

Nature abounds at Misty Mountain Inn & Cottages. Innkeeper Peg Shaw is a bird and plant person. She has created a virtual bird sanctuary amidst the gardens and woodlands surrounding the inn. Misty Mountain has a wrap-around porch and four spacious guestrooms, each with its own bath and furnished with antiques. Three have balconies overlooking the landscaped gardens. Guests in the inn enjoy a full breakfast. Morgan, a rescued basset hound, makes his home in the inn, welcoming guests and pets, which can stay in one of the six cottages. The cottages offer more privacy and are spread across four acres on the surrounding mountainside. Each has its own country eclectic décor with full bath, well-equipped kitchen and wood-burning fireplace in addition to the usual heat and air. Three of the cottages accommodate only two people; three others, up to four people. Peg and the staff proudly share their knowledge of events and activities in the North Georgia Mountains, especially the neighbor's Misty Mountain Model Railroad, which is the largest O-gauge train display in America. They are proud of the recognition they have received in *American Historic Inns* and *Pets Welcome*. For a breath of fresh mountain air and all the comforts of home, come to Misty Mountain Inn & Cottages.

4376 Town Creek Road, Blairsville GA
(706) 745-4786
www.mistymountaininn.com

Sugar Mill Creek RV Resort

Life is good at Sugar Mill Creek RV Resort, where owners and camp hosts Rita Smith and Melissa Schell look after their campground guests in much the same way as they would treat any gathering of extended family. The 48 paved RV sites are easily found just off Highway 197, yet nicely secluded in the Chatahoochee National Forest. You, your pets and your kids will appreciate this lovely wooded location cut by a bubbling creek that once served moonshiners. The 10-acre campground has a bath house, laundry room, a playground and basketball court along with facilities for many other games. If tent camping is your pleasure, pick a site along the creek. A three-level covered deck is ideal for a special outdoor event. The lower level is an outdoor bar with entertainment on weekend evenings. The general store carries camping staples as well as beer and wine. The Sautee-Nacoochee Valley surrounding the campground contains several inviting Appalachian foothill communities, including Clarkesville, Clayton, Hiawassee and alpine Helen. Water sports abound at nearby Lake Burton, the Chatahoochee River and several state parks. Golfing, horseback riding and hiking are other popular pursuits. For easy living in a country setting, set up camp at Sugar Mill Creek RV Resort.

4960 Laurel Lodge Road, Clarkesville GA
(706) 947-0162
www.sugarmillcreek.com

Trackrock Campground & Cabins

Nestled in the foothills of the Smokey Mountains and bordered by the Chattahoochee National Forest, Trackrock Campground & Cabins sits on 300 acres of scenic woodlands and meadows. In 1966, Tommie and Martha Alexander turned their family farm into an 18-site campground. They continued to make improvements over the years, and today the family-owned campground, managed by their son, features 94 shaded, level, private campsites for tents, pop-ups and RVs. There are also five fully furnished cabins for those who'd rather rock on the porch than rough it. Campers can bask in the sun on the sandy beach or swim and fish in the four-acre spring-fed lake that's stocked with bass, bream and catfish. Trackrock offers many hiking trails, a large playground, recreation room, volleyball, horseshoes, seasonal Sunday chapel services and Wi-Fi Internet access. Ice, LP gas and firewood are also available at the office. Most Saturday evenings you can enjoy hayrides, and Trackrock Stables has guided horseback riding over the beautiful property. Many evenings, you might spot such local wildlife as deer, hawks or fox. The surrounding area offers shopping, golf, antiquing and whitewater rafting. Also nearby is access to the Appalachian Trail and Brasstown Bald, Georgia's highest point. Three generations of campers have returned to this idyllic spot again and again. Bring your camera and join fellow campers while you make some memories at Trackrock.

4887 Trackrock Camp Road, Blairsville GA
(706) 745-2420
www.trackrock.com

Photos © Duane Stork Photography

Virginia Highland Bed and Breakfast

In 1996, Adele Northrup was able to fulfill a lifelong dream of owning her own inn when she opened the Virginia Highland Bed and Breakfast, a welcoming urban retreat centrally located and within easy walking distance of the famed Highland Avenue Corridor in Atlanta. This very special inn was born from the ashes of tragedy after Adele lost a portion of her historic 1920s home in a fire. Adele rebuilt the charming Craftsman-style bungalow to a new magnificence and filled it with antiques and collectibles from her travels as well as all of the comforts of home. The Virginia Highland offers three lovingly appointed rooms, including the Victoria, which is outfitted with a private entrance and private balcony overlooking the woodland garden. The lovely private bathroom has a jetted tub, heated towel rack and bidet. Guests of the inn can while away the hours in the stunning gardens, sip iced tea on the covered porch or lounge in the stately living room. Those traveling on business can avail themselves of the private corner office, which offers a fax machine, copier and high-speed Internet access. In the morning you will be gently awakened by the tantalizing smell of a gourmet brunch being perfectly prepared to order by Adele, who is famous for her double-cheese omelettes and challah-style French toast. Whether you are traveling for business or pleasure, Adele invites you to stay in comfort and style at the Virginia Highland Bed and Breakfast.

630 Orme Circle NE, Atlanta GA
(404) 892-2735
www.virginiahighlandbb.com

Hotel Indigo

Atlanta has always been a progressive city with an eye cast toward the future. It's just the right location for a new concept in lodging for discerning travelers. Hotel Indigo in Atlanta is an innovative lifestyle boutique hotel with a policy of being inclusive, not exclusive. This hotel unveils a new look every season and rooms are designed around the mathematical patterns found in nature. Guests of Hotel Indigo will discover excellent dining, exercise and business amenities. Oversize beds and pillows, warm hardwood floors and spa-style showers complete with fluffy towels give a great sense of peace. There is a pub-style area for socializing, and gourmet-fast-casual dining at the Golden Bean. The foyer is expansive and welcoming. Adirondack-style chairs provide a comfortable place to lounge in the lobby, and the space is designed to make it easy to interact with other guests or find to a private space for personal quiet time. The staff, specializing in personal service, is multi-lingual, able to communicate in English, French, German and Spanish. Pet owners can rejoice, because dogs are not just tolerated here, they are invited. A pet happy hour, dubbed canine cocktails, is served on the patio and provides all the socializing, snacks and water a pampered canine could ask for, as well as a full dog menu. Encounter your own peaceful renewal at Hotel Indigo.

683 Peachtree Street NE, Atlanta GA
(404) 874-9200
www.hotelindigo.com

Inn at Ellis Square

Those who tagged Savannah as
America's Favorite Walking City
must have started at the carved doors
of the 1853 Guckenheimer Building.
Now home to the Inn at Ellis Square,
it is one of the best places to stay in
Georgia's First City. Majestic oaks,
the City Market and riverfront views
surround the hotel. Thanks to the vision
of owner Ron Thompson, the Inn at
Ellis Square adds another charmed
destination to the historic riverfront
district. Thompson spent several million
dollars renovating the corner property,
which once belonged to wholesalers
and was called the Bargain Corner. The
inn, which opened in 2005, has earned
a Preservation Award from the Historic
Savannah Foundation. By removing
modern additions and retaining such
structural elements as brick, timber
columns and hardwood floors, the
builders unveiled a Southern beauty
with an elegant interior consistent
with the brick exterior. Everything
was meticulously cleaned, repointed
and repainted. Rooms and suites are
elegantly appointed with furnishings of
the highest quality. This grand old lady
conceals a high tech side, which includes
everything from audiovisual and
lighting systems in stately conference
facilities to wireless high-speed Internet
access, voicemail and cable television
in individual rooms and suites. Guests
appreciate the swimming pool, the
fitness center and the complimentary
Continental breakfast. After a day
of sightseeing, Dominque's Lounge
offers a relaxing drink. The hotel is
popular for parties and banquets. Steep
yourself in the romance of Savannah
with a visit to the Inn at Ellis Square.

201 W Bay Street, Savannah GA
(912) 236-4440 or (877) 542-7666
www.innatellissquare.com

Tica Cabin Rentals

Greg and Thelma Coffone, owners of Tica Cabin Rentals, know that a great place to stay can make your Blue Ridge vacation. Since 1994, Tica has been supporting stellar vacations by matching well-maintained vacation properties with eager vacationers. Tica can place you in a mountain home with panoramic views or in a cute cabin next to a trout stream. Tica's rentals are loaded with such luxuries as hot tubs, fireplaces, pool tables and satellite television. Kitchens are fully equipped, and some homes allow pets. Some rentals include use of a swimming pool and tennis courts. Tica staff members help orchestrate family reunions and corporate retreats. They can arrange activities for your group such as whitewater rafting or horseback riding. Tica's wedding planner specializes in helping brides with the details for a dream wedding and reception. You can then reserve a romantic honeymoon cottage in the area. The Coffones left South Florida in 1994 to found Tica. They started with three properties and now offer 100. They own two sister companies, Great Escape Vacations and Tica of Ellijay, and handle reservations for vacation rental companies in other parts of the country. The Coffones plan to expand Tica throughout the United States. Before visiting the North Georgia mountains, call Tica Cabin Rentals.

699 E Main Street, Blue Ridge GA (706) 632-4448 or (800) 871-TICA (8422) *www.ticacabins.com*

First Class Cabin Rentals

Before Dan and Gayle Barton opened First Class Cabin Rentals, they were themselves vacationers, regularly escaping Atlanta for the mountains surrounding Blue Ridge. Eventually, they built their own cabin and used it as a rental property, then a second cabin. In 2002, when son Nicholas was two years old, they gave up their high-stress city careers and moved north to the mountains they loved. The Bartons know what a good mountain vacation should feel like and what part a rental plays in that experience. They maintain exceptionally high standards for their properties and remain available to renters 24 hours a day throughout their stay. "Dan and I really do pride ourselves on providing the highest level of customer service in the cabin rental industry," says Gayle, who takes a motherly concern for her clients' comfort. The Bartons, who operate from a large log cabin on the old Highway 76 in Blue Ridge, manage several upscale luxury cabins. You can count on extraordinary cleanliness and high-quality amenities, whether you seek stunning mountain views, lake views or wooded seclusion. All cabins are beautifully furnished and offer fully equipped kitchens, large decks with gas grills, linens and paper products. Fireplaces, hot tubs and cable or satellite television add to the fun. Some cabins offer pool tables and game rooms. Find a vacation home that captures the charm of the breathtaking Blue Ridge area with a call to First Class Cabin Rentals.

3293 E 1ˢᵗ street, Blue Ridge GA
(706) 258-3018 or (877) 277-5409
www.firstclasscabins.com

Barn Inn at Lake Rabun

At the Barn Inn at Lake Rabun, you come as a guest, but you leave as a friend. Directly across from Lake Rabun in a grand and forested historic neighborhood, the Barn Inn is a great place to escape the trials of daily life. Owners Jan Timms and Nancy Gribble have turned Barn Inn into a tranquil, peaceful getaway. Well-traveled and familiar with bed and breakfasts along the coast, Jan and Nancy purchased the 1920s rock and timber inn in 2005 and opened it to visitors the next year. Formerly the pride of Coca-Cola heir Samuel Candler Dobbs, this North Georgia treasure was once a stable for prize horses. Today, Jan and Nancy welcome prized guests who stay in one of five rooms named after triple-crown winners. The Secretariat Room has a king-sized bed. Seattle Slew offers calm, relaxing colors. Seabiscuit features linens soft as silk. Man O' War on the first floor has rock walls that remind you of the building's origins. The Citation Room invites guests to remember when they were young and climbed onto Grandma's wonderful, tall bed. A large deck allows guests to breathe the fresh air and to view the surrounding landscape. The guest lounge brings people together for conversation, television or games. Jan and Nancy also open their bed and breakfast for weddings and other special occasions. If you need time out or an overnight stay after a day of adventure, call the Barn Inn at Lake Rabun.

31 Barn Inn Road, Lakemont GA
(706) 212-9995
www.barninn.com

The Stovall House
Country Inn & Restaurant

Break yourself from the habit of rushing about and relying on technology with a leisurely stay at the Stovall House Country Inn & Restaurant. Nestled in the picturesque Sautee Valley among the mountains of northeast Georgia, the inn features five private guest rooms that are intimate, welcoming and free of distractions. Each room comes with a private bath, and all guests receive a complimentary Continental breakfast. At the restaurant, which is open to the public Thursday through Saturday, you can enjoy perfectly prepared entrées that are made with fresh local ingredients. The Stovall House can also accommodate special occasion parties and provide catering services for your next event, given advance notice. Owner Hamilton Schwartz purchased the vintage 1837 home in 1983 and received two prestigious awards just two years later: Best Adaptive Use of a Residence from the Georgia Trust, and Restoration Project of the Year from the Georgia Mountain Regional Planning Commission. In 2005, Schwartz put the home and its surrounding 26 acres into a land trust to better preserve the integrity and historic value of the property, which was owned by several of the area's most prominent citizens during the past 160 years. Discover the magic of this preserved piece of rural Georgia, located in one of the top small arts communities in America. It's a Country Experience.

1526 Highway 255 N, Sautee GA
(706) 878-3355
www.stovallhouse.com

Beechwood Inn

You'll experience the true hospitality of the North Georgia mountains when you stay at the Beechwood Inn, Georgia's premier wine country bed and breakfast. This is no ordinary inn; it is a fantasy woven from the arts and crafts of the 1920s and reflects the comfortable mountain setting in which it is located. The inn straddles a hillside of century-old terraced gardens and patios. It is filled with antiques and primitives, yet it is rustic and homey. While the past is ever-present, the Beechwood offers every convenience of our sophisticated, modern era. The inn's owners have a love of fine wine and foods that secures the inn's character. *Inn Traveler* magazine readers have honored the Beechwood Inn four years running, naming it number-one in North America for a weekend escape from 2003 to 2006. Food and wine enthusiasts will enjoy the wine weekend packages and culinary events at the inn, when celebrated wineries, winemakers and chefs from around the world collaborate to expand guests' epicurean horizons. Nearby mountains, trails and rivers offer activities that provide a lifetime of memories. You can raft the Chattooga River, hike to a waterfall or drive along bucolic country lanes. Romantic guest rooms have fine linens and cozy privacy. Most have private porches or balconies, fireplaces and wonderful views. Innkeepers David and Gayle Darugh warmly invite you to join them for the experience of a lifetime at the elegant Beechwood Inn.

220 Beechwood Drive, Clayton GA
(706) 782-5485 or (866) 782-2485
www.beechwoodinn.ws

Savannah Harbor

The Westin Savannah Harbor Golf Resort & Spa on Hutchinson Island feels miles away from city bustle. In fact, it's only minutes from the culture and excitement of Savannah—the ferry ride to the mainland takes all of 90 seconds. This resort offers spectacular river views and a host of luxury amenities. Rooms feature the signature Heavenly Bed and Heavenly Bath. The golf course will challenge golfers of all skill levels. It was designed by Bob Cupp, a prolific golf course designer, and Sam Snead, one of the world's premier golfers and winner of the PGA Tour Lifetime Achievement Award. The 18-hole championship course is host to the Liberty Mutual Legends of Golf Tournament. After a few holes or a tennis match at one of Savannah Harbor's four tennis courts, enjoy a cocktail at the Midnight Sun Lounge downstairs, or indulge in a spa treatment at the onsite Greenbrier Spa. If you need to stay in touch, the resort offers full business services. Guests can relax in the riverside Jacuzzi, take a dip in the year-round heated pool or sign up for a charter fishing excursion. Charter boats leave right from the deepwater dock alongside the resort. The resort's acclaimed restaurant, Aqua Star, serves up juicy steaks and fresh seafood nightly in an elegant and understated atmosphere. Savannah Harbor's accommodating staff is happy to help you plan a fun and relaxing stay, whether you'd like a day trip to Savannah for shopping and sightseeing or pampering in a spa and sampling fine cuisine. For a resort and spa that has it all, book your next vacation at The Westin Savannah Harbor.

1 Resort Drive, Savannah GA
(910) 201-2000
www.westin.com/savannah

Pura Vida USA

The transformational practice of connecting mind, body and spirit with nature is the focus of Pura Vida USA, a wellness resort and yoga retreat. On a hilltop amid 72 acres of woods, guests disconnect from the noise and discord of the modern world in order to reconnect with their internal selves. None of the 11 guest rooms in the main house has a telephone or television. The eight cottages, each designed as a petite suite with a cozy sitting area and full bath, lack these modern contrivances as well. Instead, with the Blue Ridge Mountains as backdrop, visitors turn to the sights and sounds of nature for inspiration, entertainment and solace. Walking trails and an open-air Jacuzzi, perfect for relaxing under the stars, encourage play and peaceful thoughts. The resort features daily yoga in a hall built specifically for that purpose. The spa on the premises sees to the total wellness of the individual. The vegetarian and modified vegetarian fare prepared daily is healthful and delicious. Pura Vida USA joins Maya Tulum in Mexico and Pura Vida Costa Rica as the newest in a family of wellness resorts in spectacular settings. For a meaningful experience in beautiful surroundings, consider a stay at Pura Vida USA.

400 Blueberry Hill, Dahlonega GA
(706) 345-4900 or (866) 345-4900
www.rrresorts.com

Happy Acres Farm

Happy Acres Farm offers a tranquil four-season vacation retreat that features panoramic mountain views. Originally the childhood home of sisters and current owners Faye Walker Housley, Carolyn Walker Cabe and Geneva Walker Betzold, the farm has been in the Lee/Walker family for 136 years. The farm was originally purchased by their great-grandfather R. M. Lee in 1870, and the home was built in 1929 by their parents, Captain and Liller Lee Walker. After the death of their mother in 2000, the property passed to the seven children. The other siblings were willing to sell, so Faye, Carolyn and Geneva purchased their interests with the idea of sharing the farm's beauty with guests. The spacious home offers three double occupancy bedrooms and a fully equipped kitchen. Although the sisters provide television with VCR and DVD, they recommend viewing the breathtaking scenery from comfy rocking chairs on the wraparound front porch instead. A working farm up until 1993, the property still features verdant pastureland dotted with cattle and such wildlife as deer and turkey. Nestled at the foot of the Blue Ridge Mountains, the 114-acre farm offers hiking, trout fishing and easy access to North Georgia wineries as well as proximity to shopping and points of interest in nearby Dahlonega, home of the first major United States gold rush and mint. For a restful retreat in stunning surroundings, treat yourself to tranquility at Happy Acres Farm.

5475 Black Mountain Road, Dahlonega GA
(706) 864-3863 or (706) 864-3573

Black Forest Bed & Breakfast and Luxury Cabins

In fashioning themselves as romantic getaway specialists, the innkeepers at the Black Forest Bed & Breakfast had heart-shaped Jacuzzis installed in the Honeymoon/Anniversary rooms. Mother Nature provided other things, such as the clear, intoxicating mountain air. Black Forest Bed & Breakfast is located in Helen amid the picturesque foothills of the Blue Ridge Mountains. As beautiful as the setting is, you may be tempted to spend your whole time indoors. Beyond luxurious rooms and suites, you will find such luxury-themed cabins as the Victorian Honeymoon and Tropical Honeymoon, which come not only with a Jacuzzi but with an in-room waterfall, fireplace and deck with a mountain view. These romantic extras are in addition to such standard amenities as luxurious bedding and bathrobes. Couples staying in the Country Cabin receive even more pampering. They'll be provided with everything they need to sip champagne and nibble chocolates while snuggling in a king-sized sleigh bed. All guests are served a gourmet breakfast on the patio where a 20-foot waterfall and koi pond provide the backdrop. When you are ready to venture from your romantic paradise, you will find the shops and restaurants of Helen within walking distance of your room, suite or cabin. Pull the shades and let romance take it from there at the Black Forest Bed & Breakfast and Luxury Cabins.

8902 N Main Street, Helen GA
(706) 878-3995
www.blackforest-bb.com

Blue Sky Vacation Rentals

People come to the alpine village of Helen to enjoy everything from mountain solitude, golf and outdoor adventures to shopping, fine dining and dinner theater. Whatever your vacation preference, Blue Sky Vacation Rentals can rent you private lodging to suit your needs. Need a season-long rental for a large family? A weekend retreat for two? If you want to spend time on the Chatahoochee River, why not stay in a cabin right on the water, with fishing, tubing and canoeing just outside your door? Perhaps you prefer the convenience of a swimming pool or an entertainment room with a panoramic mountain view and a remote location. Blue Sky offers rentals five to 10 miles from Helen or right in the resort town, which has 200 specialty shops for the shopper in the family. Shane and Helen Burnett opened Blue Sky in 2005. Shane discovered his calling in the rental business after his father, discouraged with how his Helen property had been handled, put Shane in charge of renting out the property. Blue Sky's properties range from tidy rustic cabins to luxury dwellings with hot tubs, pool tables and fireplaces, all comfortably furnished and designed to make your vacation in the foothills of the Blue Ridge Mountains a highlight of your year. Blue Sky understands that a vacation rental should be well-maintained and equipped for easy food preparation and comfortable relaxation. Assure a trouble-free vacation with the services of Blue Sky Vacation Rentals.

8160 S Main Street, Helen GA
(706) 878-5306 or (877) 857-3107
www.blueskyofhelen.com

James Madison
Inn & Conference Center

A brand-new boutique hotel anchors the multiple offerings of Madison Markets, a set of turn-of-the-century cotton warehouses converted into a fashionable shopping and gallery neighborhood. Everett Royal owns the James Madison Inn & Conference Center, which opened in 2007. His wife, Jane, owns the markets. The neoclassical inn, patterned after hotels of the late 19th century, contains 19 luxurious guest rooms, each named after one of the town's historic homes. The hotel also includes six private residences. Modern amenities mix beautifully with antique accents at the inn. Each accommodation features a private balcony, fireplace, flat-screen television and wireless Internet access. Suites offer complete kitchens. A media room is decked out in antiques and antique reproductions. A horse-drawn carriage offers a romantic exit for newlyweds or a tour of Madison, a town hailed for its livability and antebellum mansions that were spared by Sherman's army. The inn is prepared for corporate retreats and can serve up to 200 people at outdoor weddings. Let one of the inn's spa packages relax your every muscle, or tighten those muscles up in the exercise room. Experience the essence of Madison with a stay at the James Madison Inn & Conference Center.

260 W Washington Street, Madison GA
(706) 342-7040
www.jamesmadisoninn.com

Tara Inn & Suites

Tara was the beloved home estate of one of the most famous southern belles the world has ever known, Miss Scarlett O'Hara. At the Tara Inn & Suites, Owners Jeff Kashani and Hossein Horati have created a fitting tribute to Tara with luxurious suites, complete with kitchenettes and Jacuzzi tubs. One-bedroom luxury suites and studio apartments come with a high-speed data port in every room. There is a spa and a swimming pool for relaxation and meeting rooms and a banquet hall provide everything members of a business conference could ask for. All local calls are free. The area attractions are all fewer than 30 minutes away. Nearby draws include the Gone with the Wind Museum, the Ashley Oak Mansion and the 1867 Jonesboro Depot, all within five minutes of the inn. The Hartsfield International Airport is only 10 minutes away. Downtown Atlanta, Turner Field and the Atlanta Motor Speedway are 15 minutes from Tara Inn. If amusement parks interest you, Six Flags over Georgia and Stone Mountain are about a half an hour away. All of this makes Tara Inn & Suites a convenient home base and restful interlude in the hub of the city. Call for reservations and put off your troubles to tomorrow.

628 Southside Commercial Parkway, Jonesboro GA
(678) 647-1360 or (888) 647-1360

Old Clayton Inn

Imagine a large Southern mansion right on Main Street in Clayton in the North Georgia mountains. This is the historic Old Clayton Inn. The hotel has 30 guest bedrooms, each with its own individual décor. In the living room lobby, you'll find comfortable furniture and a cheery fireplace. Next to the lobby is the main restaurant, which seats 80 for breakfast and lunch. A special dinner buffet on Fridays and Saturdays stars Angie Jenkins playing Broadway piano. Next to the dining room is the Clayton Banquet Hall, which can accommodate up to 100 guests. The private Rabun Room can serve up to 20. The Old Clayton Inn can tailor its services to the needs of any group. In addition to the guestrooms, the hotel offers four small apartments and nine rooms in its extended-stay facilities. All the shops and galleries on Main and Savannah Streets are within a few blocks, and the inn is happy to arrange whitewater rafting, driving tours and golf tee times at any of four courses. The inn was built in the years 1947 and 1948 after fires destroyed earlier structures—building on the site dates back to the 1880s. The present building is the county's emergency Civil Defense Headquarters because of its reinforced concrete construction. Come stay at the Old Clayton Inn, where the staff looks forward to serving you.

60 S Main Street, Clayton GA
(706) 782-7722 or (800) 454-3498
www.oldclaytoninn.com

The Zeigler House Inn

The first time Kim and Jackie Heinz visited the Zeigler House Inn, they made an offer to buy it. That was in 2005, shortly after the 151-year-old house had undergone a full restoration. The Italianate-style home, with its 11 fireplaces and original heart pine floors, sits in the middle of Savannah's historic district on one of America's most beautiful streets, still paved in the original cobblestones. Couples and honeymooners adore the inn, which also hosts business travelers or girls' weekends away. Three of the five guest rooms offer private entrances and courtyards while two full suites inhabit the top floor of the four-story home. All five rooms offer full baths, some with whirlpool tubs, king-size beds, cable television, DVD players and either a full kitchen or kitchenette stocked with snacks and beverages as well as other amenities. Jackie, a former caterer, bakes daily to the delight of her guests. The couple finds pleasure in arranging for such extras as horse-drawn carriage rides, dinner reservations, tours and more. In two short years, some guests have already returned to indulge in the inn's pre-Civil War grandeur three and four times. "Our reward is our guest's happiness," say Kim and Jackie, who invite you to visit the Zeigler House Inn.

121 W Jones Street, Savannah GA
(912) 233-5307 or (866) 233-5307
www.zeiglerhouseinn.com

Lucille's Mountain Top Inn

With its setting in the spectacular Blue Ridge Mountains, Lucille's Mountain Top Inn makes an ideal romantic getaway. Lucille Hlavenka realized her dream of running a bed and breakfast with the opening of Lucille's in 2001. Her husband, George, a commercial architect, designed the inn to take full advantage of the panoramic views of the mountains of northern Georgia and the Sautee and Nacoochee Valleys. Together they created a delightful three-story retreat with nine elegant guest rooms filled with modern amenities. The inn treats you to a comfortable Crown Jewel bed, a gourmet breakfast and a homemade evening dessert after a day of exploration. The Bavarian village of Helen, filled with shops and restaurants, is only four miles away. You'll be surrounded with opportunities for picnics, hiking and golf. You can also decide to fish or go tubing on the Chattahoochee River. Lucille's easily accommodates family

reunions, business meetings and retreats. It's also a favorite location for weddings and receptions. Both *Southern Living* and *Inn Traveler* magazines have featured the inn. In 2004, *Inn Travelers Book of Lists* named Lucille's Best Bed and Breakfast in the USA. To further your bliss, the Mandala Spa and Wellness Center is right next door. Ditch the cell phone and disconnect from everyday life with Southern hospitality and some of Mother Nature's best work at Lucille's Mountain Top Inn.

964 Rabun Road, Sautee GA
(706) 878-5055 or (866) 245-4777
www.lucillesmountaintopinn.com

Sylvan Falls Mill Bed & Breakfast

A converted 1840s mill, complete with a 27-foot-tall waterwheel, provides pastoral lodging in the Wolffork Valley of Georgia. Depending on when you stay at Sylvan Falls Mill Bed & Breakfast, you may get to watch as the miller slowly grinds fresh flour and grits from the mill. No matter when you visit, the views of the 100-foot cascading waterfall are always gorgeous from the deck or garden bench. Hummingbirds flit and butterflies flutter through the flowers and herbs. Time passes slowly as you sit at the foot of the falls or take a walk along the quiet country road leading to Black Rock State Park. Located near four lakes, a national forest and two other state parks, the inn offers four bedrooms, each with private bath. The inn is typically filled with guests eager to pursue canoeing, horseback riding, fishing and wildflower photography. Golfing one of the nearby picturesque courses is another option, as is shopping the many antique shops, flea markets and galleries in the area. The inn is especially popular with travelers along the Blue Ridge Parkway. Owners Linda and Michael Johnson buy the ingredients for their scrumptious breakfasts locally, including cider, fruit and pork. They use organically grown whole grains to make their delicious breads. Expect to be greeted warmly and to hear a few stories of the mill's past when you are a guest at Sylvan Falls Mill Bed & Breakfast.

156 Taylor's Chapel Road, Rabun Gap GA
(706) 746-7138
www.sylvanfallsmill.com

Bernie's Nacoochee Valley Guest House

"To walk in here is to know me," says Bernie Yates of her 1920s-era inn. Bernie established Nacoochee Valley Guest House in 1989 following years of travel and research into the bed and breakfast trade. She finds that these days most of her business comes through word of mouth from those who have experienced her brand of hospitality. "We specialize in the lost art of personal service," says Bernie. Anyone who has experienced a wedding or rehearsal dinner at the guest house knows what Bernie's brand of personal service is all about. Bridal showers, birthday celebrations and anniversaries are popular reasons to plan a French country lunch or dinner at the inn. Bernie will gladly meet the special dietary needs of her guests. The menus show off fresh local produce and herbs picked from the beautiful gardens. Lodgers receive a full breakfast with their stay, and the public are welcome for lunch and dinner. The guest house once belonged to one of the area's first families. It offers three quaint rooms with full baths. Two of the rooms are located on the first floor with private entrances. Bernie has put her heart and soul into her home and the contentment of her guests. "I've found such peace in this historic valley that I want to give it back to others." Bernie's Nacoochee Valley Geust House—History, Hospitality, Fine Dining—truly a rare find you will always remember and return to, season after season.

2220 Highway 17, Sautee GA
(706) 878-3830
www.letsgotobernies.com

Photos © 2007 Azalea Inn & Gardens/Adam Kuehl

Azalea Inn & Gardens

The winsome Azalea Inn & Gardens allures guests with an invitation to rendezvous with Southern sensibilities, relaxation and new Southern cuisine in the beauty of Savannah, one of the South's most romantic cities. This 19th century bed-and-breakfast inn is surrounded by showplace heritage gardens, featured in the 2006 Savannah Tour of Homes and Gardens, and steeped in Georgia's rich Colonial history. The Victorian Queen Anne Italianate mansion was built in 1889 and is registered in the National Landmark Historic District. The home's original owner, Captain Walter K. Coney, was a competitive yachtsman and prominent member of Savannah's community. The mansion was constructed on land that became part of an antebellum garden district that includes Forsyth Park. Innkeepers Teresa and Jake Jacobson purchased the property after falling in love with the charms of the historic district during several visits to their son, who has since graduated from the Savannah College of Art and Design. The Jacobsons, with the help of master gardener Anthony Attardi of Southern Heritage Design and Landscaping, created four primary gardens with indigenous and Southern heritage plants, low volume irrigation and seasonal plantings to assure an intriguing year-round garden. The inn offers 10 accommodations, each lovingly decorated with quintessential Savannah themes, as well as snuggle-down amenities such as private baths, verandah porches, balconies and fireplaces. All-inclusive rates include free off-street parking, sumptuous breakfasts and pre-dinner fine wines. Guests traveling in groups may choose the cozy Carriage House, which features two rooms and overlooks the inn's courtyard garden swimming pool. Venture off the beaten path and bask in a picturesque Savannah setting at the Azalea Inn & Gardens.

217 E Huntingdon Street, Savannah GA
(912) 236-2707 or (800) 582-3823
www.azaleainn.com

Historic Glen-Ella Springs Country Inn

The Historic Glen-Ella Springs Country Inn offers an idyllic retreat at the southernmost tip of the Blue Ridge Mountains. Constructed in 1875 as part of Glen and Ella Davidson's working farm, the home was expanded in 1890 and again in 1905 to take in paying guests. From the early 1900s until the 1920s, the house often served as a place for wealthy coastal Georgia families to escape the threat of yellow fever during the summer. The inn ceased operations in the 1920s and passed through several owners before Bobby and Barrie Aycock began a year-long restoration of the property in 1986. The Aycocks were delighted to find that the home's features remained intact, including original heart pine floors, walls and ceilings. Electricity and bathrooms were added, and today the inn proudly offers 16 guest rooms furnished with antiques and locally made furniture. Extensive herb and perennial gardens, meadows and a large swimming pool grace the 18-acre grounds. Guests enjoy bountiful breakfast buffets. The award-winning dining room is open to the public seven nights a week for American and Continental fare with a Southern touch. Outdoor activities are close at hand, including world-class trout fishing and boating on nearby lakes and rivers. Whether you're planning a business meeting, searching for a romantic wedding site or just looking for a relaxing getaway, make plans to visit the Historic Glen-Ella Springs Country Inn.

1789 Bear Gap Road, Clarkesville GA
(706) 754-7295 or (877) 456-7528
www.glenella.com

Mountain Laurel Creek Inn & Spa

If you're looking for an idyllic mountain retreat in the North Georgia wine country, you can't do better than the Mountain Laurel Creek Inn & Spa outside Dahlonega. Innkeeper Dennis Hoover is a born artist whose skills range from pottery and graphic arts to interior design. Mountain Laurel Creek is a perfect reflection of his talent. He and his partner David bought their mountain cabin home in 2000 and immediately expanded it to include three guest suites. This year they added on again, and now boast five suites that make the perfect romantic getaway. Each suite offers a sitting room, private bath with whirlpool tub for two, a separate shower, private balcony and in-room coffee service. Your stay comes with a gourmet breakfast that may include German apple pancakes or golden egg wraps. There are no phones or televisions in the rooms, but you won't need them with the sweeping views of the Blue Ridge Mountains and close proximity to the Appalachian Trail. The Oasis Spa offers a full range of services, from massage to skincare treatments, that will elevate your stay at Mountain Laurel Creek to even higher levels. The editors of *Southern Living* heaped praise upon Dennis and David for the haven they have created, and with good reason. If you are looking for the best possible accommodations in North Georgia, make reservations at Mountain Laurel Creek Inn & Spa.

202 Talmer Grizzle Road, Dahlonega GA
(706) 867-8134
www.mountainlaurelcreek.com

Planter's Inn on Reynolds Square

While staying at the Planter's Inn on Reynolds Square, you will enjoy complimentary breakfast in the morning, wine and cheese in the afternoon, and a date with history around the clock. In a city rich with history, the Planter's Inn site shines as truly special. Several hotels have stood on this spot since 1913, including one with a notorious reputation as an upscale brothel. Before that, two of the city's leading businessmen had homes here. However, the fascinating history of Trust Lot T goes all the way back to the Colonial era, when a parsonage for the Church of England in Georgia, today known as Christ Church, was constructed. In 1739, a young man arrived to succeed the church's first pastor, Samuel Quincy. The newcomer was John Wesley, the founder of Methodism. Within steps of Planter's Inn you will find two of Savannah's oldest houses, the Pink House, now a popular restaurant, and the Oliver Sturges House. The Planter's Inn, with its 60 large guest rooms, owes much of the spaciousness that its guests enjoy today to the 1982 renovation of what was then the John Wesley Hotel. Visit Planter's Inn, where you can explore the historic Reynolds Square neighborhood, and where the inn's staff attends to you with the warmth and hospitality that is the trademark of the South.

29 Abercorn Street, Savannah GA
(912) 232-5678
www.plantersinnsavannah.com

Hamilton-Turner Inn

While all hotels provide a night's stay, the Hamilton-Turner Inn on Savannah's famous Lafayette Square affords the rare opportunity to experience the beauty and extravagance of a 19th century mansion. Once the family home and playhouse of one of Savannah's wealthiest society members, this structure, known as the Grand Victorian Lady, was built in 1873, sparing no detail of the lavish Second-Empire Victorian style. Original owner Samuel P. Hamilton and his wife, Sarah, enjoyed throwing big parties and were very style conscious. When that new technology called electricity came to Savannah, the Hamiltons had to be the first to have it. Neighbors gathered in wonder and fright for the initial illumination, half-expecting the Hamilton house to explode. Guests at today's inn may choose from 17 luxury guestrooms and suites furnished with a comfortable mixture of antiques and new furnishings. Some rooms feature romantic fireplaces, double whirlpool spa baths and 11-foot views overlooking the other architectural jewels of Lafayette Square. Rates include a full gourmet breakfast, iced tea and sweets in the afternoon, evening wine and hors d'oeuvres, and nightly turndown service with cookies at your bedside. Featured in such magazines as *The South* and *Southern Living*, the inn receives AAA's Four Diamond rating year after year. For style that once only the social elite could enjoy, stay at the Hamilton-Turner Inn.

330 Abercorn Street, Savannah GA
(912) 233-1833 or (888) 448-8849
www.hamilton-turnerinn.com

Village Inn & Pub

When George Stewart set out to develop the Village Inn & Pub on the site of his 1930s beach cottage, he vowed to preserve every tree on the property. These trees characterize St. Simons Island—live oaks draped in Spanish moss, magnolias and palms. George integrated the Mission-style façade of the original cottage into a collection of stucco buildings with half-moon balconies, creating 28 guest rooms with individual layouts to avoid tree roots. He even used an environmentally-sound alternative to standard pavement. His efforts earned him the first-ever development award from the island's environmentalist group, RUPA, as well as the respect of neighbors and the admiration of guests. The original cottage now functions as the reception area to the inn, with a breakfast room, sitting area and English pub. Guest rooms at the inn face either out to the village or inward to the pool and courtyard, which is lush with native foliage. You can kick back in a leather club chair in your room or walk a short distance to the lighthouse and quaint boutiques of St. Simons Island. The tropical landscapes of the island are popular with wedding parties, and Village Inn can provide wedding consultation services. Visit soon to see for yourself why the Village Inn & Pub won a 2003 *Coastal Living* award and has captured the attention of the national and local media.

500 Mallery Street, St. Simons Island GA
(912) 634-6056 or (888) 635-6111
www.villageinnandpub.com

Beach Bed & Breakfast

A Mediterranean-style villa with superb amenities is your site for an island fantasy. When you pull up to the front of the beautiful Beach Bed & Breakfast, you'll understand immediately why it is so often featured in travel magazines and is a member of the Select Registry, Distinguished Inns of North America. Poised on beautifully landscaped grounds on the beach at St. Simons Island, the inn overlooks the ocean. Its suites are large enough to make you feel like you're on your own private island. Enjoy your own walk-in closet, private balcony and sitting room. The refrigerator, stocked with complimentary beverages and treats, will add to the conviction that you have arrived at paradise. Guests at the Beach Bed and Breakfast enjoy the use of a spa, endless pool and a private theater. The sublime oceanfront setting, combined with special inn packages, makes the Beach Bed & Breakfast a popular destination for honeymooners and couples celebrating anniversaries. For groups larger than 20, the Beach Bed & Breakfast offers the Caribe Beach Villas and the Beachview Villas as additional accommodations. Stroll down to the shops of historic St. Simons or enjoy a leisurely breakfast on the ocean front veranda. Picture yourself basking in beauty and comfort at the Beach Bed & Breakfast.

907 Beachview Drive, St. Simons Island GA
(877) 634-2800
www.beachbedandbreakfast.com

Ocean Lodge

Rising above the beach like a magnificent sand castle, Ocean Lodge brings the luxury and service of an all-concierge boutique hotel to St. Simons Island. Opened in the winter of 2007, this graciously appointed Mediterranean-style lodge caters to the discriminating guest with state-of-the-art amenities and Old World ambience. Each of the 15 distinctively furnished suites features ocean views from a private balcony. Providing comfort with every detail, the suites include a spacious bedroom, living room and two full baths—one featuring a Whirlpool tub, captain's galley and dining bar. High-tech amenities include two wide-screen television sets, a DVD player, broadband Internet and electronic keyless entry. Complimentary breakfast is served in the parlor or outside on the Oceanview Terrace. Ocean Lodge has been designed to accommodate weddings and other special occasions. The floor plan is open and airy, offering flexible spaces for groups of varying sizes, especially on the Loggia Terrace, which boasts an appealing indoor-outdoor setting. Every evening at twilight, you'll be able to see the beacon of St. Simons' lighthouse from the Terrace or from your own balcony. It's part of the magical beauty that awaits you at Ocean Lodge, your castle on the beach.

935 Beachview Drive, St. Simons Island GA
(912) 634-1547 or (866) 634-1547
www.oceanlodgessi.com

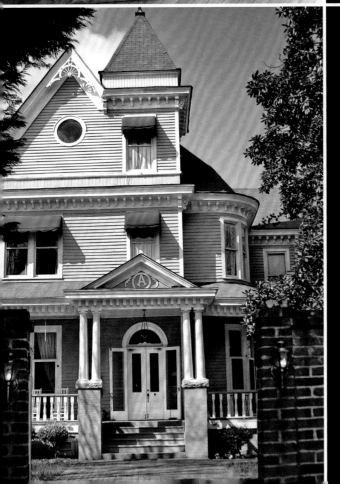

Ashford Manor Bed and Breakfast

Guests at Ashford Manor Estate Bed and Breakfast experience the privacy and privilege available only in a graceful residence without giving up the luxuries of a first-class hotel. The Ashford family owned this 1893 manor for more than 100 years. Dave, Mario and Jim Shearon purchased the five-acre estate in 1997. They can pamper guests in six romantic bedrooms that feature private baths, cable television and wireless Internet access. Guests enjoy luxury bathrobes and bath products, refrigerators and coffeemakers stocked with private label coffees and teas. Items from the proprietors' travels grace the rooms. The Safari Room includes a dog bed, and the Asian Room is decorated in Japanese antiques. Other options are the White Room, the English Room, the Garden Room and the Penthouse Suite. The gourmet breakfast changes daily, and your hosts are glad to deliver it to your room or to serve you in the dining room, where you'll find white linen tablecloths, sterling silver, china and crystal. The grounds, bordered by magnolias, redbuds and pines, offer secluded hideaways, landscaped gardens and a regal pool. Public events include an outdoor concert series, a fall wine tasting and Grace's Birthday Party, a spring fundraiser that attracts 200 dogs and the people who love them. Word is out about Ashford Manor since its appearance in *Southern Living*. The local press has named it the best bed and breakfast in the Athens area for three years in a row. Experience the charms of a venerable house and obliging hosts at Ashford Manor Bed and Breakfast.

5 Harden Hill Road, Watkinsville GA
(706) 769-2633
www.ambedandbreakfast.com

Eagle Island Lodge

They say no man is an island, but you can have an island all to yourself at Eagle Island Lodge. Captain Andy Hill is the owner of the lodge, which he opened to the public in 2003, and the 10-acre island it sits on, which is accessible only by boat. The lodge, designed by Andy's childhood friend Tripp Alsbrook, is suitable for everything from a romantic honeymoon to a family reunion. It measures 3,343 square feet, with a 1,500-square-foot screened porch and fireplace. It sleeps 10 and features two luxurious full baths and a fully equipped chef's kitchen, which Andy and his staff will stock to your liking before you arrive. Andy will even boil your shrimp for you. Though you're secluded, you'll still be able to keep in contact with the outside world by satellite television and wireless Internet. Visitors will immediately discover how beautiful Eagle Island got its name—there's a functioning bald eagle nest within sight of the house. Explore the 10-acre island on a hike or just view the ever-present wildlife while relaxing on the dock. Enjoy a warm, private night under the stars by the outdoor fire pit or soak in the hot tub with a roaring fire on the porch. The sparkling waters of the Darien River and Mayhall Creek are there for your enjoyment, with kayaking and boating from the Eagle Island dock. Andy will honor all reasonable requests and will gladly help you customize activities, food, special events and fishing charters for a very memorable getaway. You can contact Andy through the website listed below. Let Andy and his staff treat you to your own private paradise with a vacation at Eagle Island Lodge.

Darien, GA
(912) 222-0801
www.privateislandsofgeorgia.com

Photos by Richard Johnson

Forrest Hills Mountain Resort and Conference Center

From a romantic getaway to a large corporate retreat, Forrest Hills Mountain Resort and Conference Center offers lodging options and services to accommodate any group. Kraft family members opened the 140-acre oasis in 1978 and built the first six cabins themselves, using lumber culled from the property. Today, the resort offers 98 rooms in a variety of configurations. Stay in one of the rustic cabins and relax in an indoor hot tub while looking out into the wilderness, or choose a beautifully appointed Victorian cottage, complete with a candlelit dinner. Forrest Hill's lodges strike a perfect balance between privacy and group activity for large parties. When holding a family reunion in a lodge, everyone can enjoy their own rooms and come together in the large common area to reminisce and catch up with loved ones. The resort offers all-inclusive wedding packages, too. The Secret Garden wedding gazebo makes a picturesque setting for your ceremony, and you can continue the celebrations throughout the weekend with accommodations for all of your guests at the resort. During your stay, enjoy full day spa services, horseback riding or a scenic wagon ride and cookout. Just a few miles away, you'll find golf courses, great shopping and winery tours. Come to Forrest Hills Mountain Resort and Conference Center for a vacation tailored to you.

**135 Forrest Hills Road, Dahlonega GA
(706) 864-6456 or (800) 654-6313
*www.forresthillsresort.com***

Washington Plantation Bed and Breakfast

Prepare to be swept away from the nine to five routine at the Washington Plantation Bed and Breakfast, where your only assignment is to enjoy the enchanting accommodations and quiet surroundings. The Greek Revival manor, built in 1828, originally served as the seat of a plantation with more than 3,200 acres. Owners Tom and Barbara Chase retain the charm and grace of the era, with antique furnishings and period pieces in the five suites, while adding all of the luxuries of today, such as spa-like private baths and individually controlled heating and air conditioning. For guests who prefer to keep technology nearby, the inn offers cable television, phones and wireless Internet access in every room. After a restful sleep on Egyptian cotton sheets and down comforters, enjoy breakfast served on fine china. Next on the agenda, perhaps you will relax in a rocking chair on the expansive porch, tour the three fine museums in town, or go to City Square to shop. The seven acres of grounds are perfect for an afternoon stroll with sitting areas for enjoying the view. Amidst the fountains and flowers outside, the bed-and-breakfast offers a beautiful setting for a garden wedding with up to 500 guests, or you may choose to have a more intimate ceremony indoors. The plantation's mystique and hospitality recently earned it a place on the American Historic Inns' list as one of the Top 10 Romantic Inns. Come to the Washington Plantation Bed and Breakfast for your next getaway and leave the daily grind behind.

15 Lexington Avenue, Washington GA
(877) 405-9956
www.washingtonplantation.com

Sunrise Grocery and Sunrise Cabins

Tourists, locals and campers have depended on Sunrise Grocery for more than 80 years for everything from groceries and gasoline to fish bait and firewood. This steadfast landmark sits at the foot of Blood Mountain next to the Chattahoochee National Forest and Vogel State Park. Built in 1921, the tiny store served as a grill, gas station and grocery store. Its background includes back room poker games and bootleg beer. Bob and Christine Clemmons purchased the store in 1983 and subsequently added two mountainside cottages and two riverside cabins. Today, their son Jason owns and manages the store and the cabins along with his wife, Christina. The grocery sells Burt's Bees products, cheese from huge old-fashioned wheels and barbecue rubs and sauces, such as Butt Rub and Bone Suckin' sauce. You can purchase a fishing license here or take home a Foothills smoked ham. Locally produced apples and fresh vegetables join the store's boiled P-Nuts, featured in *Southern Living* magazine. Once you see this Appalachian paradise, you will want to stay and take in its charms. The cabins have a nostalgic look that's enhanced by antiques and stone fireplaces. They also feature fully equipped kitchens, satellite television and VCRs. The Clemmons can direct you to area attractions and fill you in on local history. For natural beauty, a true country store and a good night's sleep, come to Sunrise Grocery and Sunrise Cabins, where old-fashioned values still shine.

5813 Gainesville Highway, Blairsville GA
(706) 745-5877
www.sunrisegrocery.com
www.sunrisecabins.com

The Helendorf River Inn & Conference Center

The Bavarian-inspired Helendorf River Inn & Conference Center is located in the center of Helen. The inn has been in business since 1970. Many guests are the children and grandchildren of families who visited in the establishment's earliest days. While at the inn, guests may fish and tube in the river, swim in the heated pool, and relax on the private balcony or walk-out patio on the banks of the river. Charming Bavarian style furnishings create a cozy atmosphere. A short climb to the top of the inn's Rapunzel Tower reveals a quaint split-level guest room. Spacious suites each include a Jacuzzi, full kitchen and large living room with a wood burning fireplace. Over the years, the Helendorf River Inn has hosted many meetings, reunions and parties in its conference facilities. The Riverside Meeting Room, large enough to accommodate 200 people, has several sets of French doors opening to a patio on the tree-lined bank of the river. The built-in sound system, stage and catering kitchen make the room versatile. The Fireside Meeting Room features a large stone fireplace, beamed cathedral ceiling and a kitchen for catered meals or do-it-yourselfers. The Alpine Village of Helen includes many shops, restaurants, a host of scenic hiking trails, a national forest and impressive waterfalls. Visit the Helendorf River Inn and discover how the Blue Ridge Mountains can resemble the Alps.

33 Munichstrasse, Helen GA
(706) 878-2271 or (800) 445-2271
www.helendorf.com

Green Palm Inn

The charming Green Palm Inn proves the old adage that bigger isn't always better. With just four perfectly appointed rooms, the inn provides customers with impeccable service and comfort in a location perfectly suited for exploring Savannah's walkable historic district. Innkeeper Diane McCray and owner Gary Crews welcome guests as if they were family, and many visitors come to think of the Green Palm Inn as their home away from home. The suites certainly provide all the comforts of a gracious home, including antique four-poster beds and tasteful decorations. In the Royal Palm or Sabal Palm rooms, you can enjoy an evening curled up by the fireplace or soaking in a clawfoot tub. Your day at the inn starts with a filling gourmet breakfast. The inn is conveniently located just a few short blocks from the riverfront and the shops, restaurants and nightlife of the historic district. After a day of sightseeing, return to the Green Palm in the afternoon for wine tasting, a decadent dessert bar and a chance to chat with Diane or visit with the other guests. Stay at the Green Palm Inn on your next visit to Savannah and discover why people return time and time again to the place *Fodor's Travel Guides* calls a little gem of an inn.

548 E President Street, Savannah GA
(888) 606-9510
www.greenpalminn.com

Photo by Bryan Redding/Southern Distinction Magazine

Photo by Brad Fox

The Farmhouse Inn at Hundred Acre Farm

Melinda Hartney knew she was a farm girl at heart when her Uncle Ellis Johnson was developing the Farmhouse Inn at Hundred Acre Farm near Madison. Her experience in guest relations and an interior design degree helped her create an inviting atmosphere evoking the surrounding local history and farmland. Borrowing its whimsical name from Winnie-the-Pooh, the family business has grown into a charming retreat with five private guest rooms, a two-bedroom cottage and four-bedroom farmhouse. With wide plank pine floors, tall beamed ceilings and vintage interiors, the inn can accommodate a romantic evening for two as well as weddings, small retreats and luncheons. By incorporating modern conveniences such as cable television, wireless Internet and meeting rooms, the inn can also accommodate clients, corporate retreats and day meetings for area businesses. Wes Holt, a family friend, horticulturist and outdoorsman, develops and maintains the gardens, trails and barnyard, sharing his appreciation of nature with guests. Wildlife is abundant in the meadows and trails leading to the Apalachee River. Guests can take a backpack with binoculars and a trail map while viewing herons and eagles, or visit barnyard farm animals that include miniature horses, goats, sheep—and chickens that lay green eggs. Guests return often and readily make referrals. Minutes away, the historic town of Madison offers local museums, golf, antebellum homes, shopping and restaurants.

1051 Meadow Lane, Madison GA
(706) 342-7933 or (866) 253-0023
www.thefarmhouseinn.com

Attractions & Culture

Confederate soldier memorial featuring Jefferson Davis,
Robert E. Lee, and "Stonewall" Jackson at Stone Mountain Park
Photo by Peter Kaminski

State of Georgia

There is no better place to begin exploring the history and government of the State of Georgia than at the state capitol in Atlanta. The cornerstone for the Classical Renaissance building with the beautiful golden dome was laid in 1885. As many Georgia products as possible were used in constructing the building, including oak for the doors and marble for the interior finish of the walls, floors and steps. Gold for the dome was mined in Lumpkin County. The state senate and house of representatives conduct their legislative business in the assembly room. A museum on the fourth floor includes exhibits on Georgia political campaigns, Native American artifacts and state symbols. Georgia is the Peach State, so you already know the state fruit. However, what is the state flower? You'll know the answer by the time you leave the museum, and you will also know the state bird, fish, reptile and insect. The grounds of the state capitol invite visitors to stroll and learn. Memorials honoring veterans of war, a reproduction of the Liberty Bell and statues of famous Georgians are set throughout this beautifully landscaped area. What is the state song of Georgia? Of course, that is "Georgia on My Mind," made famous by Georgian-born recording artist Ray Charles. Find yourself whistling it by the time your visit to the Georgia capitol is complete.

100 State Capitol, Atlanta GA
(404) 651-7774
www.georgia.gov

The monument bears the inscriptions "COMRADES" and "TO OUR CONFEDERATE DEAD".

McDonough Hospitality & Tourism Bureau

Are you looking for a destination for a day trip outside Atlanta? The people of McDonough extend their hospitality to visitors who come for the beauty, history and thriving businesses of their downtown area. Located just 20 miles south of the metropolis, downtown McDonough is soon to be one of the largest historic districts on the National Register. Its restored buildings house many attractive restaurants, antiques shops and specialty stores. Beautiful landscaping worthy of McDonough's nickname of the Geranium City makes strolling the downtown streets a pleasure. Rich in history, the McDonough area was originally inhabited by the Creek Indian Nation. The city is located in Henry County, known as the Mother of Counties because of the many counties that formed from it. The town was named to honor Commodore Thomas McDonough, a naval hero of the War of 1812. It was the business, cultural and educational center of the area until the 1830s, when the railroad bypassed McDonough and established Marthasville, today known as Atlanta, as the commercial and social hub. After the War Between the States, the cotton industry brought a boom to McDonough. Today, as the county seat of one of the 15 fastest growing counties in the United States, McDonough looks forward to a vibrant future while respecting and preserving its past. To experience McDonough as a community, consider visiting for Music, Movies or Karaoke on the Square in the summer or for such annual events as the spring Geranium Festival.

5 Griffin Street, McDonough GA
(770) 898-3196
www.tourmcdonough.com

Marcus Jewish Community Center

Founded in 1910, the Marcus Jewish Community Center of Atlanta (MJCCA) is a non-profit organization committed to providing social, educational, cultural, and recreational opportunities that strengthen the quality of Jewish life in Atlanta. The center has more than 4 million varied interactions with the public each year. Programs include the Jewish Theater of the South, the largest theater of its kind in the region. House Mate Match is a nationally recognized housing program linking senior adult homeowners with compatible tenants. The Weinstein Center provides excellence in senior living. The MJCCA has delivered more than $4 million in humanitarian aid to the Cuban Jewish community since 2004, and it supports ongoing cultural events in Israel and Russia. The MJCCA supports some of the the largest youth sports leagues in North America. It provides the largest pre-school program in Atlanta, the Ethical Start program. More than 5,000 children between the ages of 3 and 16 attend 45 or more camps run each summer. The Florence Melton Adult Mini School, a two-year long course of Jewish study, is one of the the largest schools of its kind in the world. More than 15,000 people attend the annual Jewish Festival for music, children's programming, food, art and culture. The annual Jewish Book Festival is one of Atlanta's leading literary events. The MJCCA's kosher kitchen prepares 100,000-plus meals each year, including meals for the Meals on Wheels program and for preschool children. Rebekah Dickinson, public relations manager, invites you to take advantage of the services offered by the Marcus Jewish Community Center of Atlanta.

5342 Tilly Mill Road, Dunwoody GA (770) 396-3250 *www.atlantajcc.org*

Tellus: Northwest Georgia Science Museum

Tellus: Northwest Georgia Science Museum opens its doors in 2008. Its Fossil Gallery will transport you to the time of giant dinosaurs, where you'll meet a 40-foot replica of Tyrannosaurus Rex. A 120-seat digital planetarium will whisk you to distant galaxies. At the Transportation Gallery, you'll see the ingenious technology that engineers have used to develop automobiles, aircraft and space vehicles. The highly acclaimed Weinman Mineral Museum is moving its collection of 10,000 specimens to Tellus. Founded in 1983, the Weinman pays tribute to the rich mining history of Cartersville, showcasing the stories of the miners and beautiful gems and minerals plucked from the earth's interior. At Tellus, you'll experience physics and life sciences in My Big Backyard Gallery, a roomful of engaging hands-on and minds-on exhibits. Named after the Roman goddess of the Earth, Tellus fills a need for science education and exploration opportunities in metro Atlanta and other parts of northwest Georgia. Tellus will occupy a spectacular building with a soaring 65 foot apex clearly visible from I-75. Georgia Museums, the non-profit organization that runs Tellus, the Weinman and also Booth Western Art Museum, expects the 125,000-square-foot facility to attract at least 100,000 visitors in its first year alone. Get ready to explore the wonders of science at Tellus: Northwest Georgia Science Museum.

51 Mineral Museum Drive, Cartersville GA
(770) 387-3864
www.tellusmuseum.org

APEX Museum

Every month is Black History Month at the APEX, a museum that presents and interprets history from the African American viewpoint. APEX is an acronym for African American Panoramic Experience, a fitting name for a facility that puts the full range of human experience into perspective. Photographs, artifacts and multi-media presentations tell the African American story, from the tragedy of slavery and segregation to the victories of the Civil Rights movement and the joys of everyday life within a Black neighborhood. "My challenge, my passion, is creating an atmosphere that simulates an event from the past so that the visitor has a central experience of that time period," says Dan Moore, founder and president of APEX, which opened its doors in 1978. Exhibits invite visitors to step inside the Yates and Milton Drug Store, one of Atlanta's first Black-owned businesses. Take a seat on the vintage trolley car and watch a video about Auburn Avenue, the bustling business center of Atlanta's African American community. The museum's Hall of Achievement profiles African American musicians and artists who have placed their mark on the nation's culture. The museum also commemorates educators and businesspeople who have contributed to making the world a better place. Did you know that African Americans invented the golf tee, the hot comb and the riding saddle? An exhibit from 2006 honoring Black inventors proved so popular that it toured other cultural museums after it left APEX. Brush up on history by visiting the APEX Museum.

135 Auburn Avenue, Atlanta GA
(404) 523-2739
www.apexmuseum.org

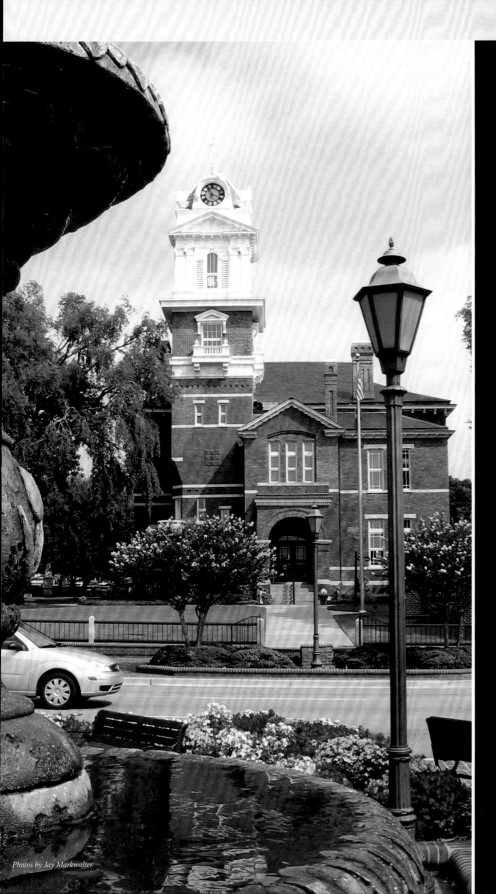

Photos by Jay Markwalter

Historic Downtown Lawrenceville

Come relax just north of Atlanta in Lawrenceville, where you will find enjoyable shopping, great dining, professional theater and one-of-a-kind events set in the history and heritage of Gwinnett's oldest city and county seat. The historic downtown square has 10 special dining establishments, including Italian, Mediterranean, classic American, good ole' home cookin', sandwich shops, coffee houses and a bakery. Music buffs can choose from several venues that provide entertainment during the week, from acoustic singer-songwriters to full live bands to karaoke. The centerpiece of downtown is the grand, historic 1885 Gwinnett County Courthouse housing the Gwinnett Historical Society, local art exhibits and the newly opened, must-see Veteran's War Museum. Events are held on the beautiful historic square and the courthouse lawn almost year-round, including many seasonal events for the family. In the spring expect Art on the Courthouse Square. Summertime brings the Moonlight & Music free concert series, Prelude to the 4th, Gwinnett Glows and the County Seat Day festival. Seasonal events include the Farmers' Market, Lighting of the Tree on Thanksgiving, the Lawrenceville Rings celebration on New Years Eve and year-round guided ghost tours. Not only the center of Gwinnett County government, downtown is also a hub of culture as the Aurora Theatre kicks off its 2007 season in the grand new home on the square. Gwinnett's only professional theater, the Aurora wins raves as North Atlanta's premier theater company year after year. Come to Historic Downtown Lawrenceville for an eventful experience.

162 E Crogan Street, Suite F, Lawrenceville GA (Tourism & Trade Association)
(678) 226-2639
www.visitlawrenceville.com

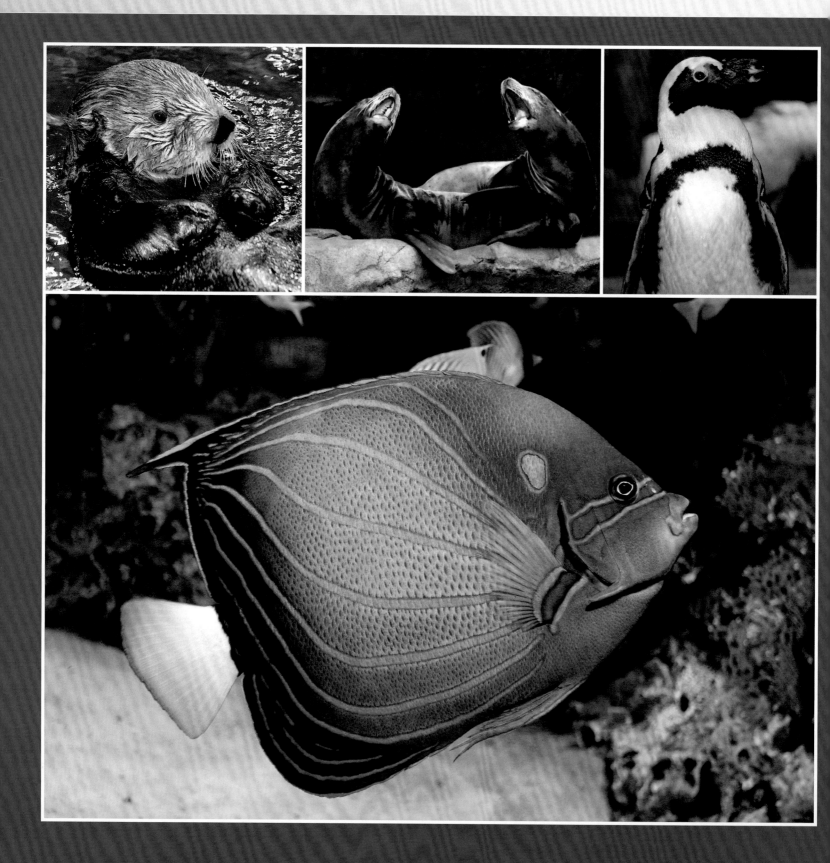

Georgia Aquarium

The Georgia Aquarium is the world's largest aquarium, with more aquatic life than any other and more than 8,000,000 gallons of water. The specifically designed whale shark habitat alone contains more than 6,000,000 gallons. The Georgia Aquarium is currently the only aquarium outside of Asia to house this gentle filter-feeding species, the largest fish in the sea. Other star attractions include gregarious beluga whales, who put a smile on the face of everyone who drops by their 800,000-gallon tank, Asian small-clawed otters and African penguins. Bonnethead sharks, one of the smallest species of hammerhead sharks, accept gentle touching. The touch pools allow guests to get hands-on with cownose rays, sea stars and scores of other animals as well. The Aquarium is composed of five distinct galleries that depict five habitats, from arctic to tropical. Consider taking in a spectacular underwater show at the 4D Theater a part of your trip to the Aquarium. The Aquarium's 4D Theater is one of the most advanced in the world. It combines digital projection with high-definition 3-D film. The food stations at Café Aquaria provide many dining options, while two gift shops offer aquarium apparel, collectibles and toys as well as books and art pieces appealing to undersea enthusiasts. For aquatic fun on a large scale, visit the Georgia Aquarium in downtown Atlanta.

225 Baker Street NW, Atlanta GA
(404) 581-4000
www.georgiaaquarium.org

Atlanta Botanical Garden

Atlanta has always attracted men and women of vision, so it is not surprising that the Atlanta Botanical Garden was established here. An oasis in the city, this botanical garden houses some impressive forms of life. The Fuqua Orchid Center, one of the world's largest orchid displays, uses new technology to simulate a cloud forest habitat. This enables rare mountaintop plants to flourish where they could not have survived before. The Dorothy Chapman Fuqua Conservatory is home to rare and endangered tropical and desert plants such as cycads and epiphytes, living stone lithops and insect-eating plants. The Center for Conservation and Education aids in identification and conservation of endangered Southeastern native plants. Twenty acres are given over to the Woodland Shade Garden and surrounding woodlands outdoor display gardens. Wander through the Japanese garden, the Parterre garden and a variety of other types of gardens. The Children's Healthcare of Atlanta Children's Garden is an interactive creation for younger children and the young-at-heart. The Garden hosts a gift shop, café and research library. Members receive benefits such as unlimited free admission for one year. This fabulous living museum provides exhibits and special events throughout the year and is available for your corporate and private events. Atlanta Botanical Garden offers the chance to observe rare sights in a dazzling, convenient setting. All areas are accessible to handicapped visitors.

1345 Piedmont Avenue, Atlanta GA
(404) 876-5859
www.atlantabotanicalgarden.org

Christian Clark and Kristine Necessary
Innoui Rossini
Photo by Charlie McCullers

Atlanta Ballet

Atlanta Ballet Dancers
S. Giocosa
Photo by Charlie McCullers

Atlanta Ballet, founded in 1929, is the nation's oldest continually performing ballet company and the State Ballet of Georgia. This famed troupe was founded as a regional dance company by a young dance teacher named Dorothy Alexander, who originally named it the Dorothy Alexander Concert Group. The local community embraced the group, and Atlanta went on to earn a reputation as the cultural center of the South. The name was later changed to the Atlanta Civic Ballet, with Dorothy as acting director. In 1946, the company became the first in the nation to help fund a symphony orchestra. In 1967, the ballet gained professional status, and in 1973, Governor Jimmy Carter named it the official ballet company of the state. Today, John McFall is the artistic director and CEO of this historically rich dance company, which continues to attract a wide audience by presenting performances that offer an intriguing mix of beloved classics and innovative new works. The Atlanta Ballet is home to the Atlanta Ballet Centre for Dance Education, which was founded in 1996 and is directed by Sharon Story. The center offers dance classes for students from the three-year-old through the pre-professional levels, along with special classes for beginning adults. Experience the poetry of motion and music at the historic Atlanta Ballet.

1400 W Peachtree Street NW, Atlanta GA
(404) 873-5811
www.atlantaballet.com

Jimmy Carter Library and Museum

The vast majority of Americans will never step foot inside the Oval Office, but anyone can gain a sense of what it feels like to be within that chamber of power by visiting the Jimmy Carter Library and Museum. The replica of the Oval Office at the museum is the most exact you'll find anywhere. Videos, photographs and personal items trace the early life and presidency of Carter, elected president in 1976. Researchers are encouraged to access the volumes of presidential materials, including files of Carter's White House staff, that are housed in the library. Members of the general public will find more than 15,000 square feet of exhibition space in the museum, much of it displaying material on the major events of Carter's presidency. The exhibit on the Camp David Summit, which produced a historic peace treaty between Egypt and Israel, is one of the most popular. From the Panama Canal treaties and the establishment of diplomatic relations with the People's Republic of China to the tense Iranian hostage crisis, the museum covers the full scope of Carter's four years. A highlight of the artwork on display is an oil painting by Mexican artist Octavo Ocampo, presented to Carter at a state dinner for Mexican president Jose Lopez Portillo in 1979. From a distance, it looks like a typical portrait of a head of state. On closer inspection, it reveals much symbolism, including 50 American flags that make up the face and neck. Spend some time reliving fascinating events of recent history at the Jimmy Carter Library and Museum.

441 Freedom Parkway, Atlanta GA (404) 865-7100
www.jimmycarterlibrary.org

Photo by Bill DeLoach

Georgia Shakespeare

"All the world's a stage," wrote William Shakespeare, who would never have guessed that his words would reverberate from a Georgia stage centuries later. Georgia Shakespeare, on the campus of Oglethorpe University in Atlanta, is a dynamic theater company. It started out with tent shows in 1986 and now offers a May-to-December season in the Conant Performing Arts Center. The company also gives roving educational performances for children of all ages. "We made a commitment early on to develop a company of artists from this region," said Producing Artistic Director Richard Garner. The vibrant company dispels the notion of Shakespeare as stodgy fare with a free season opener called *Shake at the Lake*, held at Piedmont Park. Evening shows at the company's main stage begin with an outdoor picnic outside the building. From there, patrons head into the beautiful 511-seat theater with its polished marble floors and Renaissance-meets-21st century style. The company specializes in works by the Bard but also presents the works of such contemporary playwrights as Arthur Miller and Tennessee Williams. Georgia Shakespeare is dedicated to expanding children's understanding of Shakespeare and provides many educational opportunities, ranging from play production residencies to workshops. The actors also visit schools throughout the state. If "the play's the thing" for you, be sure to visit Georgia Shakespeare.

4484 Peachtree Road NE, Atlanta GA (404) 264-0020
www.gashakespeare.org

Aurora Theatre

Big changes have come to the heart of Lawrenceville, including the arrival of the Aurora Theatre. The theater recently moved from Duluth to a beautifully renovated church on the square in historic downtown Lawrenceville, providing a center for the downtown revitalization project as well as to the city's artistic spirit. Two theaters, the flexible Discovery Point Theatre, with seating for up to 100, and the Strickland Family Theatre, featuring luxurious seating for 250, allow for a wide variety of programming. Aurora Theatre is Gwinnett's first choice for professional theatrical entertainment. As part of its expansion to the new space, the theater plans to expand its productions for children. The theater also plans an expansion of its Teatro del Sol program, a Spanish-language theater designed to preserve the cultural heritage of the area's growing Hispanic community. You can expect plenty of drama when you take part in the theater-sponsored Lawrenceville Ghost Tours. These 90-minute walking tours might even give you the opportunity to catch a ghost on camera. Experience Lawrenceville's historic downtown with a pleasant dinner followed by a play at the Aurora Theatre, where comedies, murder mysteries and musicals promise spirited entertainment.

128 Pike Street, Lawrenceville GA
(770) 476-7926 (tickets & information)
www.auroratheatre.com

Photo by NPS/Linda Byers

Martin Luther King, Jr. National Historic Site

Martin Luther King Jr. had a dream that someday, all Americans would be judged not "by the color of their skin but by the content of their character." Start your tour celebrating the life of the most famous leader of the Civil Rights movement at the National Park Visitor Center, located within the historic site and preservation district created in 1980 to honor this great man. Exhibits paint a picture of the discrimination and humiliation that African Americans endured in the segregated South, while commemorating the non-violent actions, such as the march from Selma to Montgomery in 1965, that King organized to protest the status quo. Located just east of downtown Atlanta, the historic site is anchored by three structures directly associated with King. Visitors are welcome to step inside the home where he was born, to sit in a pew of the Ebenezer Baptist Church where he preached and to pause and pray at his tomb. This hero becomes more human to you as you learn details of his life. For example, did you know that Monopoly was young Martin's favorite game? Your tour will also leave you with a profound sense of his courage and conviction. Many of the homes within the preservation district have been restored to capture their appearance in the 1930s, when King was growing up in the neighborhood. The Historic Fire Station No. 6, popular with visitors of all ages, is the oldest remaining fire station in Atlanta and holds the distinction of being the first integrated firehouse in the city. Visit the Martin Luther King, Jr. National Historic Site, and reflect on the life and times of a man whose dream of equality continues to inspire millions.

449 Auburn Avenue NE, Atlanta GA
(404) 331-6922
www.nps.gov/malu

Booth Western Art Museum

You can discover the West without leaving the South at the Booth Western Art Museum. Its galleries and changing exhibits immerse you in the myth, the landscape and real-life dramas of the American West as seen through the eyes of its finest artists. The works in the American West Gallery provide a visual feast of images from the era of six-shooters, the Pony Express and tepee villages, while the Cowboy Gallery focuses on one of the great heroic types in American history as depicted in paintings and sculptures. The Lone Ranger and Tonto gallop across the canvas of one painting in the Mythic West Gallery, which shows the influence of Western movie characters on the artistic imagination. The Reel West Gallery displays the classic posters used to advertise these movies. The museum also houses galleries devoted to Civil War art, plus presidents' portraits and memorabilia. The Sagebrush Ranch, a hands-on area for children, features art activities plus a life-size horse that young cowgirls and cowboys can sit on and a stagecoach where they can play. Dates worth marking on your calendar are the fourth weekend in October when the museum hosts the Annual Southeastern Cowboy Festival and Symposium and the second weekend in March when it hosts the Annual Southeastern Cowboy Gathering. Staff members at the Booth Western Art Museum invite you to drop by today to see art that makes it worth crossing the sagebrush plain.

501 Museum Drive, Cartersville GA
(770) 387-1300
www.boothmuseum.org

Cagle's Dairy

Urban children learn where food really comes from when they visit Cagle's Dairy, a working dairy and Georgia's sole remaining producer-processor of milk. Cagle's Dairy is also a major destination for southern Appalachia and has been cited by National Geographic. The dairy offers tours to schoolchildren and to private families and groups. School tours meet state curriculum guidelines. Family tours focus more on fun, but are still very educational. Visitors see how cattle are herded, how baby calves are fed and how cows are milked. Garden tours teach visitors how produce is grown and harvested. A special harvest tour takes place in autumn. Fall also brings one of Cagle's most popular attractions, the MAiZE. Ten acres of corn are carved into an intricate network of twists and turns, and staff members stay close to help visitors who become seriously lost. Maze-goers enjoy the fun from Labor Day to late November. When the season is over, the MAiZE is harvested for cattle feed. At Spring Farm Days in late April, the Appalachian Heritage Guild brings the past to life with demonstrations of butter churning, basket weaving and blacksmithing. Cagle's Dairy also hosts stock dog trials, where Border Collies compete at herding sheep and cattle. During the summer, Cagle's sponsors a weekly farmers' market. Mark and Kelly Cagle are third-generation owners of the farm and are assisted by their children. Don't wait 'til the cows come home to plan your visit to Cagle's Dairy.

362 Stringer Road, Canton GA
(770) 345-5591
www.caglesdairy.com

Tanglewood Farm

Nestled in the rolling hills of Cherokee County, just on the edge of Alpharetta, Tanglewood Farm in Canton is home to more than 100 friendly miniature farm animals and a colorful reproduction Wild West Town. Visitors can stroll through the 10-acre farm, petting and feeding its tiny inhabitants, which include miniature horses, donkeys and Jersey cows, plus miniature African pygmy and Nigerian dwarf goats. You'll find miniature pot-bellied pigs, Manx cats, Shetland and Babydoll sheep, chickens and even a miniature buffalo. In addition to up-close-and-personal encounters with the farm's sociable animal residents, visitors can enjoy hayrides and panning for gemstones all while exploring the town's 15 buildings, including a schoolhouse and livery stable. Tanglewood Farm is a favorite destination for families as well as school field trips. Each month the farm offers seasonal festivals celebrating everything from Pioneer Days to holidays, with special treats and activities for the children. Named one of Atlanta's best attractions by Turner South, Fodor's *Around Atlanta with Kids* and *Atlanta* magazine, Tanglewood Farm also offers birthday parties, corporate events and traveling barnyards. Step back into the 1800s with a visit to Tanglewood Farm's Wild West Town filled with friendly miniature animals.

171 Tanglewood Drive, Canton GA
(770) 667-MINI (6464)
www.tanglewoodfarmminis.com

Photo courtesy of Georgia Department of Natural Resources/Etowah Indian Mounds

Etowah Indian Mounds State Historic Site

Etowah Indian Mounds State Historic Site commemorates a spot where Native Americans arrived at the Etowah River more than 1,000 years ago. At this location, they built earthen mounds of cultural and religious significance. One of the last great cities of the Mississippian Culture flourished here. Today, archeologists are working to unlock the mystery of the mounds that these people left behind. The State of Georgia preserves this very important prehistoric site and invites visitors to ponder the purpose of these mounds as they stroll the grounds. Excavations reveal that Mound C was a burial mound, where nobility in elaborate costumes are accompanied by items they would need in the afterlife. But how did the people use the other six mounds? Did they hold ceremonies on them? Did high-ranking people live atop them? Some archeologists have characterized the largest mound as a temple mound, and remnants of a stairway to the top suggest possibilities. People must have walked up and down, from the base to the summit 63 feet above the city's plaza. How long did it take to build a mound of this size, with a top that covers about an acre? The mounds have been drawing curious visitors at least since 1540, when Hernando de Soto led his Spanish conquistadors through the area. Let your curiosity lead you to the remains of a great city at Etowah Indian Mounds State Historic Site.

813 Indian Mounds Road SW, Cartersville GA
(770) 387-3747
www.gastateparks.org

Photo by Stu Spivack

The Whistle Stop Café

In 2002, Elizabeth Bryant left a career as an electronics engineer to purchase the Juliette restaurant made famous by the movie *Fried Green Tomatoes*. Elizabeth was catering in her spare time when Robert Williams, who established the original Whistle Stop Café in 1991, decided to sell his restaurant's now-famous name. Thanks to the movie, people come from all over the world to eat at the Whistle Stop. Thanks to Elizabeth's cooking, they leave with fond memories of Southern classics such as fried green tomatoes, barbecue pulled pork and fried chicken. People purchase extra barbecue sauce to take home, and the Bryants are in the process of packaging their sauce as well as the breading for the tomatoes. Elizabeth uses family recipes, including Big Lee's Peach Cobbler and Theo's Butter Pound Cake. Her sweet root sticks—country-fried sweet potatoes dusted with cinnamon and sugar—are favorite treats. For those who know the movie, there's no mistaking the building, which retains its creaky screen door and the window with a bullet hole. You will find wooden booths, two wooden bars and movie memorabilia on the walls. Items from the building's days as a merchandise store remain, too. The café has been featured on the Food Network and in such magazines as *Southern Living* and *Southern Distinction*. The Bryants are working on plans for a franchise operation. Follow the sound of the train whistle to the Whistle Stop Café.

443 McCrackin Street, Juliette GA
(478) 992-8886
www.thewhistlestopcafe.com

Southern Museum of Civil War and Locomotive History

Share the adventures and hardships of Civil War soldiers and learn about the important role of the locomotive at the Southern Museum of Civil War and Locomotive History. Opened in 1972 by the city of Kennesaw, the museum offers three permanent collections as well as continually changing exhibits. Hear the story of how a band of Union spies stole the locomotive General while passengers disembarked for breakfast, and experience an exciting adventure as Confederate Conductor William Fuller chases them down. Discover the important role that railroads played during the Civil War, including their vital contributions to troop movement, hospital care and supplies. In the Glover Machine Works exhibit, see how the company produced locomotives. The Southern Museum offers visitors a glimpse inside a reproduction of the factory, complete with two restored Glover locomotives, an interactive explanation of the process of assembling a train and fascinating company records. As an affiliate of the Smithsonian Institution, the museum often receives the opportunity to incorporate some of the Smithsonian's world-class collections into its exhibits. During your visit, take part in an informational program, free with admission. Subjects range from the workings of steam engines to Victorian mourning practices. Visit the Southern Museum of Civil War and Locomotive History for a look at an important era in our country's history.

2829 Cherokee Street, Kennesaw GA
(770) 427-2117
www.southernmuseum.org

Hillside Orchard Farms Country Store & Farm

Preserving the farm's bounty through canning is a long-held tradition on the family farm. The Mitcham family has turned this tradition into a modern processing facility that serves customers throughout the country. Hillside Orchard Farms is also a place where families can buy food and gifts, have a picnic and listen to bluegrass music. Robert and Patsy Mitcham started a small jelly kitchen on their farm in 1985 and opened the farm's country store in 1999. Today, they produce 500 products, including sauces, juices, relishes, pickles, jams and jellies, under such well-known labels as Hillside Orchard Farms, the Mayhaw Tree and the Jelly Shop. They grow many of their ingredients on their 100-acre farm. Families drop by in the spring to pick blackberries, visit the farmyard animals or take part in an Easter egg hunt. They come back in the fall for pumpkins, apples and gourds as well as weekend demonstrations on making syrup from the farm's sorghum crop, an operation that employs a specially made copper pan. The farm makes cider in many flavors, from traditional apple to peach and raspberry. Children can play at mining or traipse through the corn maze. The hayloft of an old barn holds gift baskets and handcrafted items. Exhibits include a genuine moonshine still and a blacksmith shop. Popular pepper jellies and freshly made breads featuring apples, pecans and sweet potatoes warrant holiday visits. Groups often arrange for tours and hay rides. Pay tribute to tradition with a visit to Hillside Orchard Farms.

105 Mitcham Circle, Tiger GA
(706) 782-4995 or (866) 782-4995
www.hillsideorchard.com

Cynthia Collins, Claci Miller and Judy Fitzgerald
Sisters of Swing, the Story of the Andrew Sisters
Photo by C.Tedder

Steve Coulter and Mark Kincaid
Of Mice and Men
Photo by C.Tedder

Rachel Sorsa
Dress for Dinner
Photo by C.Tedder

Georgia Ensemble
Theatre & Conservatory

Renew your love affair with the stage at the Georgia Ensemble Theatre & Conservatory in historic Roswell. Founding directors Robert J. Farley and Anita Allen-Farley, a husband and wife team, are dedicated to providing quality professional theatrical productions, educational workshops and great fun for the entire family. Each year the Theatre produces five main-stage plays, ranging from hilarious comedies and American classics to toe-tapping musicals. They also host Theatre for Youth productions and a school tour. Established in 1992, the Georgia Ensemble Theatre serves as the official resident professional theater company for the Roswell Cultural Arts Center, which is home to a stunning 600-seat auditorium, a spacious lobby and several large meeting rooms, as well as a gallery that is ideal for classes. As the only professional theater in the GA-400 Corridor, Georgia Ensemble is conveniently located within easy walking distance of numerous Roswell historic landmarks, restaurants and shops. The theater is accessible and offers free parking, which means fighting city crowds in order to enjoy great theater is a thing of the past. The Conservatory wing plays host to a variety of activities throughout the year, including workshops for children and adults that teach the three basic elements of theater performance: acting, moving and vocal technique. Discover the magic of theater, from the comedies and tragedies that touch our hearts to the American classics and musicals that have shaped our theatrical heritage, at the Georgia Ensemble Theatre & Conservatory.

950 Forrest Street, Roswell GA
(770) 641-1260
www.get.org

Henry County Library System

You don't need to live in McDonough to use the town's Alexander Library. Travelers are always welcome to stay in touch with the world by using a computer or reading the newspapers. In fact, wherever you travel in Henry County, a library will be close by. Look for branches in Stockbridge, Locust Grove, Fairview and Hampton as well as in McDonough. Of course, to take full advantage of what these facilities have to offer, including checkout privileges for the system's 108,000 books, you do need to be a resident. If you have just moved to Henry County, you can get a library card at any branch. When choosing a book to take home, you are not limited to what you find on the shelves, because Henry Country libraries are part of the Public Information Network for Electronic Services (PINES), a lending network for 249 Georgia libraries. In addition to its checkout services, the Henry County Library System offers children literacy programs, GED preparation and English as a Second Language instruction. Storytelling for children and other activities with a focus on learning are scheduled throughout the year. Henry County's commitment to public library service dates back to 1900, when the Board of Education appropriated $50 to establish a public lending library. Mingle with other citizens of the world—visit a Henry County library today.

1001 Florence McGarrity Boulevard, McDonough GA
(770) 954-2806
www.henry.public.lib.ga.us

Prospect Park

When the new retail shops of Prospect Park in Alpharetta open in the spring of 2008, shoppers will be greeted by a panoply of international designer names, one-of-a-kind restaurants, top U.S. luxury brands, local specialty stores, class A+ office space and a groundbreaking theater complex. Surrounding the shopping, you'll find the Stanbury Hotel, a new world-class boutique hotel; the Stanbury Residences, ultra-luxe condominiums; and a beautiful 85-acre setting of parks and green spaces. The boutique hotel will contain just 156 guest suites, complete with fireplaces, disappearing plasma television screens and a décor scheme that calls to mind the best of the Old South. The residences consist of 82 spacious luxury condominiums where homeowners have access to all amenities and services of the hotel, such as a 60,000-square-foot spa, 24/7 maid service and an on-call chef. You'll be able to shop, stay and live at Prospect Park. You can work there as well, in the professional office space built above the retail shops or in the mid-rise offices that feature lush landscaping, convenience services and all the latest technology. This project, one of the country's newest and most exciting mixed-use developments, is the creation of Thomas Enterprises, a visionary real estate company. Alpharetta, a suburb of Atlanta, has an average household income almost double the U.S. average. Come to Prospect Park, where you'll find a new way of living.

Georgia 400 and Old Milton Parkway, Alpharetta GA (678) 423-5445 (media contact)
www.prospectparkonline.com

Air Atlanta Helicopters, Inc.

Today, more people in Atlanta are thinking of learning to fly a helicopter than two years ago. That's because of people like Blake Moore, who started Air Atlanta Helicopters, Inc. Blake's company provides helicopter tours, helicopter flight training and charter flights for couples, business clientele and celebrities. Air Atlanta Helicopters operates seven helicopters and one fixed wing aircraft, and it has a flawless safety record. Air Atlanta Helicopters' certified flight instructors are experts at clearly communicating complex aviation principles. Even those with no desire to become a pilot will get a kick out of looking down on Atlanta during a helicopter tour around the city. You can choose from a dozen sightseeing ventures and destinations as diverse as the City of Atlanta, Buckhead, Stone Mountain, the Chattahoochee River and Lake Lanier. Air Atlanta Helicopters also specializes in aerial photography and has flown for many television series and movie productions. All of the pilots are as personable as they are skilled, so if you need some help in orchestrating the right moment to pop the question to your girlfriend or to fly Santa to a special event, you've come to the right place. After Blake's first helicopter ride many years ago, he knew that he was meant to be a pilot. Blake is also on the board of directors of Angel Flight of Georgia, an organization that in 2006 provided 1,760 flights for children in urgent need of medical care. Let Air Atlanta Helicopters take you to the skies.

1951 Airport Road, Atlanta GA
(770) 458-7771
www.airatlantahelicopters.com

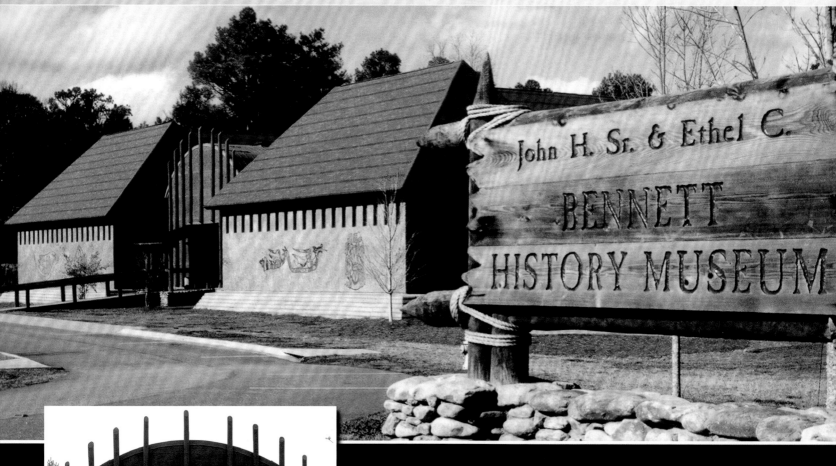

Funk Heritage Center

The Funk Heritage Center at Reinhardt College is Georgia's official Frontier and Southeastern Indian Interpretive Center. Enter the Bennett History Museum through the Childre Family Grand Lobby, a longhouse inspired by Native American architecture. Start your visit by watching a 15-minute award-winning video about the Southeastern Indians. The Hall of Ancients, which covers over 12,000 years of history, includes artifacts, interactive stations and displays depicting settlement life. The Rogers Contemporary Native American Art Gallery includes sculptures, paintings and beadwork in addition to woven baskets, jewelry and leatherwork. Still another collection, the Sellars Gallery of Historic Hand Tools, features thousands of different tools of the trade, some dating all the way back to the 17th century. Take a walk down the Northcutt Trail and enjoy the native plants. The Appalachian Settlement is a highlight of any visit here. Log cabins, 19th century farm buildings, plants, a pond and an activity area are all on hand. Executive Director Joseph Kitchens, Ph.D., keeps Georgia's Native American history alive with school programs, summer teacher workshops and school field trips to the center. The popular Suitcase Program brings museum staff to your school or community group to increase awareness of the Southeastern Indians and the Appalachian frontier history. Look back at Native American and frontier life in the Southeast with a visit to the Funk Heritage Center.

7300 Reinhardt College Circle, Waleska GA
(770) 720-5970
www.reinhardt.edu/funkheritage

Ashley Park

Take a trip south of Atlanta on Interstate 85. Before long, you're in the gently rolling terrain of Coweta County, where the pace is a little more relaxed and the living is decidedly more gracious. At Newnan, Exit 47, leave the highway. You're about to experience shopping, dining and entertainment the way you like it, with plenty of choices, in a center that's easy to navigate and pleasant on the eyes. It's Ashley Park, and as the name implies, the development is punctuated with green spaces and populated with some of your favorite things. You'll find Best Buy, Georgian Cinemas (with 14 screens, stadium seating and state-of-the-art sound system), Cold Stone Creamery and Honey Baked Ham. Gandolfo's New York Delicatessen is there for those who want to put a little North in their South. You can enjoy Dick's Sporting Goods, Cambridge Coffee and La Parilla. A brand new Dillard's, along with Barnes & Noble and Ulta, open in the fall of 2007. Ashley Park's developer is Newnan-based Thomas Enterprises, a visionary company that specializes in creating dynamic places where commerce, life and leisure intersect. Their projects include master-planned communities as well as retail, hotel, residential and office developments across the United States and in Europe. You'll want to return to Ashley Park again and again as more fabulous new shops and restaurants continue to open.

Newnan Crossing Bypass E, Newnan GA
(678) 423-5445
www.ashleyparkshopping.com

Fräbel
Glass Art Studio

For nearly 40 years, Hans Godo Fräbel has been the name people think of when they ponder superior glass artwork. Presidents, royalty and celebrities from around the world collect this master-craftsman's work, and Fräbel has often presented completed pieces to them personally. Now everyone can view the work of Fräbel and other master artists at the Fräbel Glass Art Studio in Atlanta. Fräbel, who originally lived in Jena and Mainz in Germany, founded the studio in 1967. He completed his training as a scientific glassblower at the legendary Jena Glaswerke and moved on to Georgia Tech where he began using molten glass to express his artistic vision. Later, he attained international recognition in the field of glass art when selected as the Absolut Vodka artist of the year, the first glass artist to be honored with the award. The Sculpture Gallery houses one of the planet's largest collections of fine flameworked sculpture. Traditionally, the gallery displays around 300 pieces at a time ranging from tiny, delicate flowers to major sculptures. The studio is also known for its stunning, custom designed state pieces such as a crystal palm tree presented to Queen Elizabeth II. Replicas of such pieces are displayed in a special section of the studio. Fräbel Studio shows visitors how the process works by allowing them to view the artists at their craft first-hand in the hot glass work and the annealing and mounting sections of the studio. Discover for yourself the whole new world that exists within each of these magnificent pieces—discover Fräbel Glass Art Studio.

**689-695 Antone Street NW,
Atlanta GA
(404) 351-9794 or (800) 843-1450**
www.frabel.com

Photo by Yasuko Rudisill

Photo by Charley Akers

Southern Tree Plantation

Some families visit Southern Tree Plantation every year to buy pumpkins in October or to cut their own Christmas trees starting on Thanksgiving. The McCombs grow about 30,000 Christmas trees and harvest about 5,000 pumpkins each year on their Blairsville farm. They also keep families amused with hayrides, pony rides and rides on a miniature train. A permanent wooden maze offers a safe way to get lost in the barnyard. Everybody enjoys getting to know the pot-bellied pig, two very sweet sheep, donkeys, turkeys, goats and the pet deer. The Holiday Barn houses a crafts shop and a refreshment stand. Each fall, Howard McCombs, the director of operations, gives his famous pumpkin talk to thousands of school kids. Howard's mother and father, Pat and Rodney, purchased the 60-acre property 33 years ago and ran cattle on it. In 1982, they planted their first Christmas trees. They remain part of the operation, along with their sons, Howard and Byron, and the son's families. In recent years, the McCombs have opened their property to church groups, school groups, company picnics and weddings year-round. The newly built Plantation Porch Pavilion can seat up to 250 people and includes a commercial kitchen that can handle everything from a barbecue to a formal dinner. Groups can roast marshmallows or play volleyball and horseshoes. An inflatable slide adds to the fun of the kids' play area. You can bring a picnic or cast your fishing line into a pond. The McCombs invite you to enjoy a day at Southern Tree Plantation.

2531 Owltown Road, Blairsville GA
(706) 745-0601
www.southerntreeplantation.com

Photos © Southern Tree Plantation, Inc

Teaching Museum North

For those who revel in history, Teaching Museum North is a special destination in Roswell's Historic District. Housed on the site of the original Academy, Roswell's first school, the museum has been in operation for 16 years. It features hands-on exhibits that display the history of the United States, Georgia and the city of Roswell. Political, social and historical themes educate visitors both about significant world events and Georgia history. An authentic log cabin and a turn-of-the-century courtroom provide dynamic lessons in the region's pioneer life and times. Exhibits on U. S. presidents and first ladies offer a fascinating glimpse into the lives of our nation's most illustrious families. A featured exhibit explores World War II, and a dramatic Holocaust remembrance offers insight into the war against an entire people. Admission is free, but reservations are required. Call ahead to confirm hours and admission. Curator Jacque Coxe, Museum Specialist Marge Nettuno and Building Specialist John Elam create programs of educational merit and invite folks of all ages to enjoy learning at Teaching Museum North.

791 Mimosa Boulevard, Roswell GA
(770) 552-6339
www.fultonschools.org/dept/teachingmuseumnorth

Agatha's—A Taste of Mystery

Love a mystery? Love to laugh? Love to eat? Then Agatha's—A Taste of Mystery is for you. Agatha's is a mystery dinner theater. The production is an original murder mystery comedy that takes place in the dining room during a five-course meal. What makes the evening particularly special is audience participation in the performance. When you arrive, you are given a new identity and assigned some brief lines or instructions. Two professional actors guide the show. By the very nature of the event, the professionals must improvise and help the amateurs. Participation is low-risk, and even shy guests will soon lose their inhibitions as they participate in solving the mystery and uncovering the villain. Agatha's begins a new show every 13 weeks. Caterina Angerami and Rick Warren, previously managers and now owners, continue a tradition of campy good humor that dates back to 1988. The excellent meal begins with buffet hors d'oeuvres, and the main course is served relatively late in the evening. Choose from among five entrées, including fish, chicken and beef. Wine is served with dinner, and a cash bar is also available. Agatha's growing popularity has forced a move to new premises, opened in the summer of 2006. For a high spirited night on the town, try Agatha's award-winning dinner and a murder.

161 Peachtree Center Avenue, Atlanta GA
(404) 584-2211
www.agathas.com

The 755 Club

The 755 Club has what it takes to make your next event a home run hit, whether it's a wedding or a corporate function. The club opened in 1996 at Turner Field, the home of the world-famous Atlanta Braves. Guests thrill to the panoramic view of the field and of the majestic Atlanta skyline. The 755 Club has five meeting spaces that total more than 24,000 square feet. Whether you're putting on an event for 75 people or 500, you'll find the space both luxurious and comfortable. Indeed, an event at the 755 Club provides you and your guests access to the entire Turner Field Stadium, including the Interactive Scouts Alley, the Braves Museum, and even tours of the Braves Clubhouse and dugout. Indoor wedding parties can enjoy the amenities of the club and the sense of history that permeates the Braves Museum. Baseball lovers will enjoy the many pictures of the Braves that line the walls, depicting the team's history. Head out to the terrace to enjoy the best view. The 755 Club, renowned for its steak and seafood, also offers an extensive catering menu. Whether you're looking for brunch with eggs, ham and filet of salmon, or sandwiches and other finger food, or an extensive dinner, you'll find it here. For a truly unusual experience, you can actually hold your wedding ceremony outdoors at home plate on Turner Field. Let the 755 Club help you make your next event a grand slam.

755 Hank Aaron Drive, Atlanta GA
(404) 614-2177
www.755club.com

Turner Field

Turner Field, the home of the Atlanta Braves, is one of the greatest baseball stadiums in the country, but it is also much more than that. With places to hold meetings and events of every variety, a first-rate museum and other chances for recreation and fun, this is one of Atlanta's prime entertainment and business resources. The stadium was first built for the opening and closing ceremonies and track and field events for the 1996 Olympics. Later, it was retrofitted to serve as the home of the Braves. The Ivan Allen Jr. Braves Museum & Hall of Fame covers the history of both the stadium and the team. The museum contains more than 600 Braves photos and artifacts that trace the team's history from its Boston beginnings to the current day. Want to see how the team operates? Take a tour of the stadium, including a visit to the Braves Clubhouse and dugout. Want to hold a memorable event? Check out the 30,000 square feet Lexus Level. This luxury facility can accommodate more than 3,000 guests or between 75 and 100 trade show booths. If you're holding a smaller gathering, the Braves Chophouse overlooks right field and offers indoor and outdoor space. The Top of the Chop is the newest addition, hosting up to 300 people and featuring a cabana bar. You and your guests can test your batting and pitching skills at Scouts Alley. These are just some of the attractions at Turner Field—and of course you can see the Braves. Visit Turner Field for great functions, great baseball and a great tradition.

755 Hank Aaron Drive, Atlanta GA
(404) 522-7630
www.braves.com

Mark of the Potter

Mark of the Potter started in 1969 in an old mill on the banks of the Soque River in the mountains of Northeast Georgia. Generations of visitors, young and old, continue to return each year to see what's new as well as to feed the enormous trout that congregate at the base of the shoals. Mark of the Potter has a staff of four potters and supports more than 25 regional potters as well. To compliment their work, there's a wide selection of metal, glass, jams and jellies, T-shirts and local books. Watching a potter work at the wheel remains a part of the Mark of the Potter experience. Many of the mugs, pitchers and vases produced here are coveted by the most discriminating collectors. Among the display shelves full of decorative and functional pieces, you are bound to find something that you will cherish for many years. The shop is open seven days a week, except Christmas Day. Experience the timeless art of pottery on a memorable excursion to Mark of the Potter.

9982 State Highway 197 N, Clarksville GA
(706) 947-3440
www.markofthepotter.com

City Market

An anchor attraction in historic downtown Savannah, City Market is a destination for dining, entertainment and delightful browsing. A commercial hub throughout its long history, City Market once referred to a single grand building, built in 1872, where merchants and farmers traded animals and vegetables. The site, known as Ellis Square, served as a public market even before the construction of that building. Today, City Market refers to a four-block area of restored warehouses adjacent to that original site. St. Julian Street, which runs through the heart of City Market, is closed to vehicular traffic, making the market a stroller's delight. Entertainment is featured at various times throughout the year, and outdoor courtyards provide the perfect venue for special events. The livestock and produce stalls of yesteryear have been replaced by an eclectic blend of restaurants and specialty shops. City Market boasts a vibrant art scene. Explore the many galleries and studios throughout the district and appreciate the diversity of arts and crafts on display. With working artists occupying nearly a third of the 65,000 square feet of retail space, City Market truly lives up to its billing as the Art and Soul of Savannah. On your trip to Savannah, put a stroll through City Market on your must-do list.

219 W Bryan Street, Savannah GA
(912) 232-4903
www.savannahcitymarket.com

Planter's Inn on Reynolds Square

While staying at the Planter's Inn on Reynolds Square, you will enjoy complimentary breakfast in the morning, wine and cheese in the afternoon and a date with history around the clock. In a city rich with history, the Planter's Inn site shines as truly special. Several hotels have stood on this spot since 1913, including one with a notorious reputation as an upscale brothel. Before that, two of the city's leading businessmen had homes here. However, the fascinating history of Trust Lot T goes all the way back to the Colonial era, when a parsonage for the Church of England in Georgia, today known as Christ Church, was constructed. In 1739, a young man arrived to succeed the church's first pastor, Samuel Quincy. The newcomer was John Wesley, the founder of Methodism. Within steps of Planter's Inn you will find two of Savannah's oldest houses, the Pink House, now a popular restaurant, and the Oliver Sturges House. The Planter's Inn, with its 60 large guest rooms, owes much of the spaciousness that its guests enjoy today to the 1982 renovation of what was then the John Wesley Hotel. Visit Planter's Inn, where you can explore the historic Reynolds Square neighborhood, and where the inn's staff attends to you with the warmth and hospitality that is the trademark of the South.

29 Abercorn Street, Savannah GA
(912) 232-5678
www.plantersinnsavannah.com

Blue Ridge Scenic Railway

If you haven't heard the words *all aboard* for a while, then you probably haven't taken a trip on the Blue Ridge Scenic Railway. Trains depart from the 100-year-old depot in Blue Ridge. The standard trip is a 26-mile, three and one-half hour excursion through mountainous terrain along the Taccoa River. The train makes one stop at the quaint sister towns of McCaysville and Copperhill on the Georgia-Tennessee state line, where passengers have ample time to grab a bite to eat, take a picnic to the river or shop for crafts and antiques. Along the way, rail hosts share the history of the line, which was laid in 1888. You can sit back and take in the scenery from vintage air-conditioned coaches or open-air cars, depending on the season. Locomotives from 1951 and 1961 power the train; coaches were built between 1924 and 1968. Snacks and souvenirs are available in the concession car. The popular railway began its excursions 10 years ago. Every season offers its own allure. Visitors interested in one of the seasonal specialty trips should make reservations well in advance, since such trips as the fall foliage excursion or the Santa Train sell out quickly. From May to October, adventurous travelers can book a combination train trip and rafting trip, guided by Rolling Thunder. New trips are added often, so check the website for all the excursions. Evoke old memories and make new ones on the Blue Ridge Scenic Railway.

241 Depot Street, Blue Ridge GA
(706) 632-9833 or (800) 934-1898
www.brscenic.com

Hillcrest Orchards

Farm life has a universal appeal. Just ask the families and schoolchildren who visit Hillcrest Orchards during the fall apple harvest. Hayward and Ellen Reece started with 15 acres in 1946, selling apples from a shed behind their house. Today, their daughter Janice Hale and her husband, Lynn, manage 80 acres that produce 22 apple varieties. For many families, a pilgrimage for fresh apples, mountain honey and crafts at Hillcrest's farm market is a yearly event. During festival weekends in September, farm-style entertainment includes wagon rides and the chance to pick your own fruit. You can watch corn grinding at the grist mill and visit the bakery for freshly made fried apple pies and apple cider doughnuts. Children adore the petting zoo, live pig races and contests in apple bobbing and corn shelling. The farm life builds an appetite, so Janice and Lynn prepare for their visitors with an outdoor food court featuring barbecue, burgers and hot dogs, plus apple ice cream and fudge. The Hales continue to add attractions, including the new pedal cart track and Moonshine Museum. Thousands of schoolchildren tour Hillcrest each year, gaining valuable insight into food production and hands-on experience in feeding farm animals or milking a cow. For a memorable day on a working farm, visit Hillcrest Orchards.

9696 Highway 52 E, Ellijay GA
(706) 273-3838
www.hillcrestorchards.net

Whiskey River Entertainment Complex

You would have to go to Atlanta to find a nightclub in Georgia larger than the one at Whiskey River Entertainment Complex in Macon. Owner Ernie Shepherd, who has been keeping the party going at Whiskey River since 1979, can be found on most nights mingling with his guests. "It's a lot of fun," says Ernie, who has kept Whiskey River popular by adapting to changes in the public's musical tastes. He remembers the Urban Cowboy period and the days when Top 40 was the rage. The current format at Whiskey River favors a mix of country, dance, Top 40 and Southern rock, delivered both live and by disc jockey. A few years ago, Ernie answered his customers' requests for more room by completely rebuilding Whiskey River. At its current 22,000 square feet, the nightclub is a grand location for pure party pleasure. In 2004, Ernie opened a comedy club next door. It stages the best regional acts as well as comedians seen on Comedy Central. A typical week at the comedy club might include one night of improv, another night of comedy with a political edge and another with a hypnotist. Go to Whiskey River Entertainment Complex, where bigger is definitely better.

4570 Pio Nono Avenue, Macon GA
(478) 785-3155

Old Clarkesville Mill

Old Clarkesville Mill is the newest travel destination in the Northeast Georgia mountains. This six-and-a-half acre former textile mill has been converted into a huge shopping, dining and entertainment center. The man behind Danny's Big Adventure, Danny Otter, is also the person who transformed the vacant 275,000-square-foot CMI Clarkesville Mill into the thriving antique, manufacturing, retail and recreation facility known as Old Clarkesville Mill. Most of the floor space is devoted to deals on furniture and home décor. The mill's Art and Antique Mall blends the Art-Full Barn's fine art, supplies and classes with antiques and collectibles. The Family Fun Center offers bowling, billiards and inflatable parties. You can grab a slice of pizza, sub sandwiches, coffee, fudge or ice cream at the snack bar. "The Family Fun Center has become a great place for social activity," Otter says, adding that wireless Internet will be available. "Currently in the works is the Grand Ballroom," Otter reports. The nearly 20,000-square-foot planned ballroom with 20-foot ceilings will compete with anything this side of Atlanta. "We will be able to comfortably seat 1,000 people." Other businesses located in Old Clarkesville Mill include Custom Signs and Shapes, Erin London, Hilton Head Vacation Services, Kent Studio and The Nutrition Shoppe. Additionally, a large section of the mill is devoted to climate-controlled mini-storage.

583 Grant Street, Clarkesville GA
www.oldclarkesvillemill.com

City Segway Tours Atlanta

Now there's a new and fun way to see the sights in Atlanta—with the trademarked Segway electric personal transportation device. Your knowledgeable City Segway Tours guide shares the history, current-day information and fascinating stories about the area as you zip along, up close, through the parks and sidewalks of Atlanta. The company offers two tours, each three hours long. The History of Atlanta tour takes you to all the major hotspots. Beginning in downtown Atlanta, with its spectacular shopping, dining, history and entertainment, you proceed to the Georgia State Capitol and then onward through the Sweet Auburn historic district, through Centennial Olympic Park, to the famed Georgia Aquarium and many more of Atlanta's top sights. The Ghosts and Legends evening tour takes you through downtown Atlanta's Fairle-Poplar district. You learn of legendary sinister characters, then continue on to Peachtree Street, where you'll hear spine-tingling tales of Atlanta hauntings and ghost sightings on the Georgia State University campus. Both tours are limited to groups of eight to ensure an intimate experience. Be sure to bring your camera. You can also arrange private tours for small groups and urban expeditions for larger groups. City Segway Tours Atlanta welcomes you to enjoy one or both of its superb tours. Oh, and the ride is a hoot.

50 Upper Alabama Street, Suite 256, Atlanta GA
(678) 482-9966
www.citysegwaytours.com

The Forum on Peachtree Parkway

The Forum on Peachtree Parkway is more than great shopping and dining—it has become a community gathering place. Its wide Main Street, punctuated with open green mini-parks and lush landscaping, invites shoppers and their families to stay awhile. The distinctive offices over the stores and restaurants house professional firms, making The Forum a town center for the northeastern Atlanta suburbs. The Forum boasts such retailers as Ann Taylor Loft, Banana Republic, Coldwater Creek, Old Navy, Talbots and Belk. You'll also find local specialty stores such as J. Harrington and fab'rik, a boutique with one-of-a-kind finds. Phase 2 of The Forum is now open and features Trader Joe's, a unique purveyor of fine foods, plus one of only two Merrell footwear and sportswear stores in the country. You have a fine choice of restaurants, with Ted's Montana Grill, Thai Spice, Jason's Deli and locally owned Grace 17-20. Do you seek books and music? Visit Barnes & Noble. Seeking a new look for your home? Drop by Designer Antiques, Pottery Barn or Bombay. For the children's rooms, check out Pottery Barn Kids. Gifts and accessories are easy to find at Brighton Collectibles, Swoozie's and Chickweed's. The developer of Forum on Peachtree Parkway is Georgia-based Thomas Enterprises, a visionary company that specializes in creating dynamic places where commerce, life and leisure intersect. Its projects include master-planned communities as well as retail, hotel, residential and office developments across the U.S. and in Europe.

5155 Peachtree Parkway, Norcross GA
(770) 368-8811
www.theforumshopping.com

Ted's Montana Grill

Ted's Montana Grill, a gathering place for family and friends, offers time-honored American favorites, hand-made with fresh ingredients. The founders of the grill are restaurateur George McKerrow, Jr. and Ted Turner, creator of Cable News Network and the Turner Broadcasting System. The grill provides a 21st century twist on the classic comfort foods you'll remember from family dinners or church suppers. At Ted's Montana Grill, authenticity is a way of life. The restaurant makes every menu item from scratch. All dishes are prepared to order. There are no pre-made salads, pre-packaged French fries or onion rings and no microwave. In fact, the only freezer on the premises is for the ice cream. Ted's proudly serves naturally raised bison, which is nutritious, lean, rich in iron and a healthy alternative to other meats. But, whether it's bison, beef, chicken or fish, at Ted's Montana Grill it's all 100 percent fresh all the time. That's the way they do it. Ted's Montana Grill has been featured on television and radio and in newspapers across the country, including the *New York Times*, the *Wall Street Journal* and the *Atlanta Journal Constitution*. Come see what the buzz is about.

5165 Peachtree Parkway, Suite 205, Norcross GA
(678) 405-0305
www.tedsmontanagrill.com

Grace 17-20

What is grace? A seemingly effortless beauty or charm of movement, form or proportion; an excellence or power granted by God; a short prayer of blessing or thanksgiving said before or after a meal; and now, a fine restaurant at The Forum on Peachtree Parkway. The innovative team at Grace 17-20 blends diverse backgrounds and philosophies into one common goal: to present a unique dining culture where casual elegance is expressed in everything from the creative, ingredient-driven menu to the comfortable, stylish atmosphere and gracious care in service. At Grace 17-20, striking private spaces provide a beautiful backdrop for inspired celebrations. The staff proudly offers two private dining options. The Tower Room accommodates up to 30 guests for a seated luncheon or dinner. For something more intimate, the Chef's Table, adjacent to the main dining room, seats 10. For private rooms, special menus and festive wines, come to Grace 17-20.

5155 Peachtree Parkway, Suite 320, Norcross GA
(678) 421-1720

Spa Sydell

Spa Sydell's goal is to improve the appearance, health, knowledge and state of mind of its clients. Co-chair Sydell Harris founded the company in 1982 at a single shop in Buckhead under the name of Sydell–Skin Care Salon. Today, reflecting the growth and direction of the industry, the business is known as Spa Sydell. Spa cognoscenti consider Harris to be one of the leading experts in the region. She has trained, either directly or indirectly, a majority of Atlanta's skin care technicians. During the past two decades, she has turned her original skin care spa concept into the most successful day spa in Atlanta. Spa Sydell is the pacesetter in the evolution of skin care in today's booming day spa concept. Services range from massages and the latest in body treatments to signature facials and manicures. With eight strategic locations, including The Forum on Peachtree Parkway, you'll have no trouble planning a rejuvenating visit to Spa Sydell.

5155 Peachtree Parkway, Suite 330, Norcross, GA
(404) 255-SPAS (7727)
www.spasydell.com

Brighton Collectibles

In 1991, the Brighton brand was launched with a single collection of belts. Over the years, Brighton has become an accessories company with something for everyone. Brighton added handbags to the line in 1993, followed by small leather goods, watches, footwear, fragrance, jewelry, home accessories and eyewear. The collection also includes men's belts, wallets, watches and other leather accessories. Brighton's line of accessories features products that coordinate from head to toe. You might choose a lipstick case that matches a wallet, earrings that match a pair of sunglasses, a handbag that matches footwear, or an entire coordinated collection of multiple accessories. Each piece in the Brighton collection is a unique, original design. The Brighton Collectibles shop at The Forum on Peachtree Parkway is one of only about 50 all-Brighton stores in the United States. Visit Brighton Collectibles, where you'll find Hearts In All The Right Places.

5145 Peachtree Parkway, Suite 448, Norcross GA
(770) 582-0696
www.brighton.com

Designer Antiques

Designer Antiques has been a family-owned business since 1977, and the mainstay of its business has always been antique English and Irish pine furniture. Designer Antiques also builds furniture to order. The firm developed its custom work to deliver high-quality furniture that would fit the specific needs of its clients. The firm takes great pride in providing its customers not only with one-of-a-kind furniture, but also a pleasant shopping experience. When you visit, you'll see a wide selection of custom and reproduction furniture in cherry, pine, walnut and mahogany. Of course, you'll also find a wide variety of English and Irish antique pine furniture and decorative accessories. The shop carries wonderful prints and needlepoint pillows by Atlanta artist Anne Hathaway. If you're thinking about upgrading your living room, dining room or bedroom furniture, make sure to stop by Designer Antiques at The Forum on Peachtree Parkway.

5145 Peachtree Parkway, Suite 457, Norcross GA
(770) 840-0027 or (866) 208-5633
www.designerantiques.com

The Grape

The Grape offers a non-intimidating and pleasurable atmosphere where customers can enjoy great wines and food at reasonable prices. The Grape presents 120 to 150 deliciously individual wines, which are available by the bottle, glass or The Grape's own special Grapes by the Bunch tasting flight. The Grape bases its presentation on its copyrighted Classification Guide, which classifies wines by the taste. The firm's motto is Your Taste Is All That Counts, and it practices what it preaches by bringing you superb wines from all over the world. Every patron has the right to taste any wine before purchase, either in the Retail Seller shop or the Wine Bar. Many of the wines are virtually exclusive to The Grape. In addition, The Grape serves a full menu of small-plate gourmet fare designed to complement the wine list. To fully appreciate The Grape, experience it in person at The Forum on Peachtree Parkway.

5145 Peachtree Parkway, Suite 470, Norcross GA
(770) 447-1605
www.yourgrape.com/aboutus/loc_forum.htm

Swoozie's

Swoozie's is a distinctive store that celebrates celebration. Swoozie's doesn't just define itself by its gifts, papers and printing services, but by its unending commitment to customer satisfaction. Its associates are all experts in the art of gift giving and enjoy helping customers find the right present for any occasion. The associates are experts on social paper as well. Swoozie's has one of the largest selections of designer invitations in the country, covering all occasions. To extend your options, it also offers lithography and thermography printing. With these services, Swoozie's can help you design great invitations for your wedding or other special occasion. In fact, custom bridal invitations are a specialty, and you can talk to a bridal expert any time the shop is open. Corporate celebrations are a specialty as well. Corporate customers consult Swoozie's for gifts and social paper throughout the year. During the holiday season, the shop is a major supplier of custom-printed corporate holiday cards. From the products on the shelves, through the music in the air, to the bows on the presents and most importantly to the staff in the black aprons, Swoozie's overlooks no detail. With a distinctive product mix and superior customer service, Swoozie's guarantees happiness on each and every visit. Stop by soon and you'll see why.

5131 Peachtree Parkway, Suite 1015, Norcross GA
(770) 441-9779
www.swoozies.com

Talbots

Talbots represents a tradition of excellence. Founded in 1947, Talbots was soon known as the store with the red door. That first shop is still located in a 17th century colonial frame house in Hingham, Massachusetts. The following year, the company launched its direct mail business by distributing 2,000 black-and-white fliers to names obtained from the *New Yorker*. Today, Talbots is a leading national specialty retailer. Its collection for women features modern classic styles in apparel, shoes and accessories. Talbots provides head-to-toe wardrobing for all occasions—from work, through the weekend, to special occasions. Its broad range of sizes includes misses, petites and women's petites. Talbots has a long-standing commitment to serving both its customers and the community. The Talbots Charitable Foundation supports the company's philanthropic objectives. A recent example is the Talbots Women's Scholarship Fund. The synergy between Talbots' customer and community service is best summarized by the company credo: Do What is Right for the Customer. Visit Talbots in The Forum on Peachtree Parkway, and let its attentive staff do what's right for you.

5151 Peachtree Parkway, Suite 725, Norcross GA
(770) 729-1430
www.talbots.com

Snip-Its

Getting your kid's hair cut shouldn't make you want to pull out yours. That's why Snip-its was created—to untangle the hair-care challenges of parents trying to find a stimulating and enjoyable hair-cutting solution for their kids. At Snip-its, the friendly and knowledgeable staff, animated gadgets, computer games and character-filled entertaining environment are all geared to make sure your child leaves with a great-looking haircut and, better yet, a great big smile. Many come to Snip-its for a fantastic kid's hair cut, a special-event hair style or an afternoon outing. Snip-its also offers spa treats and fun birthday parties. You might stop by to purchase items from the all-natural line of fruity hair-care shampoos, conditioners and style aids. Maybe you just want to browse the cute games and toys or watch the Animated Show. Whatever draws you in, Snip-its offers a safe, comfortable and entertaining setting that makes your visit Snip-tacular. You'll want to come back to Snip-its in The Forum on Peachtree Parkway again and again.

4880 Peachtree Corners Circle, Suite 1110, Norcross GA
(770) 246-0450
www.snipits.com

Limetree

No matter what the occasion, Limetree has the perfect gift. Limetree is Atlanta's hippest, most fabulous place to shop, a locally owned boutique offering a wide variety of gifts at every price point. Limetree distinguishes itself from other area gift stores by providing its carefully selected merchandise in a fun and comfortable atmosphere. Everything at Limetree is centered on creating the perfect gift experience, from the eye-popping displays, through friendly greeters at the front door, to the checkout process. The boutique is filled with stylish home décor, functional and whimsical items for the kitchen, casually chic tableware and pottery, novelties for the pampered pet, collegiate items, and luxurious bath and beauty products. If that weren't enough, there's Lil' Squeeze, where little limes shop for the best in children's apparel, accessories and gifts. You'll enjoy your visit to Limetree in The Forum on Peachtree Parkway.

5185 Peachtree Parkway, Suite 104, Norcross GA
(770) 622-LIME (5463)
www.limetreegifts.com

K-la Boutique

A favorite among Atlanta's fashion addicts, K-la Boutique is a one-stop shop for all of the latest fashion trends. Most of the clothing found at K-la is brought in from Los Angeles, thus offering customers unique styles found nowhere else in Atlanta. Here, customers will find a spectacular little dress that's perfect for every season, comfortable casual wear that begs to be worn day in and day out, and accessories with a one-of-a-kind attitude. In addition to the interesting mix of merchandise, K-la Boutique's success is driven by the store's laid-back, fun atmosphere and its knowledgeable sales team, which is always ready to help customers create distinct looks tailored to their individual styles.

5145 Peachtree Parkway, Suite 445, Norcross GA
(678) 205-5377

Courtyard Home

Ed Thompson and Dale Goforth are the geniuses behind one of The Forum on Peachtree Parkway's most artistically designed shops, Courtyard Home. Located next door to Mambo Italiano restaurant, you can't miss its overflowing window and courtyard décor. Venturing into this shop is like walking into a wonderland. Make sure you have a few hours of leisurely time to spend. There are surprises in every nook and cranny. The merchandise is refined, upscale, fun and affordable. The shop artistically showcases stellar brands such as the Cucina line of fragrances for the kitchen, Vera Bradley bags and accessories, and Casafina and Vietri dinnerware. Baskets filled with whimsical and pretty trinkets will delight you. Look carefully to the back of the shop and you'll notice a fabulous array of fresh flowers. You can pick up a bouquet for a special occasion or order custom arrangements for the most formal affair. Spice up your life with a visit to Courtyard Home, formerly Courtyard Flowers & Gifts.

5165 Peachtree Parkway, Suite 215, Norcross GA
(770) 446-7389

Bakeries, Treats, Coffee & Tea

Photo by *Vicki Hunt*

Mittie's Tea Room Café

At Mittie's Tea Room Café, you can take time for tea, the most healthful beverage on the planet. The shop was owned by Lynn Brooks until recently, when the ownership was transferred to family members. It is now owned by Dr. Kate Brooks, a naturopathic physician who loves the concept of Mittie's, and Khalil and Aura Brooks, both lawyers, who are excited about continuing the good work that Lynn began. Mittie's is dedicated to healthful dining and makes most menu items from scratch, using organic products whenever possible. Dairy products are from cows raised without antibiotics and hormones. Mittie's also cooks only with healthful oils, such as olive oil. The shop uses natural cleaning products that are safe and nontoxic. At the same time, Mittie's has received numerous awards for the tastiness of its cuisine, including a 1998 Atlanta tourism award and acclamations by the annual Taste of Atlanta and by *Bon Appétit* magazine. Many customers consider Lynn's chicken salad to be the best they have ever eaten. Wraps, salads and quiches are best-selling items. Mittie's recently celebrated 20 years in Roswell and has moved into a historic stone cottage. Plans are in the works for formal gardens, patio dining and evening openings featuring boutique wines and delicious foods. Mittie's caters and hosts birthday parties and other after-hours events. For adult par-teas, Mittie's can serve luncheon or high tea. The popular Teddy Bear Par-tea, where children bring their favorite stuffed friends, is a favorite birthday party for children ages four to eight. Mittie's is named after Mitti Bullock, a local resident and mother of President Theodore Roosevelt. Come to Mittie's Tea Room for good-tasting, healthful food in a dramatic atmosphere.

25 Plum Street, Roswell GA
(770) 594-8822
www.mitties.com

Southern Sweets Bakery

Southern Sweets Bakery is where Nancy Cole loves to bake. After landing an account of 40 pies a week baking out of her own home, her business was born from word of mouth and the kinds of referrals that only come when you have a very tasty product to offer. At Southern Sweets Bakery, Nancy's many awards hang on the walls alongside her expansive personal collection of art. The cozy café showcases Cole's award-winning pecan tart. Some of her newest taste sensations are the caramel cake and a coconut layer cake with boiled custard. In addition to the famed baked goods, Southern Sweets offers delicious soups, fresh salads, tempting sandwiches and wraps. Vegan desserts are also available whole or by the slice, as are all of the other desserts. This is a fully family-operated business. Daughter Ashley Nelson is the wedding cake creator. She achieves the kind of dreamy confections every bride looks forward to on her special day. Nancy's son David is the front house manager, and son-in-law Matt Nelson is the technical coordinator. The bakery is actually five businesses in one. It is a wholesale bakery, retail bakery, café, corporate lunch caterer and wedding cake creator/designer. With all of this talent, you know where to go when you are looking for the best. Take a journey to Southern Sweets Bakery for your own special treat.

186 Rio Circle, Suite A, Decatur GA
(404) 373-8752
www.southernsweets.com

Juices Wild

Citizens of Atlanta concerned about their health value Juices Wild, the city's only organic juice bar and an unusually fastidious one at that. Unlike most national juice bar chains, Juices Wild uses only fresh organic fruit and vegetables in its juices and smoothies—no sugar syrups or prepackaged purées. The juice bar uses triple-filtered water to rinse the produce and to make ice for the smoothies. The wheat grass is locally grown. Owners Dan and Michele Honorè have designed the menu with a nutritionist's expertise, classifying their blends and boosters according to whether you want to detox, energize, heal or relax your body. The cheery bar, with its orange countertop and red barstools, opens through an archway into an adjoining vitamin and supplement shop. Dan says he enjoys providing a gathering place for local health nuts, who can order custom blends of juices and supplements with the same cheerfulness with which coffee house junkies pursue their favorite brew. Dan takes pride in "opening up a whole new world of health for people, as there weren't any natural foods stores in the area." He and Michele will energetically explain to visitors the necessities of detoxification and the benefits of green superfoods, which advocates say can help prevent cancer and disease. Whether health foods are a new world or your world, come see what Juices Wild has in store for you.

4450 Nelson Brogdon Boulevard, Suite C-6, Sugar Hill GA
(678) 714-7747
www.juiceswild.net

Magnolia Bakery Café

The Webb family enjoys serving their community and takes pride in a business that features baked goods made fresh daily. Magnolia Bakery Café started in 1994. Today, owners Mike and Vickie Webb, along with son Chris and family friends Marylin and Michael, operate three Magnolia Bakery locations in Gwinnett County—in Norcross, Duluth and Suwanee. All locations open up each morning with hot, fresh cinnamon rolls and sticky buns. Loaf breads and baguettes are ready by about 9 am. You can order pastry and fruit trays the day before for delivery to your breakfast meeting. Many locals plan on eating breakfast or lunch at this popular restaurant. The butter croissants and other pastries make any breakfast selection extra special, while hot or cold sandwiches feature the bakery's fresh bread or bagels. A small, freshly made cookie accompanies your sandwich. Look for baked potatoes, salads and soups plus popular specialty coffee drinks. The bakery, set amid magnolia décor, is a gathering place for businesspeople, families, men's and women's groups and Bible study groups. The food and the atmosphere, which lends itself to conversation, are an irresistible combination. Mike and Vickie donate their leftovers to charity and offer 10 percent discounts to schools and churches. For a café experience that combines baked goods with a warm welcome, visit Magnolia Bakery Café.

5175 S Old Peachtree Road, Norcross GA
(770) 449-1861
3545 Peachtree Industrial Boulevard, Duluth GA
(770) 622-3887
1160 Old Peachtree Road, Duluth GA
(678) 584-1030
www.magnoliabakerycafe.com

Northern Star Coffeehouse

At Northern Star Coffeehouse, owner Bill Luebben has found a way to combine his four great passions: coffee, community, art and music. Located in the historic village of Norcross, 18 miles northeast of Atlanta, the Northern Star invites patrons into a warm atmosphere with glossy hardwood floors, red brick walls adorned with art and comfortable leather chairs. The menu offers numerous espresso and specialty drinks. Consider the chocolate raspberry latte, a dreamy Mint to Be or a cool Caramel Frosty Star. In addition to coffee, the Northern Star serves tea drinks, hot chocolate and soft drinks. Walk up a few stairs to the counter, and you will be enticed by a glass display of freshly prepared pastries and desserts. A popular monthly wine tasting event presents samples from an extensive wine list, featuring fine wines from many countries. The coffee sold at the Northern Star is organic and fair trade, so the growers get paid a fair wage. Bill opened the Northern Star to make a positive impact on the community; his efforts include hosting a community service project one Saturday each month. The Northern Star offers live music by local musicians every Friday night, an open mike every Tuesday night and a monthly singles night. On Saturday nights, movie lovers sit on the spacious outdoor patio to watch classic films projected onto a big screen. Drop by Northern Star Coffeehouse for a relaxing visit, or check out the calendar of events posted on the Northern Star Coffeehouse website.

45 S Peachtree Street, Norcross GA
(770) 840-8071
www.northernstarcoffeehouse.com

Miss Scarlet's Chocolat Emporium

Everything at Miss Scarlet's Chocolat Emporium, from the guilty pleasure of the decadent desserts to the soothing effects of chamomile tea, is designed to make you feel good. Suzie Hubbell, head chef, chocolatier and owner of Miss Scarlet's, does many jobs here and does them all well. Inside her historic home, Suzie offers patrons healthful lunch options such as homemade tomato basil soup with fresh bread or strawberry and walnut salad tossed with raspberry vinaigrette. To accompany your meal, Miss Scarlet's serves 24 varieties of hot tea, seven flavors of coffee and seven flavors of hot chocolate, with tempting names like Chocolat Candy Cane and Raspberry Truffle. These sweet beverages hint at the sweet things to come, including a four-layer fudge cake and other sinfully delicious desserts, sure to satisfy any sweet tooth. If you just cannot decide between the caramel turtle brownie and the French silk pie, try the dessert tray, with several desserts for sampling. Miss Scarlet's is an ideal spot to hold a birthday party, baby shower or other special gathering. Children and adults alike love the Victorian-themed tea parties. Suzie also prepares custom-made desserts for your special occasions, which she designs with an artist's eye, a baker's heart and a mother's love. Come to Miss Scarlet's Chocolat Emporium in historic downtown Acworth for a lovely meal and heavenly desserts.

4480 Park Street, Acworth GA
(678) 574-6449
www.missscarlets.com

Teacup Cottage

With a coffeehouse on every corner, you might forget about that more varied and subtly addictive beverage of the ages—tea. In Acworth, the love affair with this leafy delight is in full bloom, thanks to Kim Cerny. Her Teacup Cottage is a quaint tea room and a popular destination for tea enthusiasts from the Atlanta area and beyond. Kim, a former pediatric nurse, hit upon the idea of a tea room while traveling with her husband in 1996. Her newfound dream became reality in 2002, after she extensively remodeled an old cinema to create the tea room. Open Tuesday through Saturday, Teacup Cottage is an ideal place to slip away for an afternoon with friends while enjoying the country French ambience along with exceptional cuisine and welcoming Southern hospitality. This charming hideaway is also the perfect place to host a variety of day and evening special events, including bridal and baby showers, reunions, birthdays, meetings and rehearsal dinners. Teacup Cottage offers more than 40 loose-leaf teas together with a traditional menu of tempting treats and culinary masterpieces. The house specialty is the Hen's Nest, a delicious made-from-scratch chunky chicken salad topped with toasted almonds and served on a bed of Chinese noodles. It comes with frozen fruit salad, the famous pumpkin bread and homemade cheese crackers. Other popular favorites include the Shop Hound Cheese Bake, savory gourmet sandwiches and fresh soups du jour. They also offer a divine assortment of desserts that are sure to please. All teas can be purchased in their gift shop, which is brimming with teapots, cups and saucers, tea accoutrements, linens, tea stationary, books on tea and much more. Tea trays are available Thursday through Saturday with 48-hour advance notice. Indulge in your craving for life's finer things with an afternoon at Teacup Cottage.

4851 N Main Street, Acworth GA
(678) 574-6011
www.teacupcottage.com

Café Intermezzo

Café Intermezzo, the European Coffeehouse, provides an authentic step back into 19th century Europe, when the kaffeehaus was the place for pondering, for planning one's day and life while enjoying the culinary pleasures of the Hapsburg cities of Vienna, Prague and Budapest. Following this rich tradition, Café Intermezzo proudly presents more than 100 different and scrumptious tortes, tarts, cakes, cheesecakes and pies. You can also browse the restaurant's Beverage Book to select any of the scores of coffees, teas and other non-alcoholic beverages, or the hundreds of beverages which contain alcohol. An international *Speisekarte* (menu) lists a universe of lunch, brunch, dinner and late-night culinary offerings. Owner Brian Olson's love of German and Austrian coffeehouses, and his former work importing espresso coffee machines from Europe, sparked the idea for Café Intermezzo. Former partner Renate Stender's experiences growing-up in Hamburg, Germany helped nurture the concept. They opened the first Café Intermezzo in the Atlanta suburb of Dunwoody in 1979. An historic old building on Peachtree Road just north of Midtown eventually became the second location, opening in 1987. Known by locals as a wonderful place to escape into world of another time, the cafés have become a destination for quiet reflection, or for a rendezvous. Enjoy your next cappuccino seated on the serene Terrace Patio or amidst Old World charm at linen-covered tables in the café, bar or loggia. You are invited with a hearty Hapsburg welcome to enjoy the European kaffeehaus tradition at Café Intermezzo.

4505 Ashford-Dunwoody Road, Atlanta GA
(770) 396-1344
1845 Peachtree Road, Atlanta GA
(404) 355-0411

Café Campesino

In Americus, business is not just business and coffee is not just coffee. The city that gave rise to Habitat for Humanity International is leading the way again with Café Campesino, a Fair Trade coffee business that operates by the Golden Rule, not the rule of gold. Founder and co-owner Bill Harris got to thinking about coffee while building houses with Habitat for Humanity in Guatemala. There he learned the importance of coffee to peasant farmers and how international traders keep prices low. Furthermore, pressure to increase production led to the clearing of native trees and erosion. The Fair Trade revolution counteracts these trends with guidelines that ensure fair prices and support sustainable farming practices. Café Campesino—meaning small farm coffee—goes one step further by cutting out middle men and importing coffee directly from growers. Bill's brother and partner Lee, an accomplished chef, roasts the gourmet-quality, certified organic coffee in small batches on the premises. Their long-time friend and third partner, Tripp Pomeroy, then ships the coffee by the pound to wholesale and retail buyers across the nation. Walk-in visitors can tour the roastery and sample blends from Mexico, Guatemala, Nicaragua, Colombia, Peru, Bolivia, Ethiopia, Sumatra and Timor-Leste. You'll also find teas, gifts and books. Stop by Café Campesino for coffee you can feel good about buying as well as drinking.

725 Spring Street, Americus GA
(229) 924-2468
www.cafecampesino.com

Perk Place Coffee Shop

Perk Place Coffee Shop is a fixture of the charming small town of Hapeville. Chartered in 1891, Hapeville's location made it a favorite getaway and attracted a variety of businesses. Ford Motor Company came to town and Coca-Cola magnate Asa Candler built a racetrack, which is now the airport. The only access to the airport from Atlanta was Highway 19/41 through Hapeville, right past a building known as Victory Cab Company, now Perk Place Coffee Shop. In the 1960s the interstate highway system cut Hapeville off from its financial lifeline, and Hapeville was virtually forgotten. For over 40 years the town languished, but by 2000, things had begun to turn around. Ironically, today the old Victory Cab Company now serves coffee to many of the cabbies and limo drivers who work out of the nearby airport. Perk Place serves sandwiches and goodies to visitors and locals who love the small-town, family-owned charm that comes with every order. If you are ever in the Atlanta area, treat yourself to a day of participating in the wonderful

metamorphosis of Hapeville. The town also has bookstores, eclectic shops, great dining and a lovely historic bed and breakfast. Perk Place Coffee Shop is located three miles north of Hartsfield-Jackson International Airport off Interstate 85, exit 75. Y'all come!

673 N Central Avenue, Hapeville GA
(404) 768-5678
www.perkplacecoffee.com
www.hapeville.org

Antique Sweets

When Antique Sweets opened on Madison's downtown square in 2004, it was a good fit. After all, the square is historic and the store offers old-style candies made on the premises. Antique Sweets, which serves up molded chocolates, peanut brittle and divinity, is located in a late 19th century building that retains its original doors, windows and hardwood floors. When you enter, proprietor Patrick Alligood's first question is: "Would you like to try a sample of fudge?" His second question is: "What kind?" The Bulldog Bites, a version of the turtle, may be the most

popular sweet at the store. Few can resist the Georgia pecans smothered in caramel and chocolate. Fine, fresh ingredients characterize each offering. Truffles are made with a bittersweet shell of Guittard chocolate and filled with a *ganache* flavored with liqueurs such as amaretto, Kahlua, Frangelico, Bailey's Irish Cream and peach schnapps. Holidays feature specialty items that include Christmas suckers shaped like old-fashioned Santas and for Valentines Day, a solid chocolate heart box. Patrick and his mother, Patty, are co-owners. At the shop you might also meet Mike, Patrick's father, because the entire family takes a hand in creating and serving the shop's tempting selections. The Alligoods invite you to experience happiness with a visit to Antique Sweets.

132 E Washington Street, Madison GA
(706) 342-0034

The Serene Bean

The Serene Bean provides a place for the community to come together to enjoy great coffee, tasty foods and live entertainment. Owners Lara and Bill Randall opened the shop in 2004 in Woodstock's newly revitalized historic district, with an eye toward creating a place where people feel comfortable enough to grab coffee and a muffin and stay a while. The spacious 3,000-square-foot shop offers plenty of seating, from traditional tables and chairs to couches for lounging. The room at the side of the coffeehouse serves as a multi-purpose gathering area, used for scrapbooking get-togethers and business meetings. Healthful lunch options include the Mediterranean wrap, with hummus, roasted red peppers and feta, and the chicken salad sandwich, served on a butter croissant. The Serene Bean uses hormone-free chicken and meats free of MSG. Try a fresh fruit and green tea smoothie with your meal or one of the specialty espresso drinks to kick-start your day. Come by on Friday and Saturday nights to enjoy live music. Patrons are clearly enamored with the coffeehouse's warm ambience, great food and friendly service. The Serene Bean has been voted Best Coffee Shop for three years by *Around Woodstock* magazine. Come to The Serene Bean, a neighborhood café where everyone feels like a friend.

105 E Main Street, Suite 100, Woodstock GA
(770) 924-8433
www.theserenebean.com

Pappy's Fudge & Gifts

Pappy's Fudge & Gifts offers fudge in more than 30 flavors as well as an extensive selection of reasonably priced quality gifts. This divinely rich fudge, made with real cream and butter, comes in seasonal and specialty flavors, such as pumpkin pie, chocolate cheesecake and Creamsicle. You will even find a sugar-free version. Co-owner Rhonda Melton worked for Pappy's from the day it opened in 1995 in Pappy's Plaza, a rustic cluster of little shops built alongside the Nottely River five miles south of Blairsville. When the shop became available, Rhonda and her mother, Barbara Horne, eagerly purchased the cabin-style structure and opened up walls to expand the space from 1,200 to 1,600 square feet. Their expansion allowed them to add five listening centers where customers can listen to all types of music, from bluegrass to opera, before making purchases. Besides offering music that customers may not find elsewhere, Pappy's offers Minnetonka moccasins, Henschel hats for men and an entire line of themed socks. An array of colorful handmade quilts, Heritage lace and home décor items will appeal to those looking for a thoughtful gift. Souvenir seekers will discover an abundance of printed T-shirts and other Georgia mementos. Rhonda and Barbara delight in turning strangers into friends, so stop by Pappy's Fudge & Gifts for freshly made fudge, a profusion of gifts and a warm Southern welcome.

2763 Pappy's Plaza, Blairsville GA
(706) 781-6565

Douceur de France

Mention of France conjures up images of cozy couples at curbside cafés, Paris in the fall and, of course, luxurious pastries and tasty breads, such as the ones you will find at Douceur de France. Owner and chef Luc Beaudet and his wife, Danielle, opened this charming patisserie in 2000 and have since established Douceur de France as one of the area's most highly regarded culinary destinations. Chef Beaudet first learned his trade at his mother's side in the Poitou region of France. He formalized his training in the art of pastry making with a degree in culinary arts. Later, he enrolled in the famed Les Compagnons du Devoir du Tour de France, an organization whose members tour Europe to learn the pastry techniques of each region. After completing his seven-year tour, Beaudet spent two years in Japan and then five years as a pastry chef in Dallas, Texas. Douceur de France began as a wholesale business, but by 2004, Beaudet's delectable pastries and sweets were so popular that the couple transformed the company from a small pastry shop to an upscale French bakery and café. Today, they offer a full breakfast and lunch menu, featuring a wide range of traditional, homemade dishes, as well as their signature pastry and dessert line. For a taste of France, visit Douceur de France, where the cuisine is made from quality ingredients, and the pastries are made in the French tradition.

367 Glover Street, Marietta GA
(770) 425-5050
www.douceurdefrance.com

The Crimson Moon Café

At The Crimson Moon Café, the creative spirit shines and inspiration abounds. The specialty organic coffee promotes conversation, and the custom omelettes, pizzas, eclectic sandwiches and delicious entrées bring smiles. Owner Dana Marie LaChance has designed a gathering place that celebrates Southern cuisine with a menu six pages long. The café has also become one of the South's most intimate music venues, hosting some of the nation's finest performing artists and songwriters of all genres. The Crimson Moon Café is located in the circa 1858 Parker-Nix Storehouse, the second-oldest building on Dahlonega Square, which is listed on the National Register of Historic Places. LaChance purchased the historic building following a successful career in the outfitting industry. In 2001, she opened The Crimson Moon Café as a gallery of eclectic art by local artisans. The gallery soon evolved into a café with build-a-bagel sandwiches, homemade soups and salads, and live music on the weekends. LaChance, a songwriter and poet herself, now blends all her entrepreneurial and creative talents into a purpose-filled music venue that draws people from all over. If you enjoy a smoke-free atmosphere that supports creativity, with gourmet food, great coffee and select alcoholic beverages, then make The Crimson Moon Café your place to go in Dahlonega.

24 N Park Street, Dahlonega GA
(706) 864-3982
www.thecrimsonmoon.com

Hofer's of Helen

Hofer's of Helen is a café, bakery and a *Konditorei*, which in Germany is a bakery that specializes in fine cakes and pastries. The café serves full breakfasts and lunches, along with German coffee, beer and wine. The award-winning bakery has been recognized for its excellence in products and service by trade publications and magazines such as *Southern Living* and *Atlanta Magazine*. Locals and travelers alike crave its baked goods such as the Black Forest cake, apple strudel, Linzer tortes and more than a dozen varieties of Old World German breads. Hofer's combines Old World quality with modern European bakery equipment. The breads are baked in a stone hearth oven, giving them the nice thick crust usually only found in Germany. Hofer's is often visited by celebrities and sports figures, so you never know who you might sit next to. Hofer's has built a reputation for wedding cakes that have been featured in many national magazines and were recently part of the Food Network show, "The Secret Life of Wedding Cakes." The café's furnishings and decorations are German imports. It displays a 30-foot mural depicting the history of bread baking, created by German artist Josef Mahler. While at Hofer's, be sure to check out the Gift Vault, an authentic bank vault filled with imported gifts. Hofer's Bakery was founded by Gerda and Horst Hofer, a nationally renowned master *Konditor* and baker. The Hofer family came to the United States from Schwabach, Germany in the late 1950s. Today, Hofer's is owned and operated by their son Ralph. Visit Hofer's of Helen for coffee, confections, conversation and a memorable experience you will be talking about for years.

8758 N Main Street, Helen GA
(706) 878-8200
www.hofers.com

Cecilia Villaveces Cakes

Cecilia Villaveces began baking cakes out of her home in 1990. Since then, her business has expanded many times over while earning lavish praise from the local press. "Cecilia Villaveces Cakes are works of art," said *Athens* in 1997. The *Athens Daily Tidings* praised the "succulent moistness" of her cakes, while *Southern Living* called Cecilia "one of the most talented and inventive bakers in the South." One look at her menu, and your taste buds will perk up. Whether it's the caramel cake with hard caramel icing or the Fruit Basket with alternating layers of custard and fruit mixed with whipped cream, you've never seen selection like this. Many of Cecilia's layered, creamy recipes hearken back to her Latin roots, such as the Tres Leche cake soaked in three kinds of milk and the classic Tiramisu. Cecilia is also inventive, however. Consider the Chocolate Baileys cake with a Baileys Irish Cream custard filling, or the Hummingbird, a banana, pineapple and pecan cake topped with pecan cream cheese. Cecilia uses only the freshest ingredients for that inimitable homemade taste. Now managed by Cecilia's son, Enrique, Cecilia Villaveces Cakes is in high demand for weddings. Visit the website to view the impressive gallery of wedding cakes decorated with flowers and fruit and groom cakes in such custom shapes as a briefcase, lighthouse or a pair of boots. Bring your sweet tooth along and enjoy the exceptional creations at Cecilia Villaveces Cakes.

610 N Milledge Avenue, Athens GA
(706) 543-3308
www.ceciliacakes.com

Feddeaux

Pauline Feddo always had a passion for wine and food. In 2004, she left a corporate career to open Feddeaux, a combination bakery and wine shop. Feddeaux's retail location at the Shops at Hamilton Mill is half carry-out bakery and half fine wine shop. Customers return regularly to sample the vast array of pastries, including fruit-and-cream cheese croissants, toffee pecan swirls, key lime cheesecake bar cookies and custom cakes. Pauline formally introduces her wines every Friday night through themed wine tastings at Feddeaux. She makes tasting notes and offers delicious appetizers to pair with the wines. Feddeaux also makes custom gift baskets that pair wines with gourmet foods and treats. One of the most significant additions Pauline has made to her business is her partnership with Cecilia Villaveces Cakes. Pauline has found that beautiful, delicious wedding cakes are in high demand in the Southeast. Together, Feddeaux and Cecilia deliver over 450 wedding cakes a year. Customers can also enjoy cake by the slice at Feddeaux, which features two different choices every week from Cecilia's dazzlingly inventive menu. For food, wine and sweets that will make your mouth water, visit Feddeaux.

3521 Braselton Highway, Dacula GA
(770) 904-2212
www.feddeaux.com

Baron York Tea Room Café & Gift Shop

The Baron York Tea Room Café & Gift Shop is truly an elegant escape. This tea room answers a prayer for owner Dea Irby. Her customers feel blessed, too, once they have sampled a bottomless pot of tea and scones with house-made lemon curd and mock Devonshire cream or tried the daily soup and sandwich. The house special is Dea's own chilled Baron York Tea, made with 10 fruit juices. If you can correctly guess all the fruits in the tea, you win a free bottle of it to take home. Popular lunch entrées include the Frango Surprise, a Brazilian chicken pastry, and the Balkan Sendvic, a flatbread roll-up with a Macedonian paté. Dea offers a large assortment of loose teas and graces her popular tea parties with a cake shaped like a teapot. Dea long wanted to open a tea room, and she knew what it needed to offer. The chances that something would meet all her requirements seemed unlikely until Jerry and Monika Schulte bought the historic Baron York building and remodeled the upstairs to expose original heart pine floors. In 2003, Dea and her husband, Tom, opened the Baron York in this space. Because everything was done right, Dea's guests enjoy an interlude out of another era. The Schultes even found the exact music and sound system that Dea had admired in another shop. Be sure to sign Dea's guest book when you stop by the Baron York Tea Room Café & Gift Shop.

1444 Washington Street, Clarkesville GA
(706) 754-3044
www.baronyorkcafe.com

CCBerries

At an early age, rather than face Christmas without cookies when his mother went on a diet, Skip Manley, owner of CCBerries, grabbed the recipe cards and learned how to make his favorite treats. Soon he was churning out enough cookies to satisfy his sweet tooth and those of his friends. Years later, he made chocolate-covered strawberries to take to a volleyball tournament (sort of as a joke since the players are pretty dirty after a day of play). The crowd went wild and his friends asked him to bring them every weekend. Taking these responses as a good sign, he decided in 2002 to take a shot at going professional and opened a candy store specializing in long-stemmed chocolate covered strawberries. Skip's repertoire still includes these strawberries. He also bathes cherries and raspberries in white, dark and milk chocolate. His truffles come in dozens of flavors, and his assorted fudge is made with real butter. Skip's strawberry creations can be personalized with holiday messages, slogans and corporate logos using a unique overlay process. If you can't make it to Marietta, visit to the store's website. There you can choose from hundreds of gift boxes and tins. Since no chemical preservatives are used, all berry orders are shipped overnight. Chocolate addicts can get satisfaction at CCBerries every day except Sunday. Just make sure you leave room for dinner.

2200 Roswell Road, Suite 130, Marietta GA
(770) 509-0280
www.ccberries.com

Vintage Tea

Civility reigns at Vintage Tea, where guests participate in the time-honored ritual of afternoon tea, served in floral-patterned cups of fine china. The selection of more than 80 teas probably exceeds what the Queen keeps in her pantry at Buckingham Palace. A variety of tea sandwiches and other dainty treats arrive at your table beautifully presented on a three-tiered tray. "My grandmother Ella Mae Day's poppy seed cake recipe has been passed down in my family, and is a very important part of my tea room," says owner Brenda Lain. Vintage Tea was created as an environment where families can flourish and friendships can be made. Guests can choose to have tea in the Victorian Parlor or Magnolia Room. The décor feels as though you are in an old home complete with wood floors, chandeliers, a fireplace and period furniture. "We want people to feel as though they have stepped back in time," says Brenda. She invites guests to select from a collection of antique hats and stoles to adorn themselves while taking tea. *I Do for Brides* magazine recommends Vintage Tea as the place for your bridal shower. "If a truly traditional and elegant setting is what you are envisioning for your party, then this Alpharetta tearoom could not be more perfect," it notes. Spend an afternoon at Vintage Tea, enjoying one of the true pleasures of civilization.

3005 Old Alabama Road, Alpharetta GA (770) 752-8422 *www.vintagetea.com*

Fashion & Accessories

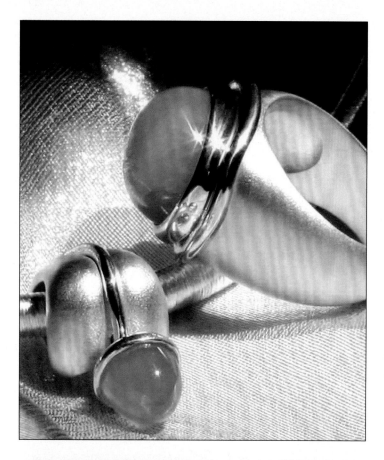

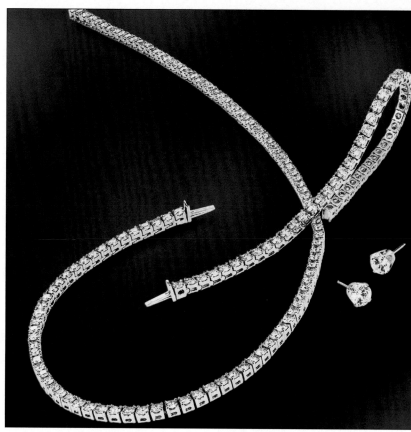

JWR Jewelers

With three decades in the jewelry business and a Graduate Gemologist diploma from the Gemological Institute of America, John W. Reed knows jewelry. What his customers have learned is that he is committed to people, too. He and his wife, Patti, have owned and operated JWR Jewelers since 1993. They have developed long-term relationships with customers, and folks around Athens know that whether you've come with a question or to make a purchase, the Reeds and their staff are happy to see you. Their display cases are loaded with gold and silver jewelry from respected companies. The exquisite unset diamonds and colored gemstones raise the possibility of custom jewelry designs. Once you've experienced the services and products at JWR Jewelers, you'll never need another jewelry store. As a full-service shop, JWR offers jewelry repair, engravings and appraisals. Fine watches, clocks and jewelry boxes from JWR Jewelers will be treasured for a lifetime. The Reeds belong to the American Gem Society and the Independent Jewelers Organization (IJO). Their highly trained staff includes Tony Cruz, an JA certified professional jeweler, and C. Paul Henriques of Jamaica, who became a master jeweler in Germany and brings 40 years of experience to the store. For a jeweler with a commitment to excellence, come to JWR Jewelers.

196 Alps Road, Athens GA
(706) 543-9800
www.jwrjewelers.com

Topaz Gallery

Topaz Gallery features the work of independent jewelry artists from Atlanta and across the nation. Owner Peter J. Embarrato is proud to carry the work of more than 100 highly talented jewelry designers. Their one-of-a-kind, handcrafted pieces feature colored gemstones such as rubies, emeralds and sapphires. Many pieces use high-karat gold and platinum; others rely on silver. Fine jewelry aficionados who are searching for masterfully crafted, highly distinctive pieces to add to their collections will be dazzled by the vibrant and majestic jewelry at this diverse gallery. Styles range from traditional to contemporary. Some of the jewelry is fascinatingly elaborate, while other items are sparse and bold. Peter says that the name Topaz means "Be joyful and spontaneous and know that you are a spark of God." The spirit of this statement animates the gallery. In addition to the wonderful gemstone creations, the gallery offers expert jewelry repair, restringing and custom design. It also provides ear piercing using pain-free and sanitary Inverness products. The shop has pierced the ears of everyone from infants to grandmothers. Topaz Gallery stays open until 9 pm every third Thursday of the month for a casual gathering of artists and jewelry lovers. Jewelry, especially unique and non-traditional jewelry, needs to be held, touched and admired. You can get a close look at marvelous gemstone creations when you visit Topaz Gallery.

3145 Peachtree Road NE, Atlanta GA
(404) 995-0155
www.topazgallery.net

The Treasure Chest

The best stores welcome visitors to a world of wonder, and offer not only the opportunity to shop but the possibility of delight and education as well. With its collection of 25,000 rare and exotic gems, the Treasure Chest in Savannah is one such store. Owner and President Mike Lepper is certain that he carries the largest selection of colored gemstones and gemstone jewelry in the entire Southeast. Dazzling examples of amethyst, emeralds and smoky topaz are just a few of the beautiful stones on view at the store. You will also find Fabergé eggs, crystals for metaphysical healing and 350-million-year-old fossils that have been fashioned into distinctive jewelry. Besides providing a showcase for these exquisite items, the Treasure Chest is also a full-service jewelry shop, offering remounting, jewelry designing and repairs. Often one of the shop's experts will fix your watch or necklace before you even have time to admire all the displays. Mike Lepper has been gem-struck since the age of 10, when he began his career at a clock shop and jewelry store. His fascination with the earth's beautiful riches has led him to travel the world, buying gems at the mining or cutting source in Thailand, Israel, Brazil and beyond. The Treasure Chest houses the headquarters of Saravana Gems International, direct importers of diamonds and colored gemstones, with offices on four continents. For jewelry shopping, repairs and delightful browsing, visit the Treasure Chest.

32 Barnard Street, Savannah GA
(912) 238-0664
www.treasurechestsavannah.com

Divas and Dames Boutique

Ladies, get ready to get your glam on with a visit to Divas and Dames Boutique, where owners Shana and Jay Gould offer up a dazzling array of creative clothing and accessories that are, after the shop's motto, a little bit funky, a little bit trendy, but oh so chic. This spectacular shopper's paradise features a diverse collection of fashions, in sizes from zero to three extra large. Divas and Dames carries a choice selection of designer goods by such companies as Seven Jeans, Kenzie Shoes and Spanx Hoisery. Look for Brighton accessories, along with fun, fabulous jewelry, shoes and girly doodads that will delight divas of all ages. Shana adds stunning pieces created by local artisans, who craft original artwork and apparel that fits in beautifully with the shop's glamorous inventory. Let your little diva celebrate her next birthday or class party in style at Super Diva's, Shana's latest enterprise, located just upstairs from the boutique. The super friendly and welcoming staff at this charming enterprise magically transforms your darling and her pals into princesses, movie stars or models for a day, complete with gowns, accessories and makeover, as well as a photo shoot and a glamourous gift bag. Parents may bring refreshments, but don't be surprised if your special ladies are having too much fun to stop for cake. Add pizzazz to your day, your home and your wardrobe at Divas and Dames Boutique, where indulging your inner diva is always in style.

4809 S Main Street, Acworth GA
(678) 574-4777
www.acworth.net/divas.htm

Whidby Jewelers

The Whidby family has been providing quality jewelry to the public at fair prices since 1901. Ben and Heather Whidby seek to provide their loyal clientele with only the best products and customer service. This couple, the third generation to own and operate this self-described mom and pop jewelry shop, consider Whidby Jewelers to be more than a livelihood. Helping lovebirds pick out engagement rings, wedding rings, then anniversary gifts, then watching their children grow up and come in for jewelry of their own—this is its own reward, they say. In the shop's friendly and warmly decorated environment, you can find everything a jewelry enthusiast's heart might desire. Shoppers can celebrate every occasion with something from this store, from diamonds, watches and pendants to crystal, fine china, baby gifts and custom-designed pieces. The Whidbys also carry a variety of designer lines. They can keep a copy of your wish list or wedding registry at the store for you. They also offer in-house repairs, engraving and appraisals. In short, they can take care of all your jewelry needs. Visit Whidby Jewelers to see why this family-run shop has built such a loyal following in the community.

177 W Jefferson Street, Madison GA
(706) 752-0105
www.whidbyjewelers.com

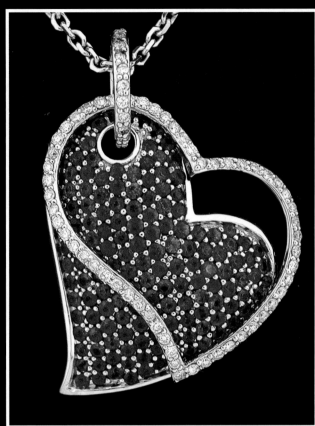

Redfern Jewelers

Thao Gibson's native Thailand plays an important role in her jewelry designs, which have been delighting St. Simons Island customers since Redfern Jewelers opened in 1987. Thao's creations dance with color and light, thanks to her use of brilliant gemstones, including rubies and sapphires mined in Thailand. Thao's homeland is the gem capital of the world, and Thao grew up fascinated by gems like those her older sister sold in her own shop. She studied to become an accredited gemologist, but first worked as an interpreter at the U.S. Embassy in Bangkok, where she met her husband, John, an American immigration officer. Thao's interest turned back to gems when the couple returned to the states. Their twin daughters, Lucy and Kim, were infants when Thao opened the shop. Today, the girls help in the shop, and like her mother, Kim is now a graduate gemologist and jewelry designer herself. John works as the goldsmith for the shop and specializes in laser welding. Redfern Jewelers also offers pearl re-stringing, engraving and appraisals. Thao buys gems for her jewelry in Thailand and has the jewelry custom-made there while she visits with her family. "I am fortunate to work in a business where we deal with happy people," says Thao, who especially enjoys helping customers pick out gifts to surprise their loved ones. Make your loved one happy or simply celebrate the beauty of gems with a visit to Redfern Jewelers.

209 Redfern Village, St. Simons Island GA
(912) 638-5314
www.redfernjewelers.com

Zïa Boutique

From the exotic and contemporary to the classically understated, Zïa has it all. You'll find home interior accents, exclusive accessories and a wide variety of fine sterling silver and gold jewelry by 48 designers. Each designer featured within the plush walls of Zïa Boutique hails from a far-away place, such as Brazil, Thailand, the Netherlands or Mexico. Zïa, the hip 26-year-old owner, strives to provide one-of-a-kind pieces his customers can't find anywhere else, which is why he searches the world over for undiscovered talent. His stellar taste matches that of celebrities such as Cameron Diaz, Jessica Alba, Kirsten Dunst and Eva Longoria. All have been spotted wearing pieces by Anika Inez, a designer also featured at Zïa Boutique. For a handbag that will make your outfit, a standout gem or accent piece for your home, Zïa Boutique is sure to have the latest to suit your stylish lifestyle.

325 W Broughton Street, Savannah GA
(912) 233-3237
www.ziaboutique.com

Photo by Fernando Weberich

BleuBelle Boutique

With designer clothing from BleuBelle Boutique, you won't have to worry about seeing your dress on somebody else. BlueBelle carries just a few of any style and can even track your upcoming occasion to ensure your gown will be unique. Whether you are looking for denim or a cocktail gown, owner Heather Burge and her yorkie-poo Chloe will give you the undivided attention you deserve. (She may be just a pup, but Chloe is BleuBelle's general manager.) Along with such designer lines as Trina Turk, Ella Moss and Susana Monaco comes a gracious Southern hospitality that puts customers at ease. *Savannah Magazine* named BleuBelle Boutique as Best Women's Store in two consecutive years. It's been featured in many magazines, including *Town & Country* and *Deep*. Heather and Chloe recently opened a new bridal salon down the street from the boutique in Savannah's downtown historic district. Heather believes that a wedding gown exists to complement every bride and carries gowns by designers who use intricate detail and yummy silks and satins, including Vera Wang, Reem Acra and Carolina Herrera. Expect strapless silk taffeta, French tulle, Chantilly lace and embroidery. You can stop by the bridal shop, on the third floor above Paris Market, but an appointment will let BlueBelle provide the best service. For singular fashions, visit BleuBelle Boutique and BleuBelle Bridal.

205 W Broughton Street, Savannah GA (912) 443-0011 *www.bleubelle.com*
30 W Broughton Street (3rd floor), Savannah GA (912) 341-0012 *www.bleubellebridal.com*

Upscale Fashions Consignment Boutique

Upscale Fashions Consignment Boutique has been delighting Stockbridge with women's designer fashion clothing and jewelry since it opened in 1997. Owner Anita Johnson, who operates the store along with daughter Nicole and sister Ulrike Hunsicker, prides herself on bringing 20 years of retail experience and a European sense of high fashion to her shop. Upscale Fashions carries designer clothes from such labels as Liz Claiborne, Anne Klein and Ann Taylor in sizes ranging from 2 to 24. You'll find everything from lightly used evening, cruise and prom wear to casual clothing and career apparel at prices that are a fraction of what you'd pay at other stores. The jewelry and handbags at Upscale Fashions are delightful accompaniments to the ensembles sold here. The store puts on periodic fashion shows, so patrons can keep abreast of the latest trends. Anita has recently added a selection of smaller furniture, including lamps and home décor, to the store. Customers appreciate the casual elegance of the shop. If you are looking to clear space in your closet, bring your designer label clothes to Upscale Fashions, where they'll be expertly displayed to receive the best price. Consignors receive 50 percent of the selling price. Whether you're buying or selling, you can count on expert, friendly service from Anita and her knowledgeable staff. Before you pay full price for designer clothing, take a look at the quality at Upscale Fashions Consignment Boutique.

5029 N Henry Boulevard, Stockbridge GA
(770) 506-0101
www.upscalefashionsinc.net

Photo © 2006 Gary Gruby

Gogo

As a child growing up on Cumberland Island, Janet Ferguson earned the nickname "Gogo" for her ceaseless energy, which she spent scouring the landscape. It was the inspiration and love of Cumberland Island passed down by her grandmother that sparked her desire to design from nature. This hobby would become the basis for her life's work, which now appears at her shop Gogo on St. Simons Island, at her studio on Cumberland Island and internationally. At the St. Simons shop, Gogo's work is set against faux gold walls with royal blue trim and a Moroccan influence. Using the treasures she finds in nature, her creations are cast in 14 karat gold and sterling silver then combined with semi-precious stones. Gogo designed wedding rings for John F. Kennedy, Jr. and Carolyn Bessette; her customers include world leaders and Hollywood celebrities. When she is not designing, Gogo enjoys traveling the world and studying the diverse uses of nature. Celebrate art and nature with jewelry by Gogo.

600 Sea Island Road, Suite 9A, St. Simons Island GA
(912) 634-8875
www.gogojewelry.com

Galleries
& Fine Art

Fräbel Studio

For nearly 40 years, Hans Godo Fräbel has been the name people think of when they ponder superior glass artwork. Presidents, royalty and celebrities from around the world collect this master-craftsman's work, and Fräbel has often presented completed pieces to them personally. Now everyone can view the work of Fräbel and other master artists at the Fräbel Glass Art Studio in Atlanta. Fräbel, who originally lived in Jena and Mainz in Germany, founded the studio in 1967. He completed his training as a scientific glassblower at the legendary Jena Glaswerke and moved on to Georgia Tech where he began using molten glass to express his artistic vision. Later, he attained international recognition in the field of glass art when selected as the Absolut Vodka artist of the year, the first glass artist to be honored with the award. The Sculpture Gallery houses one of the planet's largest collections of fine flameworked sculpture. Traditionally, the gallery displays around 300 pieces at a time ranging from tiny, delicate flowers to major sculptures. The studio is also known for its stunning, custom-designed state pieces such as a crystal palm tree presented to Queen Elizabeth II. Replicas of such pieces are displayed in a special section of the studio. Fräbel Studio shows visitors how the process works by allowing them to view the artists at their craft first-hand in the hot glass work and the annealing and mounting sections of the studio. Discover for yourself the whole new world that exists within each of these magnificent pieces—discover Fräbel Glass Art Studio.
689-695 Antone Street NW, Atlanta GA
(404) 351-9794 or (800) 843-1450
www.frabel.com

Photo by Yasuko Rudisill

Photo by Charley Akers

Vinings Gallery

The spacious walls of Vinings Gallery frame a bright array of lively art from nationally recognized and emerging artists. More than 30 of the world's most sought-after artists contribute to the 3,000-square-foot space that also includes a new studio for custom framing. Owners Gary Handler and Denard Stalling present their colorful palette of artwork in both public and private showings. Their dedication to clients and artists, a relaxed, accessible style, and vast knowledge of art, design and composition combine to create a gallery that exudes warmth and vibrancy. Extraordinary service and attention to detail ensure satisfaction at every level. Denard himself is a nationally recognized painter whose pieces are sought after by collectors. Visitors can usually find him at the easel by the front window or designing one of his handcrafted frames in the back studio. Gary is an expert at choreographing the gallery to display just the right mix of works and artists. Together Denard and Gary broke ground on their new enterprise in 1999, working diligently to build a very personal, full-service gallery. The partners, along with Gary's mom Micky Handler, cordially invite you to discover Vinings Gallery, a one-of-a-kind art destination for collectors and artists alike.

4686 S Atlanta Road, Smyrna GA
(404) 794-7762
www.viningsgallery.com

G-Art Europe

If you are passionate about glass art, then you must make G-Art Europe in the upscale Phipps Plaza a required stop on your Atlanta itinerary. You'll meet General Manager John Archuleta, who loves glass art as much as you do and who will show you around the gallery of exquisitely blown pieces. G-Art Europe is the only gallery in the United States dedicated exclusively to showing European glass signed by the artists. It does not purchase its items in bulk from a distributor but deals strictly with individual artists. Many of these relationships date back as far as 20 years, when G-Art Europe dealt in antique glass. As its representatives traveled throughout Europe on collecting excursions, they met many contemporary artists whose work inspired a change in the company's focus. G-Art Europe works as closely with its regular clients as it does with its artists, meaning that matching artist with buyer is more than a matter of serendipity. Once John and his assistants at G-Art Europe know what you are looking for, they will go out of their way to help you find it, and they will gladly ship your purchase to your home. To behold beautiful art glass for the serious collector, go to G-Art Europe.

3500 Peachtree Road NE, Atlanta GA
(404) 812-0478

Main Street Gallery

In 1985, Jeanne Kronsnoble and an artist friend opened a studio in Clayton where they could create and display their artwork. Jeanne's interest in local folk art soon became a passion, and she began traveling the back roads to meet artists and collect their work. In 1996, the gallery moved into a historic storefront space to showcase the work of these artists. Main Street Gallery has evolved into one of the premier folk art galleries in the United States, and Jeanne has become a recognized authority in the field. The gallery has been featured in such publications as *Southern Living* and the *New York Times*. In a 2006 *Better Homes & Gardens* article Jeanne defined folk art: "It is art by artists with no formal art training. These artists have an instinctive ability to create a work of art. They are self-influenced and self-motivated. Mostly, they use readily available materials and aren't even aware they are creating art. What results is honest and touching, a compulsive outpouring—powerful and whimsical, but always close to the soul." The gallery's three floors abound with artwork by over 75 artists. The work includes sculpture using wood, metal and found objects, as well as primitive furniture, paintings and Southern folk pottery. Jeanne now carries some fine art, jewelry and international pottery, but contemporary folk art is still her specialty. Experience the work of today's folk artists at Main Street Gallery.

51 N Main Street, Clayton GA
(706) 782-2440
www.mainstreetgallery.net

Aurum Studios and Aurum Jewelry Art

Art to wear and art for your home—Aurum has a remarkable collection of both. In Athens since 1975 and Lake Oconee since 2004, Aurum is dedicated to fine design. Jewelry at Aurum is known for original looks and unusually beautiful gemstones, worked in gold, platinum or silver. The handmade wooden cases feature pieces by Aurum's own talented jewelers as well as nationally known designers such as Bellarri, Kirk Kara and J. Vincent, plus Jewels by Star, Memoire, Simon Sebbag and the Mazza Company. The Aurum eye for good work continues in the gallery of American crafts, featuring quality work by regional and national artisans, with a great selection of pottery, hand-blown glass, wood, metal and fiber pieces. Paintings and photographs by local artists complete the exceptional selection. The friendly and knowledgeable folks at Aurum would love you to visit, and you'll be glad you did.

125 E Clayton Street, Athens GA (Aurum Studios)
(706) 546-8826 or (877) 928-7860

1051 Parkside Commons, Suite 101,
Greensboro GA (Aurum Jewelry Art)
(706) 454-0444 or (866) 452-8786

www.aurumstudios.com

Roman Frances—*Peacefulness*
oil on canvas, 22.8″ x 28.7″

Monestier—*Floral*
oil on canvas, 39.4" x 39.4"

Michael John Hill —*England's Rosy Old Dawn*
oil on canvas, 60" x 48"

DE Fine Art

For more than a decade, DE Fine Art has enjoyed its role as a leading source for European original paintings for many of America's leading galleries. Its 15,000-square-foot headquarters in Northeast Atlanta on Peachtree Industrial Boulevard, five miles off of 285 and adjacent to the Atlanta Hilton NE, is now open to the public. Its huge inventory consists of more than 1,500 paintings by more than 35 European artists. Alvar Suñol of Spain, one of the most prominent, has been called a living Picasso. Giner Bueno, another Spaniard, is a modern-day impressionist. The work of Roman Frances is characterized by superb draftsmanship and feeling of light. Sandra Batoni of Florence, Italy often depicts mysterious figures in private spaces. The young French painter Monestier is a colorist above all. England's Michael John Hill is known for his English landscapes. In 2001, the Georgia Museum of Art honored Alvar with a six-week exhibition of his work. More than 15 books have been published on DE artists. Robert Harris, president of DE Fine Art, emphasizes the importance of exclusive relationships with these and other artists. Harris stresses, "We purchase every painting in our inventory, thus receiving the best price possible for our clients." Prices of the works vary widely, from $1,000 up to $200,000. Robert's wife, Pat, got him into the art business and is a co-owner. Rob Harris, their son, is vice-president. Years ago, Robert's business concentrated on decorative rather than fine art. Today a visit to DE Fine Art can be summarized by its slogan: Where Seeing is Believing.

5933 Peachtree Industrial Boulevard, Suite B, Atlanta GA
(770) 300-9733
www.de-fineart.com
www.distinctivelyeuropean.com

Crocker Pottery

Georgia folk potters represent a tradition that dates back almost three centuries. Craftsman Michael Crocker of Crocker Pottery is a top representative of that tradition. As a child, he hung around a nearby pottery shop in Lula. "It would fascinate me so much I couldn't stand it," he says. Michael began working as a potter at age 12 and has never looked back. Today, Crocker Pottery exhibits not only his work, but the products of other Georgia folk potters. Many pieces are by the famous Meader family. The collection includes jugs, churns and pitchers of all types. Decorations include whimsical faces, grapes, snakes and many other traditional themes. Folk paintings, books and related materials can be purchased at the shop. At the kiln, Michael uses only traditional materials, such as the local red clay, and traditional techniques. Michael Crocker is considered one of the top authorities on North Georgia pottery in the nation and can usually identify the origin of a piece of local pottery at a glance. His work is on display at major museums, such as the Smithsonian Museum, the National Museum of American Art and the Atlanta History Center. Michael's brother Melvin and his mother Pauline assist at the store and kiln, and Michael is training his son in the craft. To see an intriguing, age-old tradition, come to Crocker Pottery.

6345 W County Line Road, Lula GA
(770) 869-3160
www.northeastgeorgiafolkpottery.com

Gems of Africa

Wallene Jones and her son Keith Washington own Gems of Africa, a gallery of treasures gathered from across the African continent. The concept of their gallery grew from a desire to bring African art to the attention of the American public. Twice each year, they travel to Africa in search of gems. Their findings are on display in this elegant gallery filled with items you will not see elsewhere. Gems of Africa takes you on a visual journey through many countries and cultures, reflecting the rich diversity of Africa. You will find paintings by prominent African artists such as David Mbele, Ben Macala and Peter Sibeko of South Africa, and Nuwa Nnyanzi, Vincent Massudy and Yusef Musoke of Uganda, just to name a few. Shona sculptures, made by second and third generation artists, generate a great deal of interest, as do the tribal masks used in rite-of-passage ceremonies. Contemporary sculptures range from large stone floor pieces to tiny hand-blown glass depicting animals. Wood carvings, beaded jewelry and hand-woven baskets, batik textiles and paintings are all beautifully represented. Three dimensional pottery with animals, trees and flowers protruding from the sides are one of Wallene's special interests. Remember, you don't have to travel to Africa for fine African art. Come visit Gems of Africa, a gallery of treasures.

630 N Highland Avenue, Atlanta GA
(404) 876-8200
www.gemsofafricagallery.com

Laura Leiden Calligraphy

Watkinsville boasts a world-renowned artist right in its backyard at Laura Leiden Calligraphy. Laura Leiden was a Fulbright Art Scholar and has traveled the world exhibiting her paintings. A graduate of both the Rhode Island School of Design and the Massachusetts College of Art, Laura began a part-time calligraphy business in 1978, creating monogrammed stationery for sale at arts and crafts fairs. She moved to Watkinsville in 1983 and began wholesaling her work to gift stores. She is now a full-time artist with a studio and an 8,000-square-foot wholesale facility in Watkinsville. You'll find prints of Laura's hand-lettered original verses, framed and as greeting cards, in her Watkinsville store and other fine stores across the nation. Laura has not let her wholesale operation deter her from her main goal—to create fine art. Her luminescent acrylic and mixed media pieces regularly appear in galleries and area art shows. Laura's work is abstract, using brilliant colors and textures, including some fabrics. She also paints layers of transparent acrylics for the appearance of stained glass lit from within. If you look closely, you will find Laura's personal thoughts written in calligraphy and buried within each piece. Laura's artwork is a joy to behold in any form. Visit one of Laura's websites to view her work and discover where you can find her creations, or call for an appointment to visit her gallery.

1081 Industrial Drive, Watkinsville GA
(706) 769-6989 or (800) 235-3836
www.lauraleidencalligraphy.com
www.lauraleiden.com

Bowman & White Gallery

It's no wonder Bowman & White Gallery has been known as the decorator's choice for the last decade and has been repeatedly featured in the *Atlanta Magazine* "Best of" edition. Located just north of Holcomb Bridge on Spalding Drive, Bowman & White Gallery's more than 6,000 square feet provide the largest selection of designer framed art and oil paintings in Atlanta. Owners Eric and Laurie White fill the gallery with the hottest trends in fine and decorative art, including original oil paintings, limited editions, hand-colored prints, movie posters, contemporary art, and heavy ornamental frames and mirrors. The gallery found a niche when it began offering oversized art for oversized walls, and it also has Atlanta's largest collection of original European advertising posters mounted on archival linen. These collectible vintage posters date from the 1880s to the modern day. With thousands of choices, you'll be able to find that finishing touch for your home or business. Already have a special print that needs a perfect frame? The gallery stocks hundreds of high-quality custom mouldings and designer mat boards and features technology that will allow you to preview the finished product. The gallery's vast inventory allows it to pass volume discounts along to its customers. Visit the website for a virtual tour and plan your spree today. You won't find another gallery like Bowman & White.

6305 Spalding Drive, Suite D-2, Norcross GA
(770) 448-8282
www.bowmanwhite.com

Alvida Art Gallery

Expect art with a progressive spirit worthy of its namesake at Alvida Art Gallery in Savannah. Alvida was a female pirate of ancient Denmark, a scourge of the sea who became a queen. Inspired by this woman, gallery owners Anne El-Habre and Judith Metzger turned a college friendship into a business partnership that supports local artists who share their vision of art with presence. This multidimensional gallery shows a variety of fine and functional art from more than 20 artists. Along with an eclectic mix of oils, watercolors and acrylics, you will discover expressive, custom-crafted jewelry, pottery and glass sculptures. Anne and Judith also carry traditional and digital photography. Consider Alvida for custom framing, as well. With more than 800 frames from which to choose, Alvida has a selection that can satisfy every taste. Whether you are shopping for a gift or looking for a special piece to accent your home, go to Alvida Art Gallery and experience art to please a bold queen.

7303-D Abercorn Street, Savannah GA
(912) 355-5656
www.alvidaart.com

Stained Glass at Sugar Creek

When Margaret Dugan of Stained Glass at Sugar Creek creates a stained glass window, she lets the glass and the light speak for themselves. For Margaret, "light shining through stained glass speaks to the soul." She operates out of a home studio in Madison's historic district, where she builds custom stained glass pieces for individual clients and gives lessons. Margaret has been a glass artist since 1985. She is a member of the Madison Artist Guild and displays stained glass at Madisonfest each year. Her windows are on display at Southern Heartland Gallery & Frame Shop, on the square in Covington. Windows by Margaret are one-of-a-kind creations. Stained glass can fit in many areas of a home, from windows and doors to transoms and sidelights. A stained glass piece over a master bathroom garden tub allows the light to enhance the space while assuring privacy. Artificially lighted cabinet doors can also benefit from stained glass art. Margaret delights in each opportunity to create with glass, from drawing out the design and cutting individual pieces to inserting them into lead cames and soldering the joints. If stained glass artistry appeals to you, make a call to Margaret Dugan at Stained Glass at Sugar Creek.

(706) 752-1999
www.stainedglasssugarcreek.com

The Gallery at Spalding Corners

For 25 years, the Gallery at Spalding Corners has been providing its customers with custom framing, prints and original wall art. Trust the experts in this family owned and operated Norcross business to handle your conservation framing and shadow boxes with care. The toughest part will be choosing moulding and mats from more than 1,000 choices. Instead of hanging your art directly on a wall, consider a custom-made wall shelf, often called a mantel, to effectively group artwork. If you're looking for wall art, check out the selection of limited editions from some of the best artists in the Atlanta area. Take a look at the giclees, which use a special printing technique that depicts the original piece with great accuracy. Many in the art community believe giclees are better than most art prints or lithographs. Engraving, photography and paintings also hang in the gallery. If you would prefer help with your decorative decisions, the professional staff now offers commercial and residential design services.

Recommendations might include faux painting, personalized portraits or mural art, along with window treatments or new upholstery on existing furniture. To enhance your surroundings with art, visit the Gallery at Spalding Corners.

7724 Spalding Drive, Norcross GA
(770) 447-4814
www.galleryatspaldingcorners.com

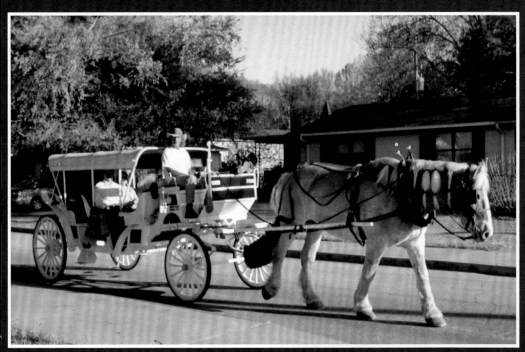

Martha's Mountain Gallery

Martha's Mountain Gallery offers an eclectic array of merchandise, ranging from stained glass, cathedral chimes and wall art to hats and tin license plates that show off your team spirit. Dutch steins and blue Delftware share gallery space with hand-painted Russian nesting dolls, local jams and Amish relishes. Owners Gabby and Martha McCay opened the gallery in 2003 as a way to showcase Martha's talents as a portrait artist. Martha's clients include corporate leaders, political dignitaries and professional sports personalities. She has been commissioned for pet portraits and portraits of homes, and works in either pastels or oils. Martha's Native American heritage has given her the desire and insight to explore jewelry design, and she specializes in creative contemporary and vintage-inspired turquoise and sterling silver jewelry. You will find Italian hand-carved shell cameos as well as turquoise and opals set off with sterling or 14-karat gold-filled wire. Although Martha's distinctive styles appeal to a wide variety of tastes and personalities, she can also create customized pieces upon request. You may even take part in Gabby and Martha's gold panning and gem grubbing operation, and Martha can turn your gem finds into a piece of keepsake jewelry. Gabby and Martha know that the beauty to be found in Helen extends well beyond their doors. With this in mind, their carriage company, Southern Comfort, offers horse and carriage rides for those wishing to take a leisurely tour of this quaint alpine village. Come to Martha's Mountain Gallery for a well rounded experience of fine art and craft.

8611 N Main Street, Helen GA
(706) 599-2425

Anne Hathaway

Anne Hathaway creates whimsical animal portraits in watercolor. Her designs also translate beautifully to home furnishings, dinnerware and textiles. You can view Anne's original artwork and other art objects bearing her designs at Anne Hathaway's gallery and studio, a cottage-style shop in mid-town Atlanta. Since 1975 Anne and her husband, Eric, have been delighting customers with products inspired from Anne's original paintings, plus custom furniture created by Eric. Anne is a versatile artist and the whimsical style she employs to capture the antics of animals and the beauty of flowers is particularly beloved. You can watch Anne apply color and detail as she works right in the middle of her gallery. You will find giclee prints here, plus Anne's designs rendered on needlepoint pillows, throws, bedding and even umbrellas. Cookbooks feature illustrations by Anne. Anne designs comforters and shams for Down, Inc. She also has her own pottery company where she creates designs and has them handpainted in Italy to be sold all over the United States. *Southern Living* has featured Anne's work in 1998 and in 2003. Two Royal Caribbean cruise ships display her paintings and giant murals in their card rooms. Anne uses a bumblebee insignia that defines her philosophy. "In nature, it is aeronautically impossible for the bee to fly, yet it defies nature and soars," she says. For art that will make you smile, visit Anne Hathaway's gallery.

22-H Bennett Street, Atlanta GA
(404) 352-4153
www.hathawaydesigns.com

Matilda's Gallery of Folk Art and Whimsy

Matilda's Gallery of Folk Art and Whimsy features three captivating cottages. The Enchanted Cottage is a wildly decorated little building crammed full of colorful folk art from local up-and-coming artists, plus a coffee shop on the back porch. The two other cottages, the Framing Gallery and the Hen House, are also galleries. Regular musical events complete the scene. When you visit, you cannot help but pick up the spirit of joy and happiness. The magic of Matilda's is clearly visible from the street, because the yard is filled with colorful objects, both decorative and useful. In 2002, Matilda's was recognized in *Atlanta* magazine as the place for the Best Whimsical Stuff. The magazine went on to say, "This colorful compound brimming with folk art, handpainted furniture and home accessories is truly magical. Owner Mary Jane Potter is the fairy godmother." Mary Jane and her husband, Mark, display the work of 50 to 60 local artists. The work is not pretentious, but it is not amateurish either. Rather, it is witty, colorful and fresh. Home & Garden Television (HGTV) has purchased artwork from Matilda's for their 2006 Dream Home. To lift your spirits, come visit Matilda's Gallery of Folk Art and Whimsy.

377 S Main Street, Alpharetta GA
(770) 754-7831
www.matildascottage.com

Artrages Gallery

In downtown Sandy Springs, Artrages Gallery offers the largest selection of artworks by top-of-the-line American craftsmen and artists in the Atlanta area. The 3,200-square-foot showroom displays the works of more than 600 artists. Artrages is the only representative in the state of Georgia for the outrageously popular Sticks furniture line. These handcrafted, colorful furniture pieces and accessories are numbered limited-edition works. Artrages regularly features gifted jewelry artists and famous lines of glass art such as Nourot and Karg. The gallery's space is artfully arranged and accented with gleaming jewels of colorful blown glass and the festive exuberance of solid painted wood. Eye-catching gold and silver jewelry is handmade by talented artisans such as Amy Kahn-Russell and Holly Yashi. The gallery is owned by Texas native Sherry Steinway, who is renowned for her distinctive hanging pots. She had a vision to offer the finest in American handmade arts and crafts and her gallery fulfills that dream admirably. Steinway has traveled the world with her husband and developed an eye for artistic treasures which she uses to good advantage to fill her gallery. Artrages Gallery was awarded the Top 100 Gallery Award of American Craft Retailers by *Niche* magazine. Artrages Gallery is your destination for an original gift or to add to your own art collection.

6035 Sandy Springs Circle, Sandy Springs GA
(404) 252-6488
www.artrages.com

The Willows Pottery

The Willows Pottery is a working studio and gallery that offers a full line of decorative and functional stoneware pottery created by both on-site artists and talented local craftspeople. Manager Emily DeFoor opened this distinctive studio for Habersham Winery in the spring of 2003 after falling in love with pottery at North Georgia College, where she took a pottery class taught by the late Bob Owens. Friend and co-crafter Betsy Ledbetter, who holds a degree in arts management and business from the College of Charleston, developed her skills after enrolling in a class at the Gibbs Museum and joined Emily at The Willows in the summer of 2003. The Willows Pottery specializes in mugs, serving pieces, kitchen accessories and dinnerware sets, along with magnificent stoneware sinks. The studio additionally offers a

Paint-Your-Own Pottery area. Here budding artists can select from an assortment of pottery pieces, then paint and glaze the pieces themselves. Customers can choose from dishware, decorative tiles and accessories, as well as terrific child-specific forms. The Willows can handle groups of 10 or less without a reservation. Emily and Betsy encourage visitors to watch them at their pottery wheels and to ask questions about the pottery-making process. Learn more about this ancient art form while painting your own pieces or purchase original pottery for your home at The Willows Pottery. It's located a half-mile south of Helen in the Historic Nacoochee Village.

7275 S Main Street, Helen GA
(706) 878-1344
www.thewillowspottery.com

Misty Mountain Pottery

The blues, greens and earth tones in Chuck Hanes' pottery evoke the natural landscape that inspires him. Even the logo of Misty Mountain Pottery is a stylization of the landscape, depicting an orange sun against the mountains, the kind of scene that makes Chuck feel close to God. Chuck's spiritual journey led him to pottery. He takes no credit for shaping the clay and gives God the glory for molding it into useful vessels through his hands. "I am merely a tool. I want to give Him the honor and praise He deserves," says Chuck, who began working as a potter in 2002. He offers his work at arts and crafts shows in addition to displaying it at his Madison store, which opened in 2005. While Chuck crafts both functional and decorative stoneware pieces, his love of cooking pushes him toward functional pieces that can be used to make and serve food and are both microwave and dishwasher safe. A visit to his studio is an opportunity

to watch Chuck create baking dishes, mugs, bowls, plates and vases. On the day we visited, we couldn't help but be struck by one of the decorative pieces, a rendition of a conch seashell, so meticulously crafted that, like nature's counterpart, we could put it to our ears to hear the ocean. For artistic folk pottery that will enhance your home, visit Misty Mountain Pottery.

271 W Washington Street, Madison GA
(706) 717-0790
www.mistymountainpottery.com

Hummingbird Lane Art Gallery

Tune in to the natural world while browsing artwork and accessories inspired by the great outdoors with a trip to Hummingbird Lane Art Gallery. This light and airy gallery is housed on the top floor of the historic Hall's Block building, which was constructed in 1883. You might hear the echo of your footsteps as you walk across the original wood plank floors of the grand old dwelling. Experience the joy of finding one captivating piece after another as you move through the 4,000-square-foot venue. Camerone Malloy first opened Hummingbird Lane Art Gallery in 1990 and quickly built a reputation for excellence by offering only the finest works of local and regional artists. Todd and Amy Strickland, loyal customers since 2000, purchased the business and took over as the new owners in 2006. They were delighted when longtime employee Deni Cobb chose to stay with the company as manager. Hummingbird Lane offers a diverse selection of handcrafted items, such as birdhouses, pottery and woodcarvings, as well as metal sculpture, rocking chairs and wind chimes. One section of the gallery is dedicated to original framed paintings from some of the 160 artists that the gallery represents. Visitors will also find intricately carved jewelry cases, stepping stones for garden paths and creations crafted from natural materials. Find exceptional art and décor inspired by nature when you visit Hummingbird Lane Art Gallery.

100 N Public Square, Dahlonega GA
(706) 864-5991
www.hummingbirdlaneonline.com

Georgia Originals

The theme of Georgia Originals is Georgia Made, Georgia Grown. Started by local artistic dynamos Kathy and Jerry Chappelle, Georgia Originals features some of the best artwork, crafts and foods that Georgia has to offer. The Chappelles, founders of Happy Valley Pottery and Chappelle Gallery, opened this ode to Georgia pride in 2005. The store was 10 years in the making, but it was well worth the wait. Here you can purchase products from 37 Georgia artisans, all hand-chosen by the Chappelles for their talent and style. Products include jewelry, pottery, stained glass, woven rugs, furniture and wood carvings, along with silk wall hangings, oil paintings, oil lamps and ornaments. Georgia Originals seems like a natural project for the Chappelles, who have worked for more than 35 years to foster not only their own artistic careers, but the talents of countless artists who have been drawn to the Athens area by their energy and vision. If you are looking for a place to view and purchase some of the most refreshing art being created in America today, make plans to visit Watkinsville, the home of Happy Valley Pottery, Chappelle Gallery and Georgia Originals.

2 S Main Street, Watkinsville GA
(706) 310-0030
www.georgiaoriginals.com

Chappelle Gallery

Chappelle Gallery is the second commercial endeavor in the amazing artistic venture started by Kathy and Jerry Chappelle in Watkinsville. Founders of Happy Valley Pottery, the Chappelles opened this gallery in 2002 in the historic Haygood House on Main Street, an appropriate locale for what is certainly an historic artistic undertaking. The Haygood House, built in 1827, was the birthplace of Bishop Atticus G. Haygood, a former president of Emery College, and Laura Askew Haygood, one of the first missionaries to China. Today the building serves as a showcase

for the Chappelles and 65 local and regional artists with national reputations. The gallery specializes in pottery and blown glass, but also features a wide variety of paintings, pen and ink drawings, photographs and more. You will find jewelry, along with pieces in wood, wrought iron, pewter, cast aluminum and fiber. Like the Chapelles, the gallery is dynamic and multi-dimensional, offering a range and depth of creativity that will inspire you when you visit.

25 S Main Street, Watkinsville GA
(706) 310-0985
www.chappellegallery.com

Happy Valley Pottery

Happy Valley Pottery is the anchor of an amazing artistic endeavor that has been unfolding in Watkinsville since 1970. That was the year Jerry and Kathy Chappelle moved from Minnesota and started a pottery studio on an old chicken farm in the country. Today Happy Valley Pottery is a thriving artists' community where you can watch many artists throwing pots, blowing glass

and painting in a variety of styles. The Chappelles came to the Athens area when Jerry took a job teaching art at the University of Georgia. They were soon followed by artists from all over the country who came to learn and create art in this bucolic setting. The Chappelles have since opened two other artistic ventures in Watkinsville, the Chappelle Gallery and Georgia Originals, creating an artistic synergy that has drawn the attention of art lovers from around the nation. In addition to making exquisite pottery, Jerry is known for creating elaborate ceramic murals for homes and buildings. Happy Valley Pottery is a thriving, dynamic endeavor that will inspire you when you see it. Make plans to visit the Chappelles the next time you're near Athens.

1210 Carson Graves Road, Watkinsville GA
(706) 769-5922
www.chappellegallery.com

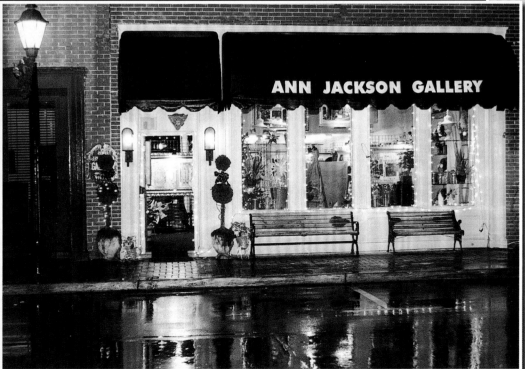

Ann Jackson Gallery

Ann Jackson opened her gallery in 1971, but the successes that led there started in the 1960s when she and a friend held a garage sale to sell their paintings. Today, three of her daughters, Valerie Jackson, Victoria Jackson and Mary Wheeless, run Ann Jackson Gallery, a cornerstone of the Roswell art scene. Victoria and her daughter Margaret Jackson Killorin show their work there along with Ann's, while youngest daughter Patricia works out of the gallery as as an interior designer. The gallery specializes in fine oils, but also carries work in other media, including acrylics, works on paper and sculptures. Ann Jackson represents both international and local artists with style and price ranges for just about every taste and pocketbook. A large exhibit of artwork by Dr. Seuss, including sculptures, has drawn deserved attention. Recently, the gallery brought in Pierre Auguste Renoir's great grandsons to speak at the opening of a show that focused on drawings by great masters. With this quality of exhibits, it's easy to see why Ann Jackson Gallery won the People's Choice award for Best Gallery in Atlanta three times. Ann and her daughters know what people like, and part of what people like is the artwork of the Jackson family. The creative gene runs strong here along with the drive and knowledge necessary to manage a superior gallery. Services include in-house art consultation, art installation and custom frame design. For artwork from people who walk the walk and talk the talk, visit the experts at Ann Jackson Gallery.

932 Canton Street, Roswell GA
(770) 993-4783
www.annjacksongallery.com

Health & Beauty

The Healing Onion

The Healing Onion offers gifts, aromatherapy and homeopathic options for better health. Suzie Hubbell, who also owns and operates Miss Scarlet's Chocolat Emporium next door, is a flower essence practitioner, trained in the art of creating plant essence blends specific to your individual needs. At the Healing Onion, Suzie offers patrons a wide selection of custom perfumes, bath salts, massage oils and other all-natural products. Lemongrass bubble bath beckons you to a long soak in the tub, and an extensive selection of aromatic candles range from invigorating to soothing scents. Just as she handcrafts Miss Scarlet's chocolates, Suzie also creates many of her own soaps and lotions, using only therapeutic-grade pure essence oils. In the gift shop, the teapots, gourmet teas and accessories are sure to be a hit with any friend in need of a little pampering. The shop offers greeting cards, gift baskets and vintage clothing. Remember to bring home some of Suzie's handcrafted chocolates and candies for nibbling later. Come to the Healing Onion in historic downtown Acworth when you need Alchemy for the Soul, and experience two unique shops sharing one convenient address.

4480 Park Street, Acworth GA
(678) 574-6449

Blue MedSpa

Blue MedSpa provides you with a results-oriented health and wellness plan, combining the relaxation and pampering of a spa with noninvasive clinical procedures designed to keep you looking and feeling your best. Owner John Stupka envisioned bringing his background in the medical industry to a luxurious spa atmosphere and succeeded to such an extent that *Condé Nast* magazine named Blue MedSpa one of the Top 55 Hot New Spas in the World. Expert hair stylists offer a full range of services, including cuts, colors and styling for special occasions. Pamper your hands and feet with a manicure or pedicure, which includes aromatherapy and exfoliation. This upscale contemporary spa provides many massage options, including Swedish, deep tissue and hot stone massage, as well as other customized therapies. For even more visible results, the Blue MedSpa medical team offers clients a variety of clinical services as alternatives to surgical procedures. Lipodissolve uses small injections to melt fat away. A revolutionary treatment that feels like a deep tissue massage, TriActive painlessly contours the body and reduces the appearance of cellulite. To smooth wrinkles without surgery, Thermage tightens the skin and delivers big results in a short time. Out-of-town guests can even get a quick touch-up of Botox, offered by some of the top injectors in the country. Whatever your needs, a visit to Blue MedSpa will rejuvenate your mind, body and spirit.

190 10th Street, Atlanta GA
(404) 815-8880
www.bluemedspa.com

Savannah Day Spa

Savannah Day Spa spans four floors of a 1826 mansion. Owner Celeste Hobson had the original three floors refurbished and added a fourth to fully encompass the ambitions of her spa. These ambitions have since paid off in national praise from such magazines as *Southern Living* and *Savannah*. *New Beauty* called it a "five-star beauty destination." Enter the Savannah Day Spa on the main floor, where Victorian elegance gleams from 14-foot ceilings, marble fireplaces and luxurious draperies. Once used for entertaining, the main floor now welcomes guests into original double parlors separated by massive arches. The garden level of the mansion contains two suites with eucalyptus steam baths, rainfall showers and jetted tubs. The third floor houses the Couple's Suite, with coffered ceilings, a stone shower and custom footbaths. Guests will find a full range of massage, waxing and skin treatments on the upper floors, which enjoy expansive views of the historic district. Savannah Day Spa also produces its own line of organic beauty products and organic cotton loungewear under the label Indulgence. Indulge yourself in the romance of yesteryear and the benefits of today's most advanced body treatments at Savannah Day Spa.

18 E Oglethorpe Avenue, Savannah GA
(912) 234-9100
www.savannahdayspa.com

Nature's Own Herb Shop

An holistic approach to health has been the foundation for wellness in many cultures over the centuries, and at Nature's Own Herb Shop you can learn more about how natural healing, herbs and vitamins can improve your health and overall well-being. Owner and operator Ardina Pierre purchased the already existing Brown's Health Food Store in 1997 and renamed it Nature's Own Herb Shop along with making many esthetic repairs. Ardina is both a registered nurse and a master herbologist, and is truly dedicated to educating and counseling her customers in proper nutrition while helping them overcome common health issues with the right supplements to ensure optimum well-being of body, mind and soul. Ardina's mission is to make a difference in the lives of those who come to her store. To that end she is constantly furthering her own education in the field of natural and holistic health. With her own radio show on WCLK and network spots on TBN with Doctor Saxon, Ardina is well on her way to spreading the news about proper health maintenance. Nature's Own Herb Shop provides an extensive selection of high-quality products such as cancer teas, antioxidants and vitamins, as well as minerals and herbs. Additionally, the shop offers treatment for chronic conditions, diabetes and weight, plus educational materials on an assortment of common issues such as allergies. Learn more and live healthier by visiting Nature's Own Herb Shop.

628 S Central Avenue, Hapeville GA
(404) 209-1969 or (800) 550-9077
www.naturesownherbshop.net

Repose MedSpa

Repose MedSpa's holistic approach promotes wellness for the clients of one of Atlanta's most comprehensive body and skincare treatment facilities. Owners Bhavya and Jayant Chaudhary offer respite from daily life and base their services on the belief that beauty is created from the inside out. Highly skilled professional estheticians express that philosophy by the treatments offered for specific parts of the body. Clinical facials use medical-grade products that not only improve the appearance of skin, but actually correct skin conditions such as fine lines, rosacea or acne. Deep tissue massages release stress and address muscular skeletal conditions. Beginning in 2007, an on-staff physician provides laser services and other rejuvenating treatments. The spa features Cosmedix and Jane Iredale product lines. The staff at Repose MedSpa is friendly but calm, in line with the Repose commitment to creating and maintaining a tranquil environment that soothes the souls of guests. Bhavya and Jayant invite you to spend a few hours or a full day regaining your inner balance at Repose MedSpa.

4520 Olde Perimeter Way, Suite 200, Atlanta GA
(770) 698-8828
www.reposemedspa.com

Pura Vida USA

The transformational practice of connecting mind, body and spirit with nature is the focus of Pura Vida USA, a wellness resort and yoga retreat. On a hilltop amid 72 acres of woods, guests disconnect from the noise and discord of the modern world in order to reconnect with their internal selves. None of the 11 guest rooms in the main house has a telephone or television. The eight cottages, each designed as a petite suite with a cozy sitting area and full bath, lack these modern contrivances as well. Instead, with the Blue Ridge Mountains as backdrop, visitors turn to the sights and sounds of nature for inspiration, entertainment and solace. Walking trails and an open-air Jacuzzi, perfect for relaxing under the stars, encourage play and peaceful thoughts. The resort features daily yoga in a hall built specifically for that purpose. The spa on the premises sees to the total wellness of the individual. The vegetarian and modified vegetarian fare prepared daily is healthful and delicious. Pura Vida USA joins Maya Tulum in Mexico and Pura Vida Costa Rica as the newest in a family of wellness resorts in spectacular settings. For a meaningful experience in beautiful surroundings, consider a stay at Pura Vida USA.

400 Blueberry Hill, Dahlonega GA
(706) 345-4900 or (866) 345-4900
www.rrresorts.com

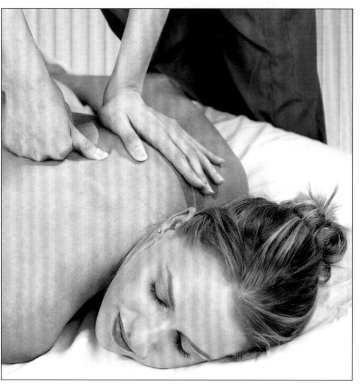

Heavenly Touch Wellness Center & Spa

Experience the difference at Heavenly Touch Wellness Center & Spa. Hattie Mercer started the spa in 1998 after extensive training in both Eastern and Western massage therapy. As a registered massage therapist, her years of experience have created the kind of health that flows from a relaxed spirit, mind and body. Discover the wellness escape treatment, featuring an aromatic Dead Sea salt treatment, a body wrap for detoxification and a 60-minute therapeutic massage. The treatment continues with a healthy lunch, reflexology and a facial. Other services include a Swedish, deep tissue, hot stone or couples massages, sports and pregnancy massages, or a personalized therapeutic massage using Ayurveda pure oils and herbs. The therapists are highly trained and accept medical massage prescriptions from various physicians. Heavenly Touch also offers classes on infant massage techniques. Company parties can be enhanced with chair massage. The spa offers organic shea butter, which protects your skin from harmful sunrays, prevents wrinkles, repairs dry skin and soothes aching muscles and even eases cold symptoms. Heavenly Touch Wellness Center & Spa has a wealth of experience to offer for the relief of pain and stress in everyday life. Hattie and her staff invite you to take a wellness break and experience the difference.

2895 Peachtree Industrial Boulevard, Suite 105, Duluth GA
(770) 418-1160
www.htouch.com

ImageSpa

At ImageSpa in Snellville, it isn't about the lights or the dazzle, it's about you. Owner Barbara McClure, RN has provided the perfect place to relax, renew and refresh. Using a formula that combines technology with wellness to create beauty, this first-rate spa has services available that will help you look and feel your best. Allow Barbara and her highly skilled staff of professionals to take you though a regime of treatments that will make you feel pampered, while rejuvenating your body, mind and spirit. ImageSpa's massage therapists are trained in sports massage, deep tissue massage, Swedish massage and neuromuscular massage. You may also treat your feet or hands with soothing reflexology, an ancient art of specialized stress-relief. ImageSpa takes pride in providing state-of-the-art services such as microdermabrasion, electrolysis, synergy cellulite treatment, permanent cosmetics and advanced skin care programs using LED light therapy. In addition, the spa provides expert facials, body treatments and hair and nail services. Between visits, you can maintain and continue to improve your skin, hair and nails with the top-of-the-line professional product lines offered at ImageSpa. When you are ready for lunch, head to the Garden Room. Come and treat yourself to all the luxury and care that you deserve with a visit to ImageSpa.

2435 E Main Street, Heritage Village, Snellville GA
(770) 978-0956
www.imagespa.net

Scarlett's Retreat Day Spa & Mercantile

Southern belles in need of some pampering sashay to a gracious and luxurious turn-of-the-19th-century home in McDonough. Here at Scarlett's Retreat Day Spa & Mercantile, the staff prepares them for the ball with soothing massages and wraps as well as nail care. Antique furniture and elegant draperies give the treatment rooms the look and feel of parlors. The Red Georgia Clay body wrap is said to be just the thing to rid ladies of Yankee attitude and get them feeling soft and kissable once again. Aunt Pitty Pat's Exfoliation and Bath Ritual includes a soak in a Victorian tub and a soft massage. For an exquisite full day at the spa, the Southern Dreams package offers a bath, massage and facial followed by a Mint Julep manicure and pedicure and a makeup application. A light lunch is included. Gentlemen unwind at Scarlett's Retreat through such packages as the Mister Butler, which combines a full-body massage with an Aromatherapy Tub Ritual. Rhett would have appreciated the complimentary liqueur and cigar that comes with it. Products in the mercantile section of the spa support the staff's philosophy of nurturing mind, body and spirit while being friendly to the environment. The building is listed as a landmark house of Henry County. Experience Southern bliss at Scarlett's Retreat Day Spa & Mercantile.

22 Jonesboro Street, McDonough GA
(678) 432-7474
www.scarlettsretreat.com

Home & Garden

Pine Mountain Loft & Gallery

Georgia and Gary Kelley are dedicated to promoting and enhancing the romance of traditional log homes. Leaders in sales of Barna Log Homes, the Kelleys have created Pine Mountain Loft & Gallery to furnish and celebrate them. The store's two floors of merchandise offer everything from decorative art, pottery and paintings to custom furniture, fabrics and flooring. A special exhibit devoted to Barna Log Homes offers interior and exterior design inspiration. The store even provides decorating services. Georgia, an experienced saleswoman with a marketing degree, grew up in the Pine Mountain area and had long dreamed of returning. Two of the Kelleys' children now work in the company's Barna Log Homes division, while the other two are artisans who show jewelry and hand-blown glass at the gallery. Georgia and Gary have immersed themselves in local organizations and they are active members of the Chamber of Commerce, the Pine Mountain Merchants Association and the Harris County Special Olympics management team. Pine Mountain Loft & Gallery is just one hour southwest of Atlanta and a world away in the foothills of the Appalachian range. Make your escape to the mountain charms of Pine Mountain Loft & Gallery and visit with Georgia and Gary.

103 Broad Street, Pine Mountain GA
(706) 663-7663 or (888) 663-LOGS (5647)
www.bestlogdecor.com
www.bestloghomes.com

Mountain Treasures

Capture the spirit of mountain living—timber-covered walls and the gentle gaze of the moose, deer and elk overhead invite you to slow down and enjoy your visit when you enter Mountain Treasures, in the North Georgia mountains. Discover furnishings from such respected companies as Old Hickory, Flat Rock, Marshfield, LaCrosse and Shadow Mountain. Find custom pieces from regional artists and one-of-a-kind antiques and decorative accessories ranging from metal and wood carvings to unique lighting, with styles that traverse time and space. What unites all of these offerings is the vision the owner, Dee Speer, shares with guests. Mountain Treasures is a place both intimate and welcoming, where families, couples and individuals will find the perfect fit for their lives and homes. Change the way you experience the mountains and make Mountain Treasures your destination for fulfilling dreams.

5711 Highway 52 E, Ellijay GA
(706) 635-5590
www.mountaintreasures.biz

Classic Expressions

Owners Tammy Williams and Bethany Henson use their backgrounds in crafts and other creative fields every day at Classic Expressions. Theirs is a multifaceted business combining a retail shop with such personalized services as event planning and interior design. The warm, inviting shop offers fine gifts and home accents, such as candles, bath and body products and jewelry. Treats for the kitchen include gourmet cookies and coffees. At times, Tammy and Bethany showcase artists and painters, as well as craftspeople who make purses and beaded items. They put their creative energies to work for customers with specific gift needs. For example, they love creating gift baskets. Just give them a theme, anything from baby to Italy, and they will assemble a beautiful and bountiful basket tailored to the request. Over the course of their 13-year friendship, Tammy and Bethany have planned and decorated scores of receptions and parties. Let them bring holiday brightness and cheer to your home, office or business with their Christmas decorating. When you need a creative solution to a gift or decorating need, consider Classic Expressions.

780 Mayfield Road, Suite 102, Alpharetta GA
(678) 319-0040
www.northfultonshops.com/classicexpressions

Lydia's, Something a Little Different

A multi-talented designer, Thea Willing de Navarro always had an eye for distinctive art and décor. With her shop, Lydia's, Something a Little Different, she discovered the worth of her talents. Lydia's began in 2004 as Lydia's Workshop, a storefront for Thea's budding landscape design business. Thea had discovered a passion for gardening while seeking solace during her husband's battle with cancer. After his death, she went on to earn a degree in environmental horticulture and tasted her first success as a designer. As Thea's career and life began to flourish again, so did her store. Eclectic garden ornamentation, home décor and gifts accumulated at Lydia's. Thea sought out local artists to supplement her collection, and they were happy to join a project marked by such appreciation and good taste. Doll artisan Peggy Briggs joined the store and worked closely with Thea to design original creations. A resident artist, Clara Howard, specialized in hand-painted screens and figurines. Thea began scavenging and renovating antique vehicles such as Civil War doctor's carriages and Model A trucks, and these too appeared at the store. By this time, Lydia's had become a landmark in Acworth for truly special finds. Then as now, success was its own advertisement. Since remarrying, to the Reverend Enrique Navarro, Thea has decided to retire. Those who found treasures in her garden shop, however, will always remember Lydia's, Something a Little Different.

4591 Dallas Street, Acworth GA
(770) 917-9965

Petal Pushers

Three Petal Pushers locations in the Washington Square area ensure you can find gifts and home accessories during the holidays and through every season. Henry and Shay Harris envisioned working together as a family in their own business, doing something they loved. In 1993, with the help of their son Jeremy, they opened Petal Pushers in the historic Fitzpatrick Hotel. The store carries a selection of whimsical gifts, furniture classics, Tiffany-style lamps, sparkling cut crystal, table-top linens and more. One year, with Christmas fast approaching, Henry and Shay transformed Petal Pushers into a winter wonderland, offering ornaments, figurines and other holiday items. The themed choices proved so popular that the couple soon opened their second store, Petal Pushers Christmas, and devoted it entirely to this magical season. Open September to January, Petal Pushers Christmas carries holiday collectibles, lighted and unlighted trees, and everything else you need for a jolly good time. You can even pick up a decorated tree, complete with your choice of motifs, such as Santa, snowmen or angels. In 2004, the Harris family opened the Antiques Orphanage. At this third site, you can find antiques, collectibles, fine furniture and some pieces deemed almost unadoptable. Come to any of the Petal Pushers locations for delightful gifts, items to beautify your home during the holidays, and antiques to enjoy throughout the year.

Petal Pushers: 10 W Square, Washington GA
Petal Pushers Christmas: 24 E Robert Toombs Avenue, Washington GA
Antiques Orphanage: 12 W Square, Washington GA
(706) 678-4400 *www.petalpusherswashington.com*

Cynthia Aiken Interiors—Mountain Cottage

You can bring classy Southern elegance to your home with design tips from Cynthia Aiken Interiors—Mountain Cottage. Cynthia has been in the interior design business for more than 20 years. She originally went to design school at the urging of friends and family, who often sought her advice for their own home design projects, due to her good taste and sense of style. During her distinguished career, she and her interior design company have received recognition from many major publications, including *Better Homes and Gardens* and *Southern Living Home Plans*. Cynthia has been featured on Home and Gardens Television, where she was a guest on the program *Dream Builders*. She has created four magnificently designed homes for the *Street of Dreams* program. Her style gracefully mixes Country French with upscale classic cottage features for comfort that is both casual and elegant. Cynthia prides herself on creating spaces that seem to say "come on in and make yourself at home." At Mountain Cottage, you can glean expert advice from Cynthia and her professional staff while you browse your way through a beautifully designed retail space filled with the latest home decorating trends in window treatments, furniture and such accessories as lamps and Trapp candles. Make your home as comfortable as it is beautiful with a visit to Cynthia Aiken Interiors—Mountain Cottage.

248 Foothills Parkway, Marble Hill GA
(770) 893-1500
www.cynthiaaikeninteriors.com

Granny's Cottage

When Colleen and Tom Mangifesta first moved to the North Georgia mountains, they found the kind of furnishings they appreciated at Granny's Cottage, which is probably why the owners called them when the store was offered for sale. Today, the Mangifestas sell handcrafted log and wood furniture, authentic Amish furniture and an eclectic mix of home accessories in a neatly arranged storefront at the intersection of US 19/129 and State Route 325, in the little community of Ivy Log. Part of the fun of a visit to Granny's Cottage is not knowing what you might unearth. You might find a stunning quilt or a one-of-a-kind lamp carved with a chainsaw. Need a handcrafted table, an Adirondack chair for the backyard or a mantel made of juniper wood? You have come to the right place. The store offers soy candles, a selection of collectible bears and museum-quality wall hangings, generated without the aid of a computer and guaranteed for 100 years. Colleen uses her decorating talents to help homeowners and realtors choose the right accessories. The Mangifestas believe in fair pricing and quality offerings. They say that the best part of the business is getting to know their shoppers and guests. Colleen and Tom invite you to spend some time at Granny's Cottage.

5893 Murphy Highway, Blairsville GA
(706) 781-6269
www.grannyscottage.com

c.a.n.o.p.y.

The delicious scent of the seasonal candles, home fragrances, diffusers and potpourri waft through the front doors of c.a.n.o.p.y., beckoning one and all to enter. It's the personal touches that differentiate one home from another, and owner Carol Sandlin ohas set out to give you plenty of choices to accessorize your home. The store carries an impressive line of monogrammed items, such as engraved soaps, candles and cutting boards, plus serving pieces, stationery and baby gifts. Carol can help you find embroidered linens and napkins along with such distinguishing touches for your table as dishes and gourmet food items. Set the mood in your interior with the shop's selection of lamps, pictures and accent pieces. Personal gifts also abound, including body lotions and sachets for women and shaving products and fragrances for men. Gift wrapping is another thoughtful touch. Carol attributes her love of retail and the public as the reason for opening her store. She operates the downtown shop with the help and support of her husband, Keith, and their three daughters. This shop deserves repeat visits, since merchandise changes frequently. For distinctive home décor and gifts, come to c.a.n.o.p.y.

21 N Wall Street, Cartersville GA
(770) 383-8883

Gado Gado Home Gallery

If you ask Indonesians to describe the country's national decorative style, they will probably say gado gado: an eclectic combination of ingredients. Indonesia has been an international trade destination for centuries, and its style represents a layering of Chinese, Indian, Arabic and Dutch influences. Gado Gado Home Gallery upholds this tradition. Founded by Jill and Setiawan Onggo, from New York and Java, this import company features handcrafted wood furniture, home accents and art by skilled artisans. No two trips to Gado Gado are ever the same. The owners travel frequently to discover new treasures and hand-select each piece. "For me the background of the piece is very important," says Setiawan, who can describe in detail the provenance, craftsmanship and style of any given item. The furniture is primarily teak and is intricately carved and refined, hand-hewn and rustic, or Asian contemporary. A kaleidoscope of woodcarvings, masks, shadow puppets, textiles and silver jewelry come from Bali, Java and beyond. Gado Gado opened its first showroom in Midtown in 1997 and its second location in early 2007 in downtown Decatur. Since then, *Atlanta Magazine* and *Atlanta Homes & Lifestyle* have featured the store. Its success reflects the growing popularity of the best styles from around the world. Step into Gado Gado and take your home to another destination.

549-4 Amsterdam Avenue, Atlanta GA
(404) 885-1818
431-1 W Ponce de Leon Avenue, Decatur GA
(404) 377-9755
www.gadogado.com

D&B Designs

Rachael Buffa and Debra Bailey turn blank white walls into Tuscan countrysides and outdated kitchen cabinets into functional works of art with antique finishes in their business, D&B Designs. Debra, a teacher at the Art Institute of Colorado at Denver, met Rachael, who had a background in interior design, when they both moved to Alpharetta. They quickly discovered that their individual talents combined perfectly and in 1994, went into business together, creating unique painted baby furniture and nurseries. Soon word of their talent spread, and people commissioned them for large-scale projects. The two continue to remain busy entirely from word-of-mouth referrals, thanks in large part to their careful attention to detail. After a paint crew does the base work, Debra and Rachael personally attend to all of the other facets of the project. Their talent has earned D&B the opportunity to work on large residential and commercial projects, such as a series of murals for the Goddard Nursery Schools in the Atlanta area. Though murals are a favorite of both women, including whimsical ones featuring children's characters by Dr. Seuss and others, the women also specialize in creating the look and feel of aged Italian plaster and elegant faux finishes. Call D&B Designs to turn your walls and architectural features from drab to dazzling.

6200 Vickery Creek Road, Cumming GA
(678) 778-5962

Details Design Center

An attention to details is what Sherry Cox has built her very successful design business on ever since she opened her doors in 1997. The Athens/Oconee area has recognized her amazing talent by voting her the number-one designer in 2006. Details Design Center specializes in creating a totally custom look for your home, office or home-away-from-home. The design team focuses on variations of classical European tradition, but as Cox states, "Our degreed designers know how to gracefully walk the line between contemporary and classic styles. We skillfully bring colors, patterns and texture into the design to create harmony and balance in the home." Details has more than 5,000 designer fabrics on-site and carries more than 100 furniture lines including Century, Habersham, Hickory White, Taylor King, Wesley Hall, Harden and Lexington in the showroom. As a result, it is able to please the most discerning customer. The design center is bursting at the seams with quality art and fine oils, not to mention the fabulous lamps, furniture and accessories to complete your design project. You will want to explore Details Design Center for all your design needs. .

3161 Hog Mountain Road, Watkinsville GA
(706) 769-8464
www.detailsdesigncenter.com

Eddy West

Eddy West is the antique store of tomorrow. The store specializes in antique reproductions, distinctive American primitives and French and Canadian country-style furnishings. The large line can be viewed at three showrooms, online, and through 2,500 different retail establishments throughout the United States and Canada. With their mix of yesteryear beauty and technological advances, the fashionable furnishings blend well in today's homes. Careful research of museum-quality pieces led owners Juliann and Craig Eddy to create an aging process that allows brand-new furniture to enjoy the warmth and character of antiques. The distressed technique, first employed by the Eddys in their Southwest primitive collection, brings an individual charm and sense of age to the furniture. Each individually designed piece is manufactured in the Eddy West plant, where standards for durability and quality assure a treasure that will last for generations. With more than 200 pieces and more than 70 color options, Eddy West has something to grace every room in the house. Tables, hutches, chests and sideboards come in a multitude of sizes and styles. Hand-painted antique reproductions and eloquent accessories help create interiors that offer relaxation and country charm. Eddy West has been featured in *Home & Garden*, *Country Living* and *Victoria* magazines. Juliann and Craig invite you to find your lasting treasure at Eddy West.

735 Mayfield Road, Alpharetta GA
(800) 829-9037
525 Plantation Drive, Clarkesville GA
(706) 754-6226
1358 Washington Street, Clarkesville GA
(706) 839-1532
www.eddywest.com

The Red Hound

Owners Candy Kane and Lori Foley are a huge part of the warm, friendly atmosphere that draws Alpharetta residents to the Red Hound. This gift shop, named after beloved dachshund Ollie, is a delightful place to shop for home and garden accessories as well as dinnerware and other artistic touches for your table. Candy and Lori are glad to create custom gift baskets from the store's extensive variety of gourmet treats and personal care items. Look for handcrafted tiles by Sid Dickens, Casafina dinnerware and handcrafted jewelry by local artists. The Red Hound can help you improve the look and function of any room with artisan-made goods and trusted brand names. Consider crushed marble figurines by Isabel Bloom, candle lamps by Shades of Light and glass serving pieces by Peggy Karr. Scentier fragrance lamps are always appreciated. Occasionally, you'll find fresh flowers, and always you'll find variety, service and reasonable prices. The shop offers free gift wrapping, a bridal registry and UPS shipping at cost. Whether you seek a corporate gift, a personal gift or something to grace your space, stop by the Red Hound for a selection that promises to please.

11130 State Bridge Road, Suite C104, Alpharetta GA
(678) 624-7733
www.theredhound.com

the Scarlet Tassel

HOME DECOR & ACCESSORIES

The Scarlet Tassel

Customers can't get enough of the Scarlet Tassel, a home décor and gift store named one of the country's top 50 retailers by *Home Accents Today* magazine. Since opening in 2003, co-owners Shelly Dozier-Mckee and Deirdre Staab have created one of Atlanta's most popular retail stores, which earned a 2006 Best of Atlanta award. As a source for great design inspiration, the store's frequently changing displays are set up to help customers visualize the merchandise in their own homes. Cozy nooks display candles, kitchen accessories, office décor and wine/bar accessories. Walls throughout the store display a wonderful range of clocks, framed artwork and the collectible memory tiles crafted by artist Sid Dickens. With excellent customer service a company creed, the Scarlet Tassel prides itself on helping customers find items not offered in the store through their special order program. "This is a customer-driven business," says Deirdre. All staff members are qualified to assist customers with design questions. It's easy to spot the staff members because they all wear red canvas carpenter aprons. Free design workshops are offered in the store during seasonal open-house events, and in-home design assistance is available if you schedule one of the store's popular accessory calls. With more than 40 years of combined experience in the catalog and home décor industry, Shelly and Deirdre have grown an idea into a successful, award-winning business called the Scarlet Tassel.

**6235-A Roswell Road,
Sandy Springs GA
(404) 843-0387**
www.thescarlettassel.com

Love Street Gifts and Gardens

Carol Scott's customers often tell her that they come to Love Street Gifts and Gardens, her beautiful Smyrna shop, just to escape their stressful day. The gift and garden shop is not far from Love Street Home, its sister business that specializes in interior design, furniture and home accessories. Love Street Gifts and Gardens is located in a charming 1920s craftsman bungalow surrounded by a garden that blooms all year. The garden contains an amazing selection of yard art, seasonal plants and containers. You can buy your greenery planted or plant it yourself. *Atlanta Magazine* has awarded Love Street Gifts and Gardens a Best of Atlanta for Best Garden Whimsy. Inside the cottage, the rooms burst with gifts ranging from the humorous, such as funny cards, napkins, plaques and refrigerator magnets, to the sublime. Tableware, hand bags and Pandora jewelry are available. Well-known lines include Vera Bradley, the Thymes and others. You will enjoy your visit to Love Street Gifts and Gardens.

1295 Concord Road, Smyrna GA
(770) 434-8578
www.lovestreetonline.com

Love Street Home

Love Street Home is a Smyrna favorite for finding affordable new or antique furniture. This pretty little shop is located a few blocks down the street from its sister store, Love Street Gifts and Gardens. Owners Carole and George Scott carry everything from shabby and urban chic to traditional items. Love Street Home is a one-stop shop for your interior design needs. George offers a full interior design service that includes upholstery and furniture. Love Street Home has a terrific mix of great designs at reasonable prices. You can find modestly priced original oil paintings and frames. Decorate your house with items ranging from iron wall décor to silk and dried flowers. Love Street Home stocks a large selection of linens for bed, bath and kitchen, including goods from Vera Bradley. Pick up a table lamp or some of the well-known Tyler Candles from Tyler, Texas. For treasured home accessories and quality furniture, visit Love Street Home.

1125B Concord Road, Smyrna GA
(678) 556-3878
www.lovestreetonline.com

La Villa

In Savannah, La Villa is the place to go to find exclusive lines of European-style tabletop decorations, dinnerware and home accessories. Owners Cristina and Tom Coughran have assembled a sophisticated collection of home décor items that can add the perfect accent to your table. The Coughrans, long-time European residents, were enchanted on a visit to Savannah by the beauty of the Low Country, its fine weather and excellent golf courses. They decided to relocate. Cristina soon noticed that there weren't any local shops stocking the European decorative items she loved. The Coughrans decided to open their own shop to introduce Savannah to these beautiful home decorations. All of La Villa's offerings have the clean lines and bright colors typical of the sophisticated European home. From exclusive Le Jacquard Francais linens to lovely Rosenthal china, La Villa stocks it all. Riedel and Schott stemware provide graceful additions to your table setting. Other featured lines include Alessi, WMF cutlery, Arte Italic ceramic ware and Blomus barware. One ardent customer describes La Villa as "a present for Savannah." The Coughrans invite you to see their unique selections and hope you too will find treasures to enhance the beauty and enjoyment of your home.

5525 Abercorn Street, Savannah GA
(912) 355-0619
www.lavillasavannah.com

Little g's Mountain Garden Center

Susan Pleasant and Jennifer Mills found the spirit to start a new life by establishing a nursery and landscape business in Cherrylog. For the past three years, Little g's Mountain Garden Center and its sister business Jennifer's Landscape Design have used plants, water features, stone walls, patios, decks and even tree houses to enhance local landscapes. Little g's specializes in landscape solutions. Whether you seek medicinal herbs, annual color or something that will grow on a red clay slope at your mountain home, Little g's offers plants that are proven performers, including native trees and shrubs. Jennifer's Landscape Design offers the services of seven professionals who can design and install a landscape that changes your relationship with the outdoors. A visit to the two businesses, in one store located midway between Ellijay and Blue Ridge, could be your excuse for a day away. You can explore a landscape filled with fountains, waterfalls and plantings as well as pottery and yard art, then stop next door for barbecue at the Pink Pig and some local bluegrass at a hall down the street. Susan and Jennifer visited Cherrylog several times before abandoning their careers in Texas. Susan left a corporate career. Jennifer's landscaping career actually dates back 30 years to her native North Carolina. The two spent four years getting to know the North Georgia area and remodeling a dilapidated building for their store. Take your dreams to Little g's Mountain Garden Center and watch them grow roots.

768 Cherry Log Street, Cherrylog GA
(706) 273-2012
www.littlegsgardencenter.com

Timpson Creek Gallery

Timpson Creek Gallery, set along Highway 76 West at the north end of Lake Burton, is home to one of the most distinctive collections of home furnishings, antiques and art, clothing, jewelry and so much more in the North Georgia mountains. Two Adirondack-inspired buildings house more than 10,000 square feet of showroom space, while the top floor of one building is the studio of master craftsman Dwayne Thompson, one of America's preeminent rustic furniture makers. His creations, worked in hickory, mountain laurel, poplar bark, antler, stone and his own bronze castings, will leave you speechless. Dwayne, along with his wife Cecile, co-own the gallery. Their daughter, Anne Neal, provides summer help to the friendly and knowledgeable staff members who are ready to assist you when you visit. Cecile is a former teacher with a flair for design. She has blended her talent with Dwayne's to assemble a collection that is worth the drive from anywhere. Timpson Creek is also North Georgia's exclusive dealer for the Genesee River Trading Company. In addition, you'll find the work of several established artists, including the paintings of local artist Libby Mathews. If you're looking to adorn yourself instead of your home you will find clothing from French Dressing Jeans, Rockmount, Scully and Double D. Also, look for jewelry by New Mexican artists Hal and Margie Hiestand, hand-selected by Cecile.

7142 Highway 76 W, Clayton GA
(706) 782-5164
www.timpsoncreek.com

Brenda Evans Designs

Somebody forgot to tell Brenda Evans that the era of house calls is over, though you won't find any homeowners in her community volunteering to enlighten her. They enjoy being able to have someone from Brenda's design company come to their place with ideas that reflect the latest decorating trends. If you make a purchase, Brenda will either waive the fee for the house call or give you a discount on what you buy. She and her team are always visiting furniture markets and seminars to stay at the top of their field. They pass on the knowledge they acquire not only to homeowners but to local builders, who count on Brenda Evans Designs to know what is in style right now. The company's interiors have been featured in real estate brochures and local magazines. Visit the showroom to see all the furniture, home accessories and bedding that this business has on offer. "We carry a good product, with good warranties, that we can stand behind," says Brenda. "That makes all the difference." Brenda is also involved in community projects and joins Alex's Army in the fight to find a cure for cystic fibrosis. Whether you are decorating a room, an apartment or an entire home, consider picking up style tips from the experts at Brenda Evans Design, where the slogan is We Make House Calls.

**2142 Tails Creek Road, Ellijay GA
(706) 635-7556**

Donna M's Custom Arts

Donna M. Hatcher will warm your home with her custom hand paintings. In business as Donna M's Custom Arts, Donna can envision any art design your heart desires. She has painted on old windows, saw blades, gourds, and even a rug that fits around your toilet. Donna can design décor for a child's room or linoleum rugs to comfort your kitchen. These designs vary from handpainted roosters to your favorite pet, or perhaps a historical sight to bring back old memories. Some of Donna's most popular designs include a linoleum rug with your favorite team, placemats for your dining room table and saw blades featuring historical sights. You will find some of Donna's creations at Trash & Treasures, a little antique store on Highway 75, en route to Helen (on the left, next to Blue Creek Bar-B-Q). You may also check with Donna for other local stores that carry her artwork. If you have just bought a cabin and want to furnish it with custom paintings, or if you want a custom painting for your home, just give Donna M's Custom Arts a call.

Cleveland GA
(706) 865-9172 or (770) 845-5842

Savannah Fine Linens

At Savannah Fine Linens, Gaye and Larry Anderson create in-house bedding collections from textiles produced by some of the world's finest weavers. Imagine slipping into soft sheets with thread counts from 300 to 1,000 in yarns as diverse as long-staple Egyptian cotton, organic linen, bamboo, silk or beachwood. Underneath you is a Hungarian down featherbed; above you, a soft cashmere blanket; under your head, an eiderdown pillow. Whether your taste runs to hemstitched duvets, matelassé or embroidery, you'll appreciate the selection at Savannah Fine Linens. The staff can help you put together your own custom look. In addition to bedding, Gaye and Larry appreciate the role of linens throughout the home and offer fine Turkish towels, imported linen tablecloths and damask table runners. You can complete an exquisite table with imported dinnerware and silver place settings reminiscent of opulent Versailles or add sparkle to a room with a Waterford lamp. The store also carries sleepwear and fragrances. For linens and accessories with European allure, visit Savannah Fine Linens.

412 Whitaker Street, Savannah GA
(912) 447-5885 or (888) 294-8489
www.savannahfinelinens.com

Outrageous Bargains

The more you need an extreme makeover for your home, the more you need the inventory and services of Outrageous Bargains. This explains why the prime time television show *Extreme Makeover: Home Edition* used the store in a show that aired in 2007. Planning your home's interior design can be a daunting endeavor without the right help and the right products. The staff members at Outrageous Bargains will listen to your dreams. They can even visit your home to help with space planning. You can count on them to consider your lifestyle, preferences and budget when making suggestions. You can also count on Outrageous Bargains to have everything you need for your makeover, including 3,000 bolts of fabric, carpet, lamps and furniture. The stores are well stocked with such accessories as mirrors, vases, wall art and

bed ensembles. Husband and wife team Patti and Kurt Gosch operate Outrageous Bargains stores at Peachtree Shopping Center in Duluth, Highway 9 Design Center in Alpharetta and on Home Center Drive in Kennesaw. For outrageous deals on interiors, come to Outrageous Bargains.

(770) 497-9577 (Duluth)
(770) 754-4443 (Alpharetta)
(770) 426-5800 (Kennesaw)
www.outrageousbargains.net

Accents

Karen Hendrix showed a natural inclination towards redecorating from her teenage years, first redecorating her own room then her family home. Today, she owns Accents, a St. Simons Island shop that specializes in home accessories and gifts. She also runs House Calls by Karen Hendrix, a full-service interior design firm that specializes in rearranging your furnishings for an entirely new look and feel. The store evokes an inviting atmosphere with individually-decorated rooms, warm colors and flowers. You'll find Italian Casafina stoneware dishes, Matouk fine linens and Hobo handbags, as well as kitchen items, soy candles and baby gifts. Accents provides gift wrapping, which it finishes with a handmade bow. Karen holds a certification in redesign from Interior Redesign Industry Specialists and is an allied member of the American Society

of Interior Designers. She can help you with window treatments and personal shopping for flooring, furniture and accessories. She also can help you arrange your home for shows to potential buyers or help you transition your things to a new home. Karen excels at working with a budget and looks forward to your visit to Accents.

1624 Frederica Road, Suite 5b,
St. Simons Island GA
(912) 638-2030
www.housecallsbykarenhendrix.com

Cobblestone Corner

The inspiration for the appealing handcrafted furniture, home décor and gifts at Cobblestone Corner started in a pile of salvage. More than 30 years ago, Dub and Edna Knight ran a salvage shop, and each day brought a new pile of material to sort through and sell in the store. One morning, a batch of woodworking tools arrived and instead of selling them, Dub began experimenting. Though he had no previous experience, he began making simple furniture for his family. Word of Dub's beautiful pieces spread, and soon friends were coming to him with special requests for their homes. Dub and Edna eventually phased out the salvage portion of the store to dedicate more time to woodworking. Now, you can find many of Dub's original designs at Cobblestone Corner, from chandeliers to dining room tables. A pie safe adds country charm and practical storage to your kitchen, and a warm Ponderosa pine bedroom creates an inviting personal retreat. Dub uses mainly birch and pine woods for his handcrafted pieces, and says that the wood shows more character as it ages. Old Village Paints, available in a variety of colors, give pieces a durable finish that stands up to daily use. After years of providing delightful items for homes, Edna and Dub are now greeting the sons and daughters of their original customers. Visit Cobblestone Corner to beautify your home with timeless furnishings from the Knight family.

2237 Whitfield Place, Kennesaw GA (770) 427-0076

Inside Design

The best time to consider your new home's interior design is before the walls go up or the paint goes on. For that kind of foresight, creativity and attention to your lifestyle, folks from Madison to the Gulf Shore of Florida trust Jennifer Hendrix and Frannie Kimsey. They're the owners of Inside Design, which opened in Madison Markets in 2004. The partners bring two decades of combined design experience to their enterprise. They have the kind of talent that shows up on the pages of *Southern Living* magazine. In June 2002, the magazine featured a new Atlanta cottage skillfully aged by Frannie. In the February 2006 issue, Frannie's personal kitchen makeover demonstrated what a new color palette and some hardworking surfaces can do for a busy young family. For the kitchen, Frannie chose her favorite colors—gold and red with touches of green and orange. When she or Jennifer work with clients, however, they make a point of reflecting a client's personal taste rather than their own. They know the top tier brands and hire dedicated employees to handle everything from renovations, installations and wall finishes to color planning, restorations and decorating for special events. Whether your taste is contemporary, traditional or downright funky, Inside Design can bring your rooms together with window treatments, fabrics and bedding as well as furniture, accents and artwork. Before they joined forces, Frannie was a partner in Kimsey-Walton Interiors, and Jennifer worked for O'Steen's Design Center. Visit the dynamic designers at Inside Design n in the renovated cotton warehouses behind the James Madison Inn.

244 W Washington Street, Madison GA
(706) 343-1457
www.insidesigninc.com

Rose Cottage Furniture

The inside of Rose Cottage Furniture looks more like an elegantly appointed home than a store. Located in a historic house in the heart of Kennesaw, Rose Cottage offers 10,000 square feet of showroom space. The care with which owners Terry and Kathy Loyd arrange each room shows in every detail. You can't help but get ideas for your home as you take it all in. The great thing is that the settings are intended to delight and inspire you, and never to impose. "We design the client's home according to the client's taste, personality and style," says Kathy, "not according to ours." Still, if you need advice, you have come to the right place, because Kathy, her mother and grandmother have been in the home design business for what seems like forever. The Christmas season, a special time at Rose Cottage, starts the second weekend in October with a fully catered open house. Drop by if you're in the neighborhood, or visit any time during the holiday season to enjoy the special arrangements throughout the store. People come from all around just to see them. For elegant, sophisticated furnishings with timeless appeal, consider Rose Cottage Furniture. As its slogan has it: The Store. The Style. The Thrill.

3008 Cherokee Street, Kennesaw GA (770) 428-9255
www.rosecottagefurniture.net

OwenLawrence

OwenLawrence is a premier gallery for luxurious home and office furniture. From objets d'art to table settings, from leather accessories to the finest in linens and porcelains, OwenLawrence Gallery brings together everything you need to make your home or office a more perfect reflection of yourself. Owners Owen Halpern and Lawrence Pritchard travel the world seeking incredible pieces to display. Because they personally visit more than 70 percent of the companies that they represent, they can often tell a client exactly how a specific piece was made. These two have a passion for all that is beautiful in life, and the art, architecture, porcelain, glass and linens at the store reflect this passion. OwenLawrence carries an extensive selection of glass, such as Dibbern China. They store was the first in the United States to introduce the glass sculpture of Australia's Ola and Marie Hoglund. The subtle scents of Slatkin & Co. Candles fill the air. Silver collectors will be delighted with the fine pieces of silver from Pampaloni, an Italian company that has been family-owned and operated for more than one hundred years. The gallery produces its own exclusive line called OwenLawrence leather, which includes beautiful, richly made tables, couches and benches. New shipments arrive several times a year and clients can either purchase items from the showroom or place special orders. Exploring this amazing shop can take awhile but is worth every moment, as you discover one exquisite piece after another. All of the staff members here understand that you their most valuable asset. Come and see what OwenLawrence Gallery has for you.

Westside Urban Market,
1200 Howell Mill Road, Suite A, Atlanta GA
(404) 869-7360 or (800) 499-3607
www.owenlawrence.com

Ambiance Interiors & Gifts

Internationally known and regionally recognized for trendsetting designs, Ambiance Interiors defines lifestyle in the South. Owners Pamela Reeves and Christi Tullis have made striking transformations to many homes and businesses all over the country since they opened the doors of their store, an 1870s historic pink house, in 1999. Whether it's residential, commercial or retail consulting, three words describe the results of their well-planned use of space—elegant, enchanting and breath-taking.

When you visit Ambiance Interiors, you'll see the Tudor Room, with its classic architectural elements layered in Old World style, complimented by leather and over-sized furniture. The Victodern (Victorian/modern) Room combines contemporary with antique to create a striking balance between different eras, showcasing original and limited edition artwork and a variety of accessories and furniture. Stepping into the Passementarie Room evokes memories of a Paris apartment. Wrapped in luxurious fabrics, trimmings and tassels, it is both warm and sentimental. The French Kitchen holds treasures galore, including themed recipe books with a companion CD of dinner music. The Tabletop Room showcases china and serving pieces to complete any party or bridal registry.

The Nursery and Girl Power rooms address the wishes of the younger generation with accoutrements, décor and gifts. The Gift Gallery spotlights the world famous polka-dot gift wrap set in custom cabinets, offered just for that special person. Highlighted in both the store and Design Center is the Ambiance Signature Paver System, which will make you think you're walking on 100-year-old cobblestone or slate.

Many national and regional publications, including *Southern Living*, *Home Accents Today*, *Gwinnett Magazine* and *Romantic Homes* have featured Ambiance Interiors. It was voted Best of the Best for Interior Design for many consecutive years by *Gwinnett Magazine* and A Favorite Shopping Experience by *Southern Living*. A destination is the best way to describe this hidden secret in North Georgia for all who enter. Have your smile on and camera ready, Dottie, the polka-dotted Hummer H2, may be around on your visit to this incredible shopping experience.

580 Buford Highway, Suwanee GA
(770) 932-1380
www.ambianceworldwide.com

Blossom Boxes

Enhance your home or garden with the latest in container gardening designs from Blossom Boxes. Owner Steve Eton and his talented team design stunning window box gardens using the latest innovative materials and a myriad of lovely plants, flowers and herbs. Steve left a career in home remodeling in 1995 to open Blossom Boxes after seeing many of his customers go crazy over his planted window boxes. He realized that container gardening would be ideal for many of Marietta's busy citizens. Urns, planters and fountains come in reinforced concrete, fiberglass, painted aluminum and iron. Blossom Boxes plants these durable containers with unusual plant assortments that meet your needs for color and light exposure. The company also offers Mind Your Manors, fiberglass window boxes with the look of handcrafted wood, ideal for a vintage home or for those who enjoy the country look. Boxes can be built to be portable or permanent. They come in standard or custom sizes and feature built-in drainage systems and 30-year warranties. The team at Blossom Boxes, which includes designer and marketing manager Chessa Azzolesi, provides such additional services as seasonal planting, weekly or monthly maintenance schedules and worry-free watering systems. Blossom Boxes has been featured at many home shows, including the Home Builders Association Expo in 1998, and it contributed to the Roswell Woman's Club Show Case Homes from 2003 through 2005. Add stylish finishing touches to your home or office with Blossom Boxes.

2291 Pine Warbler Court, Marietta GA
(770) 579-1490
www.blossomboxes.com

Casabella

Casabella is a destination worthy of a special trip. In Spanish or Italian, the name *casa bella* means beautiful home, and your beautiful home is the focus of this fresh and entertaining store. Casabella offers a large selection of Georgia gifts and furnishings, plus complimentary in-home design services, in-store floral design services and a popular bridal registry. Owner Ann VanDevelder is a hands-on owner who combines a strong artistic instinct with business savvy. After five years of selling her merchandise in a classy flea market, she opened her own store, where she displays her wares in attractive collage-style groupings that capture the imagination. Ann combines the vintage furnishings that she loves with artwork, fine china and other accessories, and she shows an uncanny ability to earmark what will appeal to her clientele. She carefully trains her seven merchandisers so that her customers receive a consistent level of service and design flair along with the store's signature cheerfulness. Her store has grown from its original 3,500-square-foot space to 13,000 square feet. Look for local artwork, an outstanding jewelry collection and any number of items that bring design into every nook and cranny of your life. Ann also extends her decorating services to several local charity events. For a refreshing shopping experience, visit Casabella. It's more than a store, it's a lifestyle.

4400 Roswell Road, Suite 128A, Marietta GA
(770) 321-1708
www.casabellathestore.com

Elegant Attic

Billing themselves as traders in uniquities and antiquities, Kathryn Umberger and Nora Maccaro use their exceptional sense of style and taste to fill Elegant Attic with stunning pieces from across the globe. A visit to the 3,000-square-foot shop is like taking a mini-vacation to the four corners of the world. Here you will find stained glass from Costa Rica, hand-blown jewelry from France, tribal boxes from Africa and custom fountains and tile from Italy, as well as a plethora of garden benches, fabrics, oddities and collectibles that are sure to charm. Nearly everything displayed at the Elegant Attic is handmade and one-of-a-kind. Often, items are created in remote areas by native artisans. The shop also works with several local craftsmen and artists to create a wide variety of custom designed art pieces. Kathryn and Nora enjoyed more than two decades of friendship before hitting upon the idea of turning their love of travel and antiquities into a business in 2006. The duo conceived Elegant Attic, the fruition of that idea, while they vacationed together in Italy. Jane Seymour visited Elegant Attic and her home collection is featured here. Fill your home with masterfully crafted and thoroughly original pieces of art and décor with an excursion to the Elegant Attic. Check out the website for special events.

1105 Canton Street, Roswell GA
(678) 261-7988
www.elegantattic.com

Earth Products

Earth Products is a family business that dates back three generations. Shannon and Mark Deveau took over from Shannon's father in 2000. The company sells stone, mulch, gravel and similar materials. Shannon has branched out to sell more decorative wares, such as glazed pots, willow chairs and birdbaths. Earth Products also offers pond kits and is Atlanta's exclusive distributor of Aquascape pond supplies. You'll find decorative wares and pond products in a new building, which Shannon refitted with cypress planking on the walls, three types of stone on the floors and a covered porch. Mark and Shannon believe that the key to their business is the detailed advice that they can offer their customers. Customers also value their quality products and timely deliveries. Earth Products offers classes, project guides and help in finding an installer or contractor. Shannon's grandfather opened the original business as Williams Nursery in 1952. In 1985, Shannon's father changed the name and focus of the business, moving from plants to hardscapes. In 2004, Mark and Shannon opened an Earth Products store in Alpharetta. A store in Pensacola bears the same name, because "My dad's idea of retirement was to open a new business in Florida," Shannon told the *Atlanta Journal-Constitution*, with a laugh. For the best in outdoor materials and accessories, don't miss Earth Products.

515 Cobb Parkway NE, Marietta GA
(770) 424-1479
4990 Highway 9, Alpharetta GA
(770) 817-1479
www.earthproducts.net

Four Seasons Pottery

Sometimes a business owner gets to have as much fun as the customer. Just ask Greg Godwin, owner of Four Seasons Pottery. Four Seasons specializes in concrete garden props customized by Greg with acids, stains and washes. Fountains, birdbaths and statuary sporting more than 20 finishes will inspire your own garden fantasies. You'll also find fixtures like paving stones, tables and benches. Greg's father Ernie started the business in 1992 as a retirement hobby. Ernie had previously sold statues through his wife's antique shop before deciding to up the scale. "You need a large piece of property to have a business like this," Greg says, indicating the massive collection. Four Seasons carries thousands of unusual garden embellishments from suppliers throughout the world, and new shipments arrive daily. Whatever your style, you will find it at Four Seasons, where you can purchase pieces as diverse as Grecian urns, Japanese lanterns and Imperial guardian lions. You will find statuary representing cupids, folksy animals, Buddha, angels and saints, all awaiting the individual touches that will bring out the look you desire. Greg figures he could make more money in some other business, but "where else could anyone have this much fun?" he says. Plan some time to wander through the selection at Four Seasons Pottery.

336 Hammond Drive, Atlanta GA
(404) 252-3411
www.4seasonspottery.com

The Heirloom Iron Bed Company and Fine Linens

You spend a third of your lifetime in your bedroom. Shouldn't it be a true expression of your personality? Terry Parker's Heirloom Iron Bed Company and Fine Linens will put you to bed in luxury with the finest luxury linens and the best quality handcrafted iron and brass beds found anywhere in the world. The distinction of these iron and brass beds is the frame, constructed of a cast iron interlocking dove-tail system, made without screws, nuts or bolts. This eliminates the shaking and squeaking common to mass-produced beds. Heirloom's beds are a reproduction of turn-of-the-century originals with improved durability through the use of the better materials available today. It also has a contemporary line that uses the same frame system as the original reproductions. The Heirloom Iron Bed Company offers a full selection of luxury linen lines from the best Italian, German, Austrian, French and American weavers. Look for Anichini, Ann Gish, Sferra and Sontuoso. Discover the Leitner, Peacock Alley, Legna and SDH linen lines. If this isn't enough, find linens by The Purists, Matouk, Yves Delorme, Pine Cone Hill and more. You can also shop online.

10800 Alpharetta Highway, Roswell GA (770) 993-7249 or (888) 993-7249
2140 Peachtree Road, Atlanta GA (404) 352-3132 or (888) 233-4002
www.heirloomironbed.com

A Certain Something

Your house announces who you are to the outside world, and at A Certain Something, the staff makes sure that your home says something good about you. The shop offers exquisite home furnishings, beautiful accents and everything else to fill a home with warmth and light. President, co-owner and designer Avra Clark, co-owner Lori Hicks and designer Mary Cooley all work together with clients to create a look and feel that suits each person's individual taste and lifestyle. With new items stocked almost daily, it's no wonder that customers always leave satisfied. They know that their beautifully decorated home, room, or guesthouse is not just as a space to share with family and friends, but a functional piece of art. Even the store itself offers an escape from the everyday, with warm tones of gold, brown, pewter and copper reflecting from lamps, mirrors and wall accents. For a serene and truly personalized experience, be sure to visit A Certain Something.

3515 Braselton Highway, Suite E2, Dacula GA
(770) 945-9181

Architectural Accents

Architectural Accents brings the glories of the past to today's homes. Owners Charles Nevinson and Maria Williamson opened the 30,000-square-foot store in the chic Buckhead district of Atlanta in 1981 and packed it with a wide selection of architectural antiques and historical replicas that will add character and distinction to your home. The large selection of antique carved wood, marble and limestone mantels, for example, ranges from the 16th century onwards, encompassing both grand and primitive styles. An affordable collection of reproduction mantels taken from antique models is also available. Hundreds of doors from Europe and America can be bought as is or framed, finished and furnished with either antique hardware or fine new hardware from such lines as Frank Allart, Turnstyle, Rocky Mountain and Bronzes de France. Unusual chandeliers, ironwork, tiles and a myriad of other architectural pieces are always in stock. Architectural Accents has become a first stop for an international clientele of designers, architects and builders. Visit the shop or the website with your requirements.

2711 Piedmont Road, Atlanta GA
(404) 266-8700
www.architecturalaccents.com

Jere's Antiques

Since 1976, Jere's Antiques has been a major source of supplies for antique dealers, auction houses, designers and individuals. Owner Jere Myers maintains his own warehouse in England and has buyers and pickers working throughout Britain and on the continent in Belgium, Holland and France. Jere unloads a 40-foot container in his 33,000-square-foot warehouse in Savannah every seven to 10 days. The constant flow of merchandise ensures that you will have a different and exciting adventure on each of your visits. You will find an amazing selection of 18th, 19th and 20th century furniture in all types of styles, woods and price ranges. Whether you seek a bar for home or commercial use, or furniture in mahogany, walnut, oak or pine, Jere has it all. You can find an 18th century chest, the finest 19th century breakfront, an Art Deco vanity and an oak draw-leaf table all lined up in a row, ready for your viewing. Jere has hundreds of chairs in sets of four, six, eight, 10, 12 and often sets of 14 and larger. The variety is fabulous. Allow yourself some time to visit Jere's. Revel in fine craftsmanship from the past and unearth something special for yourself at Jere's Antiques.

9 N Jefferson Street, Savannah GA
(912) 236-2815
www.jeresantiques.com

Stanton Home Furnishings

Stanton Home Furnishings features the latest transitional trends, the most glamorous furniture and must-have colors for the upscale Atlanta home. This store is an ideal retail solution for those who want to marry traditional and contemporary styles in their home environment. In transitional décor, furniture lines may be simple yet sophisticated, featuring straight lines and rounded profiles. Fabric can range from graphic patterns on overstuffed sofas to textured chenilles on sleek wood frames. Feminine and masculine attributes can be balanced for harmonious design. Within the broad transitional category, customers find considerable freedom to establish styles that they find comfortable. The sofa and chairs in the living room, for example, might flaunt curves that tend toward the traditional, while in the family room the accent tables and floor lamps could have a more contemporary feel. Come to Stanton Home Furnishings for timeless style and a blend of furnishings that captures your taste and lifestyle.

1250 Caroline Street, Suite C120, Atlanta GA
(404) 586-9000
www.stantonhomefurnishings.com

Uptown Gardening & Hardware

One morning in 2001, Joanie Clabbers woke up knowing what she needed to do. She needed to create a real neighborhood hardware store, the kind of old-time establishment where everyone gets helped and everyone gets greeted. In 2001, Joanie opened Uptown Gardening & Hardware, a place that stocks what the neighborhood needs and finds its customers by word of mouth.

Uptown is prepared with tools and garden accessories to help you tackle any household project. Joanie can answer your gardening questions or recommend pesticides and fertilizers. With a feel for homey charm as well as practicality, Joanie also stocks ceramic pottery, hand-blown glass tiki torches, watering cans and hummingbird feeders. Hanging wind chimes catch the breezes and send their music out into the neighborhood, where Joanie keeps an eye out for the local college kids. Uptown is located in the former church of the Branded Heart Ministries, and Joanie feels that the souls who once prayed there watch over her store in turn. Bring your home projects to that old-fashioned neighborhood hardware store, Uptown Gardening & Hardware.

509 Barnard Street, Savannah GA
(912) 234-7151

Southern Comforts Consignments

Outfit your home in style without breaking the bank at Southern Comforts Consignments, where you can find quality home furnishings, antiques and gifts at bargain prices. Owners Jenny and Mark Eid opened this destination shop in 2003 after extensively remodeling an old hardware store. Jenny had long dreamt of owning such a shop, so she could indulge her love of antiques and estate-sale shopping. Over the past several years the Eids have owned several other enterprises in Dunwoody, where they have shown a passion for providing exceptional service and for being fair to their patrons, which is undoubtedly why customers were lined up outside the door just before to the grand opening of Southern Comforts and have continued to pour in steadily since. The frequently changing inventory in this inspiring store is arranged in inviting vignettes that allow customers to better visualize a piece in their home. This improves the odds of a piece selling quickly, which means money in the bank for customers who bring items in to

be sold through the consignment process. Southern Comforts Consignments will take your gently used furniture, accessories and antique pieces, display them for quick sale, then give you 50 percent of the final selling price. After 120 days, items that are unsold and unclaimed by the owner are donated to Attic Treasures, a charity. Redesign your home with ease at Southern Comforts Consignments.

2510-C Mount Vernon Road, Dunwoody GA
(770) 901-5001
www.southerncomfortsatlanta.com

Eufloria,
Flowers & Little Luxuries

An artist seeks many manners of expression, while a businessperson seeks many ways of becoming a leader in his or her industry. It's the combination of sensibilities that makes TJ Baggett and Laurie J. Belshan such a winning team. Through Eufloria, Flowers & Little Luxuries, TJ and Laurie import flowers and plants from all over the world to make unusual floral arrangements, potted orchid baskets and outside gardens that serve a loyal and particular clientele. Instead of volume, Eufloria focuses on variety. Laurie is the floral designer of the team. She is a trained painter and sculptor who now applies her skills to floral artistry. TJ is a master gardener who designs and installs boutique gardens, such as English Shakespearean gardens that use David Austin roses and other heirloom varieties known for fragrance and Old World charm. With so much energy it is fitting that Laurie and TJ are prominent in the Savannah scene. They speak at many different gatherings, including those of garden clubs and non-profit organizations. As designers for the Savannah Film Commission, their talents are unprecedented in the floral industry. They are available for national travel and design work, and indeed their work may be seen in many parts of the United States and Europe. Stop in and visit for floral oddities and little luxuries that represent extraordinary gifts and inspired floral design.

412 E Montgomery Crossroads, Savannah GA
(912) 354-6700
www.euflorialife.com

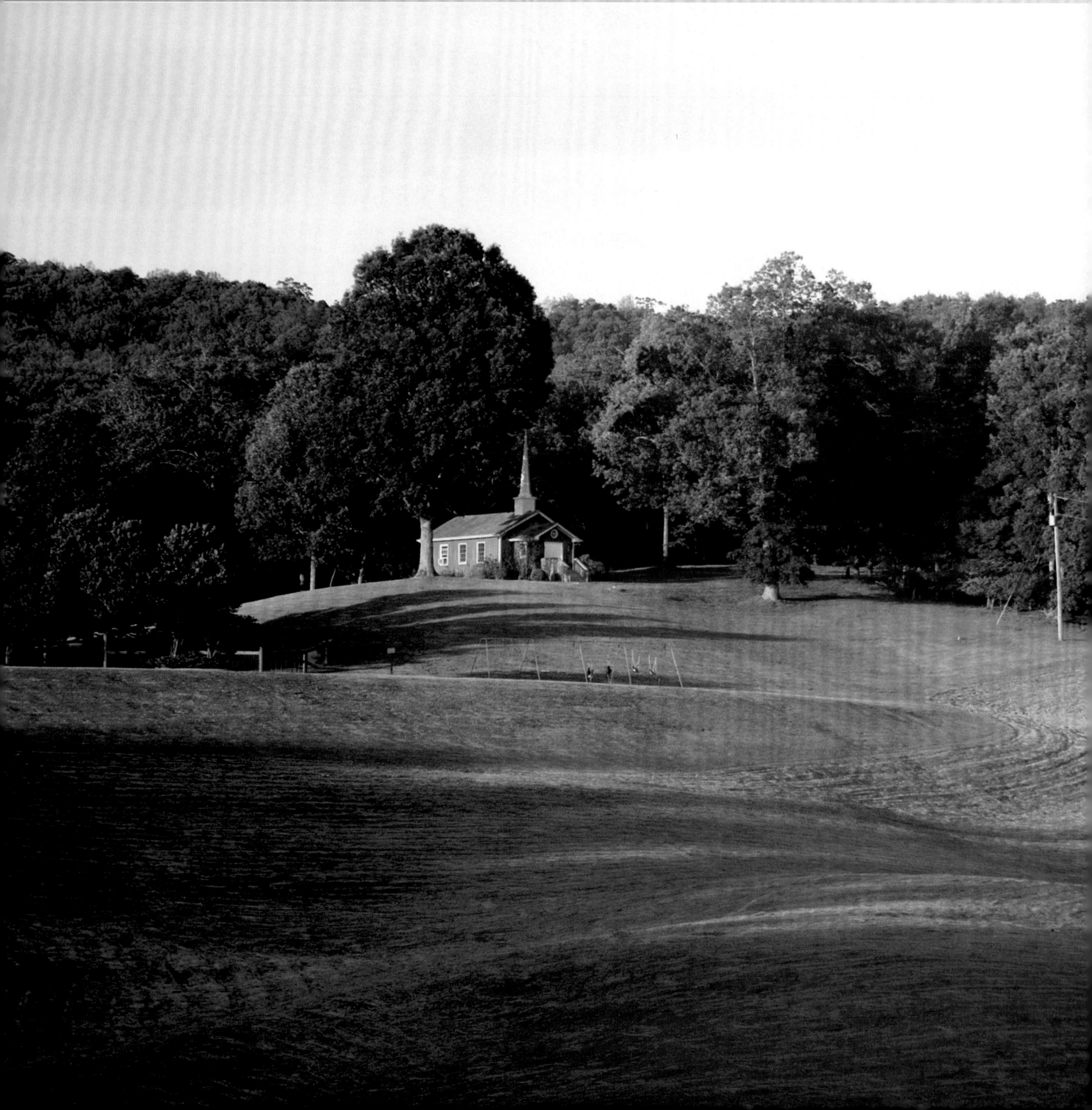

Lifestyle Destinations

First Class Cabin Rentals

Dan and Gayle Barton are Blue Ridge realtors who also manage a quality cabin rental business. As realtors, they help clients find luxury log cabins with great mountain views suitable for use as private getaways that are also lucrative rental investments. Before the couple opened First Class Cabin Rentals, they were themselves vacationers, regularly escaping Atlanta for the mountains surrounding Blue Ridge. Eventually, they built their own cabin and used it as a rental property. In 2002, the couple gave up their city careers and moved to the mountains they loved. The Bartons know what a good mountain vacation should feel like and what part a rental plays in that experience. They maintain exceptionally high standards for their properties and remain available to renters 24 hours a day. "Dan and I really do pride ourselves on providing the highest level of customer service in the cabin rental industry," says Gayle, who takes a motherly concern for her clients' comfort. You can count on extraordinary cleanliness and high-quality amenities, whether you seek stunning mountain views, lake views or wooded seclusion. All cabins are beautifully furnished and offer fully equipped kitchens, large decks with gas grills and linens. Fireplaces, hot tubs and cable or satellite television add to the fun. Whether you seek to rent or own, find a vacation home that captures the charm of the breathtaking Blue Ridge area with a call to Dan and Gayle Barton of First Class Cabin Rentals.

3293 E 1ˢᵗ Street, Blue Ridge GA
(706) 258-3018 or (877) 277-5409
www.thebartonadvantage.com

Barna Log Homes

Thirteen years ago, Gary and Georgia Kelley decided that they liked their log home so much they would sell log homes full time. Today, they operate Mountain-Lake Log Homes, Inc. and own a sister business in Alabama that specializes in log décor and more. After helping hundreds of homeowners find the right log-home package for their budget, Gary and Georgia can truly say that becoming a Barna Log Homes distributor was the right thing to do. They stand firm on their original formula for success, too—take care of the customer. Their search for a log manufacturer ended when they met Jim Barna, a respected leader in the log home industry, who has created many new technologies used in the finest log homes. Customers give a resounding thumbs-up to Gary and Georgia's choice. A Pennsylvania couple who did the building themselves credits them with the "knowledge and warm personalities that moved this project along" and calls Barna Log Homes "a standup company with a lot of integrity." Gary and Georgia traveled to Connecticut to be on-hand for one homeowner's log delivery day. They helped a parish in Wyoming with plans for a log church. Gary and Georgia's sales team is a top sales producer for Barna Log Homes and winner of the 2006 President's Gold Award for most dollars sold in the United States. Referral business is strong. Gary and Georgia pay $500 to $1,000 for a personal referral that concludes in the delivery of a log home. Let Mountain-Lake Log Homes, Inc. put you in the home or hunting lodge of your dreams.

103 Broad Street, Pine Mountain GA
(706) 663-7663
www.bestloghomes.com
www.bestlogdecor.com

BARNA
Log Homes
The experience matters

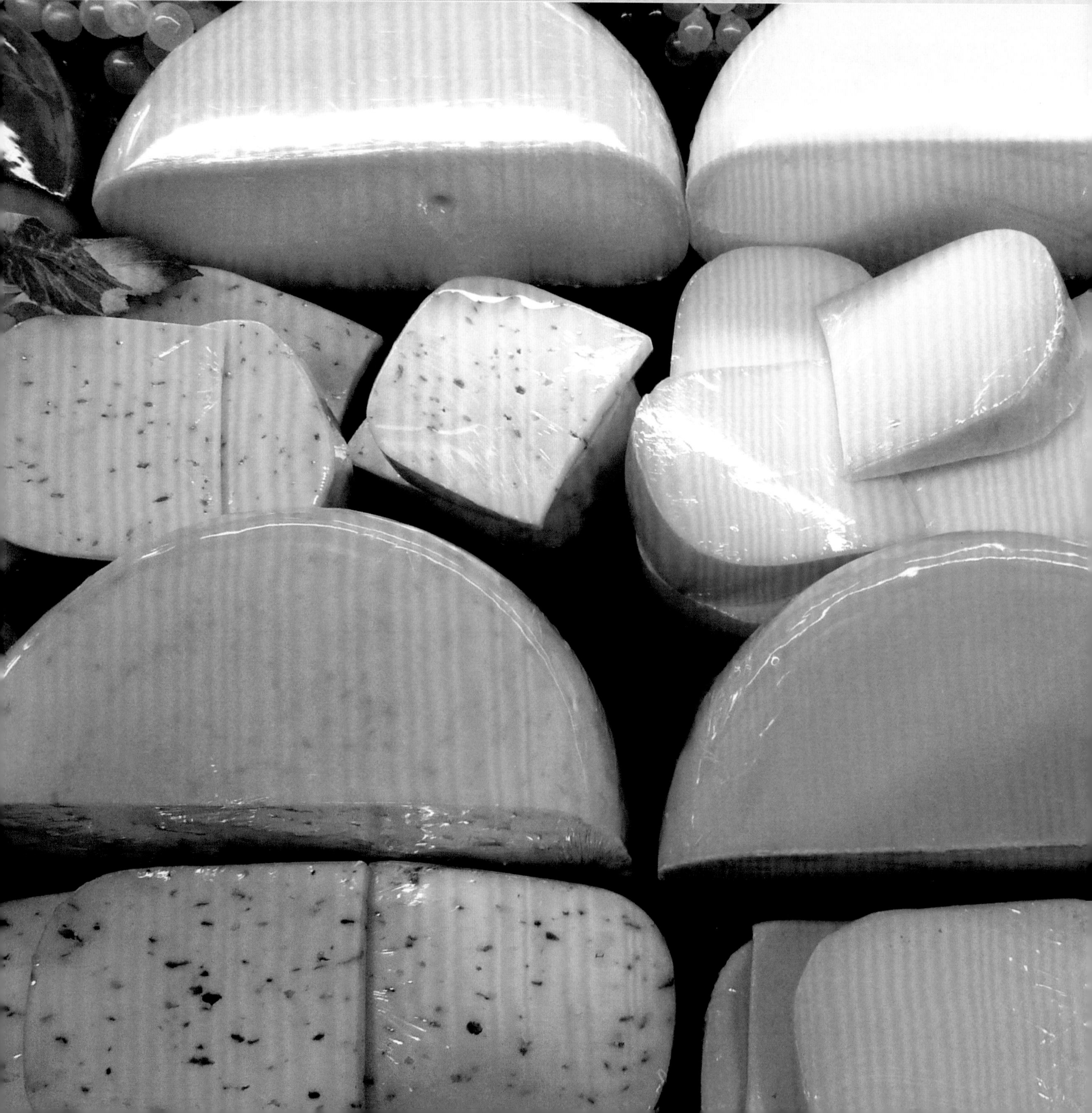

Markets & Delis

Enchanted Mountain Trout & Gourmet Meats

Tom and Karen Nunnally want their customers to leave Enchanted Mountain Trout & Gourmet Meats with natural beef, pork and poultry, free of steroids and hormones, and also with plenty of ideas for healthy meal preparation. They'll give you a free baking potato with your hand-cut steak, plus recipes to assure your success. Examples include fresh trout served with a glaze of apple, dill and rosemary or shrimp grilled in applewood-smoked bacon. The shop smokes its own meats and fish, using applewood from a local orchard. For success in the kitchen, Tom offers an exclusive line of sauces and dips that include Butcher Tom's barbecue sauce and rib rub. You can order prepared food for large gatherings or pick up a ready-made family dinner, such as pork tenderloin chili, Brunswick stew or pickled shrimp. Tom's hors d'oeuvres and natural turkeys are the stars of holiday gatherings. In 2001, the Nunnallys bought a smoked trout business and delivered the trout to local markets in a pickup truck. In 2003, they opened a small storefront in Morganton, selling fresh and smoked meat and seafood. The business expanded as families made Enchanted Mountain part of their weekly menu planning, and Tom and Karen turned their customers into extended family. Put some excitement into your meals with a visit to Enchanted Mountain Trout & Gourmet Meats.

12166 Morganton Highway, Morganton GA
(706) 374-5971

Sweet Auburn Curb Market

The people of Atlanta have come together at the Sweet Auburn Curb Market since 1918. Today, this vibrant market square is an international melting pot of culture and cuisine that caters equally to business folk, downtown and in-town residents and tourists, and hungry students from nearby Georgia State University. Two totemic sculptures, created by native son Carl Joe Williams, greet visitors at the market's entryway and usher you in to explore the exotic array of fresh produce, flowers and domestic goods. The Sweet Auburn Curb Market has chocolates, organic coffees, baked goods and seafood. It takes great pride in selling every part of a pig except the squeal. Rachel Ray's *$40 A Day* show has featured this popular and historic community landmark. President Bill Clinton fell in love with the market's signature sweet potato cheesecake in 1994. The Sweet Auburn Curb Market is also home to the busiest pharmacy in Georgia, several spirited cafés, gift shops and specialty stores with intriguing products from around the world. Enjoy a sampling of all that Atlanta has to offer at the Sweet Auburn Curb Market.

209 Edgewood Avenue, Atlanta GA
(404) 659-1665
www.sweetauburncurbmarket.com

Sevananda Natural Foods Cooperative

At Sevananda Natural Foods Cooperative, community comes first. The name Sevananda means the joy of service, and it is in this spirit that the co-op was founded, with the goal of empowering the community and improving the health and well-being of its members. With an all-organic produce department, an herbal/wellness department and a vegetarian/vegan deli-bakery, Sevananda prides itself on providing a healthy alternative to conventional foods. Produce comes from local farmers. Because it doesn't have to travel as far or be picked as early as conventionally grown foods, you can taste the freshness. Co-owned by its shoppers through a democratic membership and featuring locally grown and made products, Sevananda supports the economy of the community. The co-op was founded in 1974 as a small buying club. Today, it is an $8 million-dollar-a-year business. Three generations of families return to shop in a place with a true sense of community. As customers browse the aisles, listening to world music and sampling freshly made foods from the deli, they are sure to meet friends and neighbors. For a taste of local community spirit, come to Sevananda Natural Foods Cooperative.

467 Moreland Avenue NE, Atlanta GA
(404) 681-2831
www.sevananda.coop

Mercier Orchards

The Mercier family has devoted a lifetime to growing and knowing apples. Visitors to Mercier Orchards can pick their own apples or find out what's cooking in the bakery, restaurant and juice bar. A retail fruit and gift shop makes apples into everything from salsas, jellies and dressings to relishes, butter and pancake mixes. You can try an icy apple sorbet or choose such baked delights as fritters, pies, breads and doughnuts. Adele and Bill Mercier started out with 34 acres in 1943. Today, the family farm covers 200 acres and includes about 75,000 trees that produce more than 35 varieties of apples. You'll find peach and nectarine trees, too, along with blueberries, blackberries and cherries in a season that runs from May to December. Four generations take an active role in the orchards and farm market. Adele and Bill's son Tim holds degrees in horticulture and plant pathology that help him stay up-to-date. Tim's daughter Melissa Lillard, and Melissa's husband, David, are all part of the business. Melissa's son Zachary is now being initiated into the secrets of apples. Meanwhile, Bill still visits the orchards to check on the crop, and you might see Adele cutting apples or waiting on customers at the height of the season. The orchard is the last in the state to still operate a wholesale packaging facility. You can order apples or gift baskets at the Mercier's online store, but for a novel experience, visit Mercier Orchards in person.

8660 Blue Ridge Drive, Blue Ridge GA
(706) 632-3411
www.mercier-orchards.com

Manna to Go

It may seem unusual for a gourmet food, gifts and libations center to be located in an old service garage, but at Manna to Go, few things are ordinary. Of course, that's exactly what shop owner Michelle Wetherbee envisioned when she opened for business in 2004. As a marketing expert and gourmet food connoisseur, she sought a place that would fan the flames of the organic food movement and provide quick access to quality meals, imported wine and beer and specialty products. As a sixth-generation Clarkesville resident, Michelle celebrates the art of Southern hospitality together with an upscale retail philosophy that fosters appreciation of the earth's resources. The result is growing culinary curiosity in the community and an imaginative, fun shopping experience. You can visit the gourmet convenience store to find a zesty sauce, roasted meat, imported beers, microbrews and hard-to-find wines. Why not let Michelle create memorable corporate gifts for your employees or design custom gift baskets for special friends? While she's busy, you can shop for updated kitchenware to enhance the joy of cooking. At Manna to Go, private gourmet catering is available and fully prepared epicurean meals make life easier for on-the-go professionals and busy families. You may even want to join the Everyday Wellness to Go program that delivers calorie-controlled breakfasts, lunches and dinners to your door seven days a week, along with healthy snacks. Manna to Go is expanding to provide even more to taste and take home. Stop by today.

126 Grant Street, Clarkesville GA (706) 839-1441
www.mannatogo.com

Logan Turnpike Mill

George and Cecilia Holland would like to welcome you to the Logan Turnpike Mill. They purchased the mill in 1986 from George and Becky Rogers, who used to go around to country fairs demonstrating corn grinding. George and Cecilia carry on that tradition and have expanded to the country fair circuit to educate folks on the good nutrition and wonderful taste of freshly ground grains. The Logan Turnpike Mill carries an antique Williams grist mill circa 1916 and a 1926 Fairbanks Morse hit-n-miss engine mounted on a buckboard wagon with iron wheels. People who come here are delighted that freshly ground grains taste so good and are surprised that the old engines are so loud. Through the years the Hollands have contracted with local farmers to grow the corn sold here. The wheat comes from Montana where the cold climate and soil produce a high protein grain. The rye comes from the Midwest and the buckwheat comes from up-state New York. This company is still a family-run business. It has grown steadily through the years and now has a second location in an old homestead on the banks of the scenic Nottely River south of Blairsville. The Hollands opened this mill/store to the public in 1995 and since then the demand for products has increased, the mail order business has grown and they have even expanded to the Internet. Call Logan Turnpike Mill or visit the website today for more information.

3485 Gainesville Highway, Blairsville GA
(706) 745-5735 or (800) 84-GRITS (844-7487)
www.loganturnpikemill.com

Nora Mill Granary— Grist Mill & Country Store

Built in 1876 on the banks of the Chattahoochee River, the 130-year old Nora Mill Granary still uses its original 1,500-pound, 48-inch stones to grind grains. It captivates visitors who come for full-flavored stone-ground corn and wheat-based products and to savor a bit of living history. Ron Fain leased the run-down gristmill in the 1980s so that he and his parents could bring it back to life. Ron studied everything he could get his hands on about old-fashioned milling and became a self-educated expert on running the operation. His wife, Rita, would test recipes and products constantly to make sure all products were of the highest quality. Ron worked with his parents until their deaths. With the help of his youngest daughter, Joann Fain Tarpley, he expanded his product offerings, developed recipes, opened the gift shop next door to the mill and began selling online and through mail order. In 2001, Ron died unexpectedly, and Joann and her husband, Rich, took over operation of the mill. Rich had learned the art of milling from Ron and knew how to listen and feel the heartbeat of the mill. Today, Joann and Rich's children contribute their labor and love to the mill. A visit here is your opportunity to purchase stone-ground flour and bread as well as porridge, cornmeal and mixes to make pancakes and muffins or biscuits and gravy. Nora Mill Next Door carries thousands of gifts, including cookbooks, soaps and gourmet country foods. A kitchen here serves up samples of products from the mill and the store. Come experience the goodness at the heart of Nora Mill Granary.

7107 S Main Street, Helen GA
(706) 878-2375 or (800) 927-2375
www.noramill.com

Marietta Wine Market

Randall and Karen Heard want their customers to feel like they're visiting friends when they come to the Marietta Wine Market. The expansive high ceilings, brick walls and art from local artists provide guests with a comfortable place to shop and have a glass of wine. Twice weekly the store hosts wine tasting events. You can relax at the bar or on a cushy couch or chair while you taste, learn about wine and meet new friends. Complimentary hors d'oeuvres are served at the tastings and donation proceeds go to local charities. The Marietta Wine Market has more than 250 different wines from around the world. About half are boutique wines from smaller vineyards, as well as wines from local North Georgia vineyards. They emphasize affordable, high-value wines, with most in the price range of $10 to $35 per bottle. "This is not a wine museum, we want you to be able to buy them and enjoy them," Karen says. Don't feel intimidated if you don't know a lot about wines. They can help you select the perfect wine or gift for any occasion. Some come to Historic Marietta Square just to see Bentley, the Heard's Springer Spaniel. Bentley accompanies the Heards to work everyday, and is the store's official greeter and mascot.

18 Powder Springs Street, Marietta GA
(770) 919-1574
www.mariettawinemarket.com

Thomas Orchards, Greenhouse & Giftshop

In 1954, Jerry Thomas, Sr. planted Thomas Orchards and a business sprouted that has been growing strong for more than 50 years. Thomas Orchards, Greenhouse & Giftshop offers visitors a variety of fresh-from-the-tree delights, including 20 peach varieties and flavorful apples by the bushel. This popular roadside stop, now owned and operated by the founder's son, Jerry Jr., and his wife, Paula, is open annually from mid-March through mid-December and features a wide selection of local produce and specialty products, including gourmet preserves, downright delicious honeys and boiled peanuts. The shop is also well-known for its juicy, flavor-packed tomatoes, but it is the handmade specialty ice creams that have made the company famous throughout the county. Thomas Orchards, Greenhouse & Giftshop additionally carries an array of hard-to-find flowers and plants, as well as a choice selection of gifts for the home and garden. Jerry and Paula are always on hand to offer a warm greeting, give planting advice or help you find that ideal gift or flower selection. Skip the chain stores and savor the fruit of Jerry and Paula's labors with a visit to Thomas Orchards, Greenhouse & Giftshop.

6091 Macon Highway, Bishop GA
(706) 769-5011

Savannah Wine Shop

Located in the city's historic downtown, Savannah Wine Shop doesn't just carry Georgia wines. This tasting room plus gift and wine shop prides itself on bringing a mix of people together, so it offers a mix of wines. Here you'll find carefully chosen wines from historic regions all over the world—including Georgia, of course. The shop is lovingly tended by Stan and Daphne Ray, self-described cork dorks, who also serve a variety of cheeses from the local Sweetgrass Dairy. Patrons can taste the cheeses and buy wines by the glass. Try a wine flight (comparison tasting) to find that

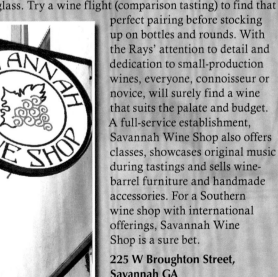

perfect pairing before stocking up on bottles and rounds. With the Rays' attention to detail and dedication to small-production wines, everyone, connoisseur or novice, will surely find a wine that suits the palate and budget. A full-service establishment, Savannah Wine Shop also offers classes, showcases original music during tastings and sells wine-barrel furniture and handmade accessories. For a Southern wine shop with international offerings, Savannah Wine Shop is a sure bet.

**225 W Broughton Street,
Savannah GA
(912) 232-3323**
www.savannahwineshop.com

Recreation & Fitness

L-R: Denise Gangone, Rosa Gangone, Jan Butler, Carolyn Fleetwood, Jackie Pharoh, Jane Sollivan, Linda Cooper, & Jacque Dale

Fleetwood Dance Center

For more than 40 years, Georgia's budding dance artists have received professional training and guidance from the Fleetwood Dance Center in Alpharetta. The company was founded by Carolyn Fleetwood in 1960 and is currently under the ownership and artistic direction of her daughter, Lynn Fleetwood Dukes. Lynn holds a distinguished background in dance, which includes instruction from the likes of Pittman Corry and Yurek Lazowiski. She also holds a bachelor of business administration degree in marketing from Georgia State University. Fleetwood Dance Center caters to both children and adults and carries on Carolyn's tradition of training dancers in all styles of dance, including musical theater, jazz and tap, as well as ballet and pointe. Many of Fleetwood's members have found professional careers in dance and musical theater, starring on stage and in television and movies. The center is home to the Fleetwood Dance Theater, which uses the art of dance to educate and entertain Atlanta's north metro area and surrounding counties. The nonprofit theater troupe works in concert with other nonprofit organizations, performing at fundraisers that benefit the local community. The troupe also provides educational workshops for local school arts programs. Enjoy beauty in motion on the stage or learn the art of dance and go on to become a part of the magic at Fleetwood Dance Center.

11164 State Bridge Road, Suite B-107, Alpharetta GA
(770) 442-5229 *www.fleetwooddance.com*

Gotta Dance Atlanta

Have you ever watched a music video and wished you had the confidence to pull off the moves of the dancers in the background or the star in the foreground? At Gotta Dance Atlanta, a dance fitness studio, you can learn how to do more than two-step with professionals. At Gotta Dance Atlanta, experts will make you lose the two left feet and extra pounds with intense but enjoyable classes. The more fluid movements of jazz and ballet are also broken down to their basics, giving anyone the opportunity to release their inner Bob Rizzo or Nuryev. For those with more experience than the local club scene, there are also classes for brushing up on technique before their next audition. Dance can burn over 60 calories for every 10 minutes you are getting your groove on. The enjoyable learning experience embodies a non-competitive philosophy. When the staff isn't teaching, they're usually busy burning up a stage at the Gotta Dance Atlanta Ensemble for local benefits, or performing individually on stages across the country with artists. If you have a passion for dance, want to get fit, or want to be better in tune to the rhythm of life, take a class at Gotta Dance Atlanta.

1778 Ellsworth Industrial Drive NW, Atlanta GA (404) 352-0420
www.got2dance.net

A Step Above Stables

Grand champion stallions, pedigreed babies and family-friendly horses make their home at A Step Above Stables in the mountains of North Georgia. More than 100 quality horses are sold each year at this full-service horse facility. The owners and trainers have the soft hearts and knowledge required to raise and train quality horses. This stable truly is A Step Above, with people who love animals, horses with great blood lines and 250 acres of riding trails and boarding land. Owner Curtis Teague is a man of integrity and drive who believes in resistance-free training that respects the horse. Curtis began working at age 12 and by 21 had purchased 20 acres of land. His daughter Kameron named the stable A Step Above at age six and continues to ensure that the stable provides a family-friendly experience. Kameron competes in equestrian sports, riding a 17-time world champion stallion. Curtis maintains an ongoing stable of no less than 40 horses. Guides use some of these horses to take small groups of visitors on rides through forest trails and overlooks of Lake Nottley. For your horseback riding session, you can request a horse with an easy walking pace or let the wind blow through your hair atop a faster steed. With an advance reservation, you can ride at the day's end and watch the sunset behind the mountains. One visit to A Step Above Stables and you will want to come back for more.

3839 S Mauney Road, Blairsville GA
(706) 745-9051
www.astepabovestables.com

Collins Hill Golf Club

Collins Hill Golf Club is one of Georgia's best-kept golf secrets. The course boasts a beautiful traditional layout with small undulating greens, varying elevations and narrow tree-lined fairways that offer a challenge to every skill level. The clubhouse is ideal for relaxation, special events and celebrations. The staff at Collins Hill seeks to exceed your expectations. Architect Perrin Walker designed the course, which was completely renovated in 2000 and rebuilt in 2007. Jim Frier manages the non-profit, semi-private club today as general manager. Seasoned pro Joe Mullins offers lessons. In the summer, golfers from 6 to 16 can attend a junior camp, with instruction, practice opportunities and supervised play. The Pro Shop provides customized club fitting and video computer swing analysis. It also sells a variety of golf equipment and accessories from vendors such as Callaway, Ashworth and AM Player, and merchandise from Slazenger, made famous in the movie *Goldfinger*. Visit Collins Hill Golf Club for outstanding golf, instruction and social activities.

585 Camp Perrin Road, Lawrenceville GA
(770) 822-5400
www.collinshillgolf.com

Outdoor Traditions

Sometimes the only thing more fun than hunting, fishing and hiking in the great outdoors is hunting and fishing for the gear you're going to use next time out. Outdoor Traditions in Dawsonville is an outdoor-lovers playground. This 25,000-square-foot mega-store is crammed wall to wall with the toys of the sporting trade. You'll find everything from the best gun selection in the region to fishing and camping gear, archery supplies, clothes and—well, everything. The store even sports an indoor archery range and a 45-foot climbing wall. The owner of this sporting extravaganza is Ginger Evans. Her goal is to offer outdoor lovers with a complete range of top-notch gear at affordable prices. Browse the website and you will see she has done that and more. Outdoor Traditions offers hints on the best places to hunt, fish and romp through the woods, along with information on how to maximize the experience when you're out there. Ginger offers free outdoor and hunter education classes, along with classes for school and scout groups. She also goes out of her way to support charitable organizations that help orphaned children both locally and abroad. There really is nothing better than getting outside and being a part of nature, but shopping in a store like Outdoor Traditions is close. High-tail it over to Dawsonville first chance you get and you'll see what we mean.

243 Stowers Road E, Dawsonville GA
(706) 216-4868
www.outdoortraditions.com

Trackrock Campground & Cabins

Nestled in the foothills of the Smokey Mountains and bordered by the Chattahoochee National Forest, Trackrock Campground & Cabins sits on 300 acres of scenic woodlands and meadows. In 1966, Tommie and Martha Alexander turned their family farm into an 18-site campground. They continued to make improvements over the years, and today the family-owned campground, managed by their son, features 94 shaded, level, private campsites for tents, pop-ups and RVs. There are also five fully furnished cabins for those who'd rather rock on the porch than rough it. Campers can bask in the sun on the sandy beach or swim and fish in the four-acre spring-fed lake that's stocked with bass, bream and catfish. Trackrock offers many hiking trails, a large playground, recreation room, volleyball, horseshoes, seasonal Sunday chapel services and wi-fi Internet access. Ice, LP gas and firewood are also available at the office. Most Saturday evenings you can enjoy hayrides, and guides at Trackrock Stables offer horseback riding over the beautiful property. Many evenings, you might spot such local wildlife as deer, hawks or fox. The surrounding area offers shopping, golf, antiquing and whitewater rafting. Also nearby is access to the Appalachian Trail and Brasstown Bald, Georgia's highest point. Three generations of campers have returned to this idyllic spot again and again. Bring your camera and join fellow campers while you make some memories at Trackrock.

4887 Trackrock Camp Road, Blairsville GA
(706) 745-2420 *www.trackrock.com*

Gold 'n Gem Grubbin

Pan for precious gold nuggets in fresh water creeks and take pleasure in gorgeous scenery as you unwind at Gold 'n Gem Grubbin. More than 100 acres of beautiful woodland, lakes and streams offer excellent fishing, picnicking and camping in a tranquil atmosphere. An authentic on-site mining operation recalls former Gold Rush days of the 1800s, an exciting adventure for gold bugs of all ages. Visitors can pan for gold and gems by the creekside like the old-timers or by the bucket, by purchasing gold and gem ore. Screen for precious rubies, sapphires, emeralds and other gemstones, both native and from around the world. When you are finished panning or grubbing, head for the Gem Shack, a large attractive shop nestled beneath fragrant pine trees by the lake. Trained staff evaluate your treasures for cutting and transformation into fine 14-karat gold and sterling silver jewelry, handcrafted by co-owner Brian Devan at reasonable mine-direct prices. An adventurer by nature, Brian left a lucrative sales position in the early 1980s to traipse along Amazon tributaries mining gold. He was totally smitten by the gold bug and eagerly purchased this gold-bearing property just outside of Cleveland in 1984. Brian and his partner, Susan Tamburino, have run the business for over 20 years. Susan's specialty is business management and she enjoys gardening. The beautiful landscaping attests to her green thumb. The couple also rescue dogs. They have a variety of breeds that are all their babies. Come and relive Georgia's gold rush with a real mining adventure at Gold 'n Gem Grubbin—as seen in *Lost Treasure Magazine* and on the Travel Channel.

75 Gold Nugget Lane, Cleveland GA
(706) 865-5454 or (800) 942-4GEM (4436)
www.goldngem.com

Unicoi Outfitters

When you call an outfitter to arrange a fly-fishing venture, the last thing you want to hear is that the guides are all booked. Unicoi Outfitters in Helen does its best to make sure this never happens by keeping a whole brigade of 22 guides on staff. These experienced professionals will take you where the trophy fish are, including places that other outfitters don't go. Indeed, through an exclusive offering by Unicoi Outfitters, a limited number of anglers can fly-fish for plump trout in the Nachoochee Bend section of the Chattahoochee River at Nora Mills. Reached by a 90-minute drive from Atlanta, this mile-and-a-half section of the river has been closed to public fishing for 75 years. The guides at Unicoi are eager to acquaint you with the secrets of this and other area trout streams. If you are new to fly fishing, the Gilligan Special provides two guests with an hour of fly-casting instruction plus two hours of guided fishing. Whether the guides are interacting with beginning or advanced fly anglers, they take their role as responsible stewards of Georgia's natural resources seriously. Serving the fly fishing community since 1994, Unicoi Outfitters added a second location in Blue Ridge in 2003. Both this store and the original shop in Helen carry a full range of tackle, clothing and fly-tying materials. Let Unicoi Outfitters be your guide to fast-flowing fun and adventure.

7280 S Main Street, Helen GA
(706) 878-3083
490 E Main Street, Blue Ridge GA
(706) 632-1880
www.unicoioutfitters.com

Adventure Trail Rides of Cashes Valley

Members of the Callihan family are born with more horse sense than most of us will accumulate in our lifetimes. The family, among the first to settle Cashes Valley, runs Adventure Trail Rides on a 400-acre property. The land has mountain views that extend beyond Georgia into Tennessee and North Carolina. Owners Misty and Derrick Callihan can saddle up adults and children as young as seven on the gentle steeds. Rides vary in length and difficulty. You can choose an hour ride with few obstacles, an hour-and-a-half ride that suits a mixed group or a two-hour ride that puts a horse through several paces as you negotiate creeks, meadows and steep terrain. Misty and Derrick use a lifetime's experience with horses to introduce you to your steed and teach you the intricacies of commanding the creature. They'll guide you to locations

that offer mountain views few people ever see. Adventure Trail Rides is one of two horseback riding facilities operated by the Callihans. The second is at Fort Mountain State Park. Between the two stables, the Callihans keep 37 horses. They also offer boarding. Derrick stays in touch with his roots through his involvement in the Alabama Cavalry, a unit that holds Civil War reenactments. To immerse yourself in the Blue Ridge Mountains, make a reservation with Adventure Trail Rides.

933 Cashes Valley Road, Cherrylog GA
(706) 258-BARN (2276)
www.adventuretrailrides.com

The Outside World

The Outside World is an equipment paradise for those who love adventure in the great outdoors. Lifelong adventurer Brent Troncalli created this 10,000-square-foot emporium to outfit, orient and train his fellow travelers between adventures. The store offers a complete line of camping and hiking gear and more than 100 models of canoes and kayaks. An experienced staff is available seven days a week to advise on equipment and demonstrate how to use it. This is especially important for such individualized equipment as kayaks, which vary widely in shape and style to accommodate different body types. Picking the wrong one off the shelf could lead not only to discomfort but to hazard when you negotiate rapids. You don't have to rely on specifications alone to make a considered choice here, because the Outside World boasts a 25,000-gallon indoor pool for testing canoes and kayaks. A wave machine creates a powerful current in the pool, turning it into the world's first indoor simulated river. In addition to demonstrations, the pool plays host to regular classes, such organized sports as

kayak football and such special events as the Paddle Expo & Rodeo. The indoor facility offers spectators a sustained look at professionals performing paddling acrobatics that would be impossible in most indoor environments. For indoor excitement and experienced support in your adventures, visit the Outside World, your friend in the wild.

471 Quill Drive, Dawsonville GA
(706) 265-4500
www.theoutsideworld.net

Pinetree Country Club

Pinetree Country Club is more than just your average private golf club. It's a first-class family destination filled with recreational adventures and culinary delights. It's also the course where Hall of Fame inductee and golfing legend Larry Nelson began his professional career. This welcoming 270-acre course first opened in 1962 and has continued to gain popularity each year due to the Pinetree's exemplary staff and family oriented atmosphere, which comes complete with a kids' campus and the state's largest private pool. The golf course itself is a classic layout designed with 14 greenside bunkers and four holes with fairway bunkers. This stunning course, which is highlighted by glorious scenery and lush, rolling green hills, was designed by Atlanta's own Chick Adams in 1960, and only Mother Nature has seen fit to alter the original design by removing some stately pines during a severe tornado in the late 1980s. In addition to offering great golfing, Pinetree also offers many special events throughout the year, including poolside dining with such themes as Wild West, 50s Night and Pirates Cruise. The club is the ideal place to host such special occasions as weddings, anniversaries and reunion parties. Ensure your family receives the pampering they deserve with the personalized attention and multiple amenities at Pinetree Country Club.

3400 McCollum Parkway NW, Kennesaw GA
(770) 422-5902 *www.pinetreecc.org*

Up the River Outfitters

If you love water, you are going to find the Chattahoochee River irresistible. Lance and Rebecca LeHew can outfit you with a tube, kayak or canoe and take most of the work out of your day, from transporting you and your boat to the put-in at Buford Dam to picking you up at the take-out. You can pack a cooler, shoot some Class One and Two rapids and take in the breathtaking surroundings. These outfitters rent canoes and kayaks from March to December, as long as the water temperature is above 60 degrees. They also sell such river-friendly supplies as fishing poles, sunscreen and waterproof shoes. You'll love the T-shirts from Life is Good, the special cell phone containers and the instant cameras. The service is as refreshing as the river, and you can count on the LeHews' knowledge for valuable insight into the river and the sights along the way. Once you know your way to Up the River Outfitters, you can find plenty of excuses to come out this way. In October, the LeHews sell pumpkins and fall decorations, and starting Thanksgiving weekend you can pick up a fresh Fraser fir Christmas tree, grown in the mountains of North Carolina. You might meet Rebecca's mom and dad, David and Jana, because they often help out. When you want to shoot the Hooch, visit the folks at Up the River Outfitters.

6144 Cumming Highway 20, Sugar Hill GA
(770) 614-3322 *www.uptheriveroutfitters.com*

Sunburst Stables

With 30 miles of trails right next to the Chatahoochee National Forest, Sunburst Stables is an ideal starting place for enjoying the mountains of North Georgia from the back of a horse. Becky and Mark Elliott purchased the long-established stables and rental cabins in 1995 and dedicated themselves to improving the facilities. Today, Sunburst offers 48 horses, suitable for all sorts of riders, and trips ranging from a half hour ride with panoramic views to 13 miles of trotting through terrain that has awed visitors from around the world. You can take riding lessons at the stables' enclosed riding arena. Sunburst can also provide boarding for your own horse. If you visit in the summer, you may see children bouncing into the pond from the water trampoline. That's one of the activities that keeps girls aged 8 to 15 involved during the nine one-week camp sessions. These revolve around horseback riding, but also include an overnight campout, tubing down the Chatahoochee, skating, bowling and swimming at nearby lakes, rivers and waterfalls. The year-round facility makes a comfortable vacation destination for families, thanks to cabins with two and three bedrooms and a bunkhouse that will accommodate a large group of up to 18 people. Cabins have fireplaces, hot tubs and fully equipped kitchens. Fall brings mountain color and hayrides for large groups. Come enjoy the horses and the idyllic setting at Sunburst Stables.

3181 State Highway 255, Clarkesville GA
(706) 947-7433 or (800) 806-1953
www.sunburststables.com

Atlanta Workshop Players

Stars are born at Atlanta Workshop Players. Just ask singer-actress Mandy Moore, Oxygen Network's head of development Amy Dean Kennedy, or *American Idol* songbird and Broadway star Diana D'Garmo—all of whom spent time learning and performing here. Artistic Director Lynn Stallings opened the nonprofit children's theater company in 1981. "Our motto is 'Kids Changing the World, One Audience at a Time,'" Lynn says, adding that the studio is committed to "using art to invoke social change and to teach character education." To do so, the theater offers a year-round theater school, in addition to performing arts camps and a professional touring company. The atmosphere at Atlanta Workshop Players is nurturing and non-competitive, with expert teachers from the fields of theater, film and television sharing their expertise. Even the shyest student can blossom into an expressive performer in such a nurturing environment. Over the course of more than two decades, the studio has produced and toured with more than 25 original musicals and offered hundreds of scholarships to children in need. Come to Atlanta Workshop Players, where your child can learn the skills to be a star.

(770) 998-8111
www.atlantaworkshopplayers.com

Photo by Don Stallings

The Studio Atlanta Dance

As their slogan has it, the Studio Atlanta Dance has been making Atlanta dance for more than 20 years. Today, locations in Buckhead and Vinings offer classes for every age and skill level. Children as young as two can start in pre-ballet training that builds coordination. Older kids go on to ballet and tap classes or participate in hip-hop classes that are taught by professionals who have choreographed and performed with such acts as Will Smith and Jay Z. The studio also features a Playball program, designed to teach kids life lessons through sports skills. Children between 7 and 12 can prepare for the stage with acting courses. The studio understands the impulse to dance shared by people of all ages and offers a full slate of classes for adults as well as children. Adults can choose from jazz, tap, modern and ballroom dance. If you would rather heat up the room with a salsa dance, the Studio Atlanta Dance can teach you the moves. Classes in yoga and Pilates promise to keep you limber and strong. Bring your fleet feet in to the Studio Atlanta Dance for an experience that will have your body and spirit dancing for the joy of it.

**1675 Cumberland Parkway,
Smyrna GA (Vinings)
(678) 556-0444
3229B Cains Hill Place,
Atlanta GA (Buckhead)
(404) 233-8686**
www.thestudioatlantadance.org

Margot's Closet

To find a costume fit for the stage, dancers and actors often travel to places like New York City, where theater and dance companies abound. Now, Woodstock area performers can find the cutting edge dance and theatrical supplies they need all behind the pink door on Main Street. Margot's Closet, named for the famed ballerina Margot Fonteyn, prepares dancers, gymnasts and actors to take to the stage in style. Donna and Alan Culpepper were inspired to open the store by their daughter's love of dance. The beautiful shop provides all the essentials for every type of dance from such well-known companies as Capezio, Danskin and Mirella. Carefully selected knitwear completes the look of today's young dancer. Moms will love the one-stop shopping experience. Everything from hair accessories to stage makeup and bags to eyelashes, you will find it here. The front case glimmers with rhinestone tiara's, diamond earrings and porcelain collectibles. Margot's has the largest selection of gifts for dancers anywhere, especially during the holidays. Ask to have it gift wrapped in pink and black, compliments of Margot's. Services at Margot's also include a multi-talented designer that can attend to all your costuming needs, and a photographer for head shots or group photos. Margot's invites dancers to keep a wish list so gift givers will know just how to please their favorite dancers. Margot's promises not to disappoint you. Come and experience the magic of Margot's Closet.

8926 Main Street, Woodstock GA
(770) 517-7917
www.margotscloset.net

Restaurants & Cafés

Dogwood Bar & Grill

Join the gang at the Dogwood Bar & Grill, where the food and drinks are first-rate and everyone at the bar knows your name. Carolyn and Chris Bates purchased the bar and grill in 2006 and their experienced staff has brought the location back to life. Enjoy hand-cut steaks, seafood, pastas and an array of specialty salads. Dogwood Bar & Grill also has homemade pot roast, spaghetti and meatballs, ribs that fall off the bone, fried chicken and pork tenderloin, just to name a few. Beyond great food, expect plenty of fun. Monday through Thursday the tavern has daily drink specials, half-price appetizers, Ladies Night, trivia and Texas Hold 'Em. Sports lovers can follow games on more than 18 televisions, including the new high-definition big screen. Whether you come for a family dinner or just to hang out on the large patio, the staff is warm and friendly and the atmosphere is casual.

12460 Crabapple Road, Suite 103, Alpharetta GA (770) 667-1112
www.dogwoodbarandgrill.com

Shoki Japanese Steak House & Sushi Bar

When Jay Kim opened his restaurant in 2000, he confidently named it *Shoki*, which means a place to which everybody comes back. And that's just what the folks in Athens are doing—coming back often to Shoki Japanese Steak & Sushi Bar for good food and the fun of tableside cooking. Kim, who came to the United States from Korea when he was 17, has been in the restaurant business since the 1980s. He is particular about every aspect of the steakhouse, from the highly trained chefs who operate the tableside hibachi grills to the quality of the food. The menu features teriyaki chicken, filet mignon, scallops, king salmon, lobster, swordfish, calamari and vegetables. Jay's wife, Diane, fashions the tiramisu and the cheesecake, tasty departures from traditional Japanese fare. You'll find a full drinks bar, including icy specialty concoctions. Shoki offers 13 tableside grills in five rooms plus a sushi bar. Jay chooses the best-trained sushi chefs he can find, then trains others in-house. Tables seat 10 to 20 people, and party rooms hold 20 to 40. The décor is Japanese with comfortable seating, lots of plants and original art on the walls. Everything about Shoki is designed to result in customer happiness, from the ample parking, to the quiet, relaxing atmosphere and the dynamic knife-wielding cooking show. Shoki is open seven days a week for dinner only. Put some excitement into your next family celebration with a visit to Shoki Japanese Steak House & Sushi Bar.

10 Huntington Road #A3, Athens GA
(706) 227-1933
www.shokisteakhouse.net

Madison Chophouse Grille

Don't be discouraged if you have to circle around the block a few times to find a parking place for Madison Chophouse Grille. It's a testament to the local popularity of this restaurant that even generous parking fills quickly. Once inside, your patience is rewarded with one delicious pleasure after another. House specialties include the fried green tomato appetizer, the prime rib and garlic mashed potatoes. The burgers are cooked to your specification with your choice of toppings. The Madison Chophouse can satisfy just about any diner with generous salads, Nathan's Famous Hot Dogs, ribs, and succulent fish, chicken and steak. The delicious Chocolate Caramel Puff dessert combines a puff pastry stuffed with chocolate and caramel cheesecake and chocolate chips and topped with fresh whipped cream and vanilla ice cream. All this satisfaction comes to you inside a charming historic building. Husband and wife Patrick and Natalie Reams bought the restaurant in 2006, but it was originally opened in 1996. Just as they know a lasting menu item when they see one, they know the value of loyal employees and have been lucky to have Manager Faye Craft stay on with them since the purchase. She is joined by a second manager, David Stone, and Kitchen Manager Josh Leshuk. Come hungry and come often to Madison Chophouse Grille.

202 S Main Street, Madison GA
(706) 342-9009

The Flying Machine

See what's flying out of the Gwinnett County Airport from a comfortable perch at runway's edge. The Flying Machine restaurant puts you near the action and creates some of its own action with good old American favorite foods and plenty of first-class entertainment. Joy and Hokey Sloan bought the restaurant in 1998 after falling in love with its unique location at Briscoe Field. Watch the planes or the sunset from the patio while eating a sandwich or a burger that has to be worth $100, which the Flying Machine nearly gives away at around $6. If you're looking for something fancier, the Flying Machine also offers steak, seafood and pasta entrées. Aviation

buffs get a kick out of the location as well as the model airplanes hanging from the ceiling. Top-flight entertainment abounds, and Hokey hops on stage occasionally to perform country music. You're in for a treat on those nights, because Hokey's a pro, having recorded his own CD with Waylon Jennings' band. For entertainment—from the corporate jets and prop planes to celebrity performers—and a party atmosphere, have your next burger in the distinctive surroundings of the Flying Machine.

510 Briscoe Boulevard, Lawrenceville GA
(770) 962-2262
www.theflyingmachine.com

Lavender Asian Bistro

Heaven is the word the *Gwinnett Citizen* recently used to describe the Chinese and Thai cuisine at Lavender Asian Bistro. Since 2003, the Lawrenceville restaurant has been providing diners with a trip to culinary nirvana with its blend of Asian flavors. Owner James Wang got his start in the restaurant business in 1979 in New York City, working his way up to head chef in 1985. James and Executive Chef Alex Lai bring their New York-honed skills to the table every day, offering food that's a treat for all the senses. "The beauty of the presentation is as impressive as the flavors," writes *Accent Gwinnett* magazine. Among the more impressive visual treats is the sticky rice, which is gathered in the center of a mountain of mangoes and

mint leaves and flavored with coconut mango sauce. The restaurant is also particularly renowned for its General Tso's Chicken. In addition to the large variety of items you'll find on the menu, Lavender Asian Bistro offers daily specials for those with more adventurous tastes. You'll enjoy watching the chefs through the windows of the dining room as they hustle about, slicing, dicing and preparing your food. The atmosphere is one of casual elegance, with bright golden colors and fine linen tablecloths. For a balance of adventurous flavors and relaxing atmosphere, visit Lavender Asian Bistro.

1195 Scenic Highway, Suite C8, Lawrenceville GA
(770) 982-3887

The Historic Green Manor Restaurant

Whether you are getting married or taking your family out to Sunday brunch, the Historic Green Manor will bring you a taste of the old South. The restaurant, which serves a lunch buffet on weekdays and a Sunday brunch buffet, resides in a gracious 1910 mansion surrounded by five manicured acres of gardens and stately trees. Owners Albert John Green and his wife, Barbara, have a special relationship to this property, which has been in the Green family since 1917, when Dr. Albert J. Green purchased it from Drewry A. Carmichael, Union City's first mayor. The property was a gift to Dr. Green's new bride and functioned as both a home and medical office, with Dr. Green's patients waiting on the expansive veranda to see their favorite practitioner. The Greens opened the restaurant in 1990, offering such Southern comfort foods as fried chicken, meatloaf, and the hands-down favorite dessert, Georgia peach cobbler. Executive Chef Odie Moore prepares this country fare to exacting standards with the help of Sous Chef Chaney Cooper and Pastry Chef Emma Bridges. If you can't make lunch, consider coming out on Friday night for a sizzling down-home barbecue buffet. CEO and General Manager Linda Johnson oversees day-to-day operations and welcomes requests for special events and catering. Linda also has a special relationship to the Green family, since she was delivered into the world by the original Dr. Greene. For warm hospitality and nostalgic charm, visit the Historic Green Manor.

6400 Westbrook Street, Union City GA
(770) 964-4343
www.greenmanor.biz

Café Hot Wing

Café Hot Wing is both the hottest and the coolest sports restaurant in the Atlanta area and a favorite for digging into wings, burgers or cheese steaks with the family. First in the hot category are the wings themselves. Owners Richard and Wan Stamey have every reason to be proud of their signature dish, named best in the area and fourth in the nation by *Wingazette Magazine*. They offer wings in 26 different varieties, ranging from mild to XX-hot and in such flavors as Cajun, teriyaki and honey mustard. The menu is big and varied and, like everything at Café Hot Wings, seeks to offer something appealing to all members of the family. Café Hot Wings is also a hot spot for karaoke, team trivia and Texas Hold 'Em. Sports lovers appreciate the 35 televisions scattered throughout the restaurant. The Stameys believe in encouraging families to spend time together, and so they welcome children. With video games in the arcade room and free WiFi, the kids will find plenty to amuse them. The café is smoke-free, and the only alcohol served here is beer—100 different bottled beers and more on tap. Beer is just one of the cool offerings here. There's key lime pie, made with real limes from the Florida Keys, and a mist system on the patio that creates an outdoor cool zone, dropping the temperature under the canopy by as much as 15 degrees. The first Café Hot Wing opened in 1987, and today seven cafés dot the metro area. For all the hot and cool good times you could want, visit Café Hot Wing.

6595 Tara Boulevard, Jonesboro GA
(770) 471-3200 *www.cafehotwing.com*

Photo by Stu Spivack

The Whistle Stop Café

In 2002, Elizabeth Bryant left a career as an electronics engineer to purchase the Juliette restaurant made famous by the movie *Fried Green Tomatoes*. Elizabeth was catering in her spare time when Robert Williams, who established the original Whistle Stop Café in 1991, decided to sell his restaurant's now-famous name. Thanks to the movie, people come from all over the world to eat at the Whistle Stop. Thanks to Elizabeth's cooking, they leave with fond memories of Southern classics such as fried green tomatoes, barbecue pulled pork and fried chicken. People purchase extra barbecue sauce to take home, and the Bryants are in the process of packaging their sauce as well as the breading for the tomatoes. Elizabeth uses family recipes, including Big Lee's Peach Cobbler and Theo's Butter Pound Cake. Her sweet root sticks—country-fried sweet potatoes dusted with cinnamon and sugar—are favorite treats. For those who know the movie, there's no mistaking the building, which retains its creaky screen door and the window with a bullet hole. You will find wooden booths, two wooden bars and movie memorabilia on the walls. Items from the building's days as a merchandise store remain, too. The café has been featured on the Food Network and in such magazines as *Southern Living* and *Southern Distinction*. The Bryants are working on plans for a franchise operation. Follow the sound of the train whistle to the Whistle Stop Café.

443 McCrackin Street, Juliette GA (478) 992-8886 *www.thewhistlestopcafe.com*

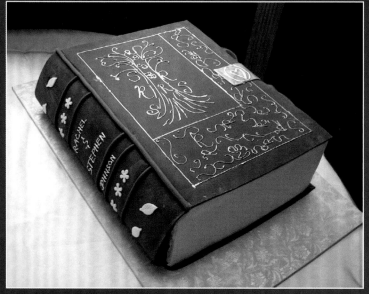

Anthony's Fine Dining

Anthony's Fine Dining is a prominent Atlanta establishment, renowned for its contemporary Southern cuisine and elegant banquet facilities. The restaurant opened in 1967 in a magnificent mansion just 15 minutes from downtown Atlanta. The Pope-Walton plantation mansion on three lushly wooded acres is one of the few remaining authentic antebellum homes. Built in 1797, the home was moved more than 100 miles in 1963, and rebuilt board by board and brick by brick. With 12 elegant dining rooms, seven fireplaces and two wine cellars, the home is designed for the special occasions in life Anthony's pastry chef can create a special cake for your gathering. Many couples have been married in this romantic house, which regularly hosts parties for 10 to 700 people. The Lady Bug banquet room with its lush red carpet, mirrors and dance floor can accommodate 200 guests for such special occasions as birthdays, anniversaries and retirement ceremonies. The Porch, a grand room surrounded in glass, is a prominent feature of the mansion. Its chandeliers beam down on the garden patio, surrounded by handmade brick walks paved in the old herringbone style and gardens of magnolia, boxwood and cherry laurel. The restaurant serves carefully prepared steaks and seafood in the New American style and offers an à la carte menu to individual diners. Many staff members have been offering warm Southern hospitality here for more than a decade. For location, food, service and a history that includes a resident ghost, visit Anthony's Fine Dining.

3109 Piedmont Road NE, Atlanta GA
(404) 262-7379
www.anthonysfinedining.com

Dillard's BBQ & Biscuits

As you drive through historic Suwanee, the tantalizing scent of authentic barbecue will tease your nostrils and set your stomach to growling until there's nothing left to do but head to the source—Dillard's BBQ & Biscuits. Ricky Dillard and his wife Sheron started this favorite eatery of the Atlanta Falcons in 1998. They use fresh ingredients and the virtue of patience to create scrumptious, slow-cooked barbecue dishes that will leave you begging for just one more bite. Ricky's brother-in-law, Greg Hunter, manages the restaurant, and the couple's daughters, Yolanda and Crystal, are always on hand to help out with everything from cooking to greeting customers. Dillard's BBQ & Biscuits features a full range of your favorite barbecued treats, such as slow-cooked pork, beef and chicken, as well as a variety of hamburgers and hot dogs. Ricky and the gang at Dillard's offer a fantastic country-style breakfast four days a week, which features tender country ham, huge fluffy biscuits and eggs perfectly cooked to order. Dillard's BBQ & Biscuits also offers a full take-out and catering menu filled with all your favorites, including an array of flavorful side dishes and desserts. In addition to gaining fame for their barbecue, the Dillards are patrons of their community and seek ways to serve it. Satisfy your cravings for true barbecue with a visit to Dillard's BBQ & Biscuits.

2 Highway 23, Suwanee GA
(770) 945-0703

Amira's Mediterranean Bistro

Opened in 2006, Amira's Mediterranean Bistro made a swift and strong impression on the Suwanee community as a place to enjoy wholesome Middle Eastern cuisine in a friendly atmosphere. Owner Michelle Bishara named the bistro after her baby daughter. One year later, despite great success, Michelle decided to close the bistro's physical location for the time being and operate it solely as a catering business. She had established a loyal base of customers who

would keep the spirit of the bistro alive while allowing Michelle to spend more time with her children while they are still young. Customers continue to enjoy her savory vegetable and meat dishes, which she makes with only the freshest natural ingredients. Her menu derives from her own upbringing and that of her husband, Neemeh, who hails from Nazareth. You'll find Middle Eastern classics such as hummus, baba ghanoush and lamb kebabs and a lavish dessert list that includes baklava and six-layer chocolate cake. The signature dessert, Mom's Phylla Basket, is an elaborate pastry filled with vanilla pudding, fresh mango and kiwi and drizzled with raspberry sauce. A review by Lori Johnson calls it "fresh and flavorful Mediterranean fare." Exotic options and addictive favorites will keep you calling back again. When planning your next event, consider Amira's Mediterranean Bistro for something distinctive, heart-healthy and sure to please.

Sugar Hill GA (678) 758-1583

Isabelle's on the Gorge

The history of Tallulah Falls, from the Cherokees and pioneers to its 19th century heyday as a resort town, has been captured and preserved at Isabelle's on the Gorge. The restaurant, located in an 1880 Victorian home, is right across the street from the falls, one of the seven wonders of Georgia. It is also within sight of a small home that once belonged to Nancybelle Almoyen's grandmother. When Nancybelle was a child, she dreamed of visiting the grand home, a vision that lasted until the day when she and her husband, Paul, leased the home and opened Isabelle's. The restaurant is named after the five generations of Isabelles in Nancybelle's family. In 2006, the couple were able to purchase the building outright. The fried green tomatoes, sweet potato

French fries and sweet tea are customer favorites at Isabelle's. Paul, who hails from New York, contributes the generous Paul's Mile High Reuben. You are sure to appreciate such special soups as the salmon chowder, along with the chicken salad and banana bread from old family recipes. Bring the family and come as you are to Isabelle's on the Gorge, where one family's dream can provide an inspirational setting for your dreams as well.

Highway 441, Tallulah Falls GA
(706) 754-5614
www.isabellesonthegorge.com

Dantanna's Surf & Turf

The three owners of Dantanna's Surf & Turf wanted their Buckhead restaurant to be driven by a fine menu rather than by sports events. "We wanted to build a restaurant based on food and reinforced by sports rather than vice versa," says David Clapp, the founder. As it turns out, David, along with Jay Kazlow and Chef Tim Williams, juggle both concepts beautifully. They serve all-natural aged steak, and the seafood is flown in twice daily. As you might guess, surf and turf combos are popular at Dantanna's. Other entrées include pork chops, roast chicken, short ribs and duckling. Customers enjoy a large choice of appetizers, salads and sandwiches. A pastry chef ensures that desserts are just as fresh as the rest of the meal. Customers can choose from among 40 beers and 100 wines, including 50 wines by the glass. A build-your-own Bloody Mary Bar adds to the fun of a Sunday afternoon spent watching your team on the bank of big-screen televisions. An adjacent cigar lounge with a walk-in humidor offers still more flat screens. You can even take your stogie outside without missing the action, because the massive outdoor patio sports seven more plasma televisions. The restaurant's name combines the names of David's two children, Dan and Anna, and the turf refers to cattle pastures and football fields. The partners have a combined 70 years of experience in the restaurant field. They also support fundraising efforts for local Boys and Girls Clubs. Update your vision of what an upscale sports restaurant can be with a visit to Dantanna's Surf & Turf.

3400 Around Lenox Drive, Suite 304, Atlanta GA
(404) 760-TURF (8873)
www.dantannas.com

Vinny's New York Pizza & Italian Grill

Vinny's New York Pizza & Italian Grill is the quintessential New York-style pizzeria, a popular and fun family gathering spot. The twist here is that owners Bill and Beth Starkey serve their authentic Italian dishes with true Southern hospitality. The 10-inch personal pan pizza is a favorite with locals. Beef lasagna, eggplant parmigiana and lobster ravioli are other headliners. The Greek artichoke salad is a hit with antipasto lovers. If you're in the mood for a sub, consider the New York Neighbor or the Philly chicken and cheese, highly favored by Vinny's regulars. Try to save room for dessert—customers laud the homemade Italian cannoli, as well as the irresistible tiramisu. Vinny's has a new special every night and a never-ending supply of heavenly hot fresh garlic rolls. The portions are generous and the prices are reasonable. The restaurant offers catering services and has on-site private rooms for large parties and special events. The entire extended Starkey family extends a warm Southern welcome to you. They invite you to visit and enjoy the delicious Italian cuisine at Vinny's New York Pizza & Italian Grill.

4977 Friendship Road, Buford GA
(678) 482-9966
115 Town Center Parkway, Hoschton GA
(706) 824-9924

The Varsity

The Varsity is a fun place to eat and a historic landmark that has been part of Georgia since 1928. Offering curbside service, the Varsity is the world's largest drive-in. Identifying cars by number is an integral part of the Varsity drive-in system. The restaurant can accommodate 600 cars and 800 people at a time. Every day, it serves two miles of hot dogs, 2,000 pounds of onions and 2,500 pounds of potatoes. Daily, 5,000 fried pies and 300 gallons of chili are made from scratch. The Varsity receives three to six deliveries per day to ensure the freshest ingredients. Many celebrities such as Clark Gable and Burt Reynolds have eaten at the Varsity. Service is lightning fast and prices are less than most quick eateries. Original owner Frank Gordy has said that he watched Atlanta grow up around the Varsity. Gordy's daughter, Nancy Simms, is the owner today. Gordy became known as the man with million-dollar taste buds. He originally called his restaurant the Yellow Jacket because most of his patrons were Georgia Tech students. The restaurant grew so rapidly that Gordy moved to the current flagship location, which takes up two city blocks, and renamed it the Varsity. Today, the Varsity has five locations in Atlanta and one in Athens—check the website for details. Come to the Varsity and enjoy the food that Georgia loves.

61 North Avenue, Atlanta GA
(404) 881-1707
www.thevarsity.com

Corkscrew Café

The Corkscrew Café in downtown Dahlonega is one of those places you'll be telling your friends about when you return home from vacation. It's the kind of place locals try to keep to themselves, but never do, because they can't help but brag. Located in an historic building that used to be the city hall and jail, the Corkscrew Café features culinary creativity and casual ambience. Owners Robert and Coleen Rotunno deserve all the credit for the vision behind their restaurant. They do with food what Picasso did with paint. Their handling of lamb, duck, seafood and vegetables have earned praise from restaurant critics throughout the region. The café's wine selection is extraordinary. The desserts are superb. Located next to the historic Holly Theatre, the Corkscrew is a magnet for the arts crowd. The restaurant seats 50 people, with outdoor seating for 60. That may seem like a lot, but believe us when we say it's not. Reservations are heartily recommended.

51 Main Street W, Dahlonega GA
(706) 867-8551
www.thecorkscrewcafe.com

Amici Italian Café

It's little wonder that Amici Italian Café is growing by leaps and bounds. Amici Italian Café offers memorable fare, a friendly and relaxed environment and quality service at four locations. Try sharing a hand-tossed Greek pizza with spinach, garlic and mushrooms topped with mozzarella, Parmesan and feta cheeses. Every ingredient is absolutely fresh. Patrons can also enjoy a selection of hot or cold deli sandwiches, choose from a tempting array of salads and appetizers, dive into a plate of pasta or homemade lasagna, and sample Amici's own dessert cannoli. The Stagecoach Catering division offers everything a hungry customer desires and takes care of all those special event details, too. The Stagecoach Catering staff will work with you to whip up a feast that will wow every guest. Petal Pushers, the in-house floral service and event design business, provides stunning arrangements to grace the tables at your special event, whether it's a wedding, holiday feast or a corporate dinner. Wherever you are or whatever you're planning, Amici Italian Café and Stagecoach Catering will serve up a meal or event to remember.

113 S Main Street, Madison GA (706) 342-0000
101 W Hancock Street, Milledgeville GA (478) 452-5003
233 E Clayton Street, Athens GA (706) 353-0000
1116 College Street, Covington GA (678) 625-3000
2946 Godfrey Road, Madison GA (706) 752-0081 (Stagecoach Catering)
(706) 474-0461 (Petal Pushers)
www.amici-café.com

Girasoles

Chef José Zambrano combines the provocative flavors of the Mediterranean with intriguing New World concepts to create a thoroughly tantalizing array of dishes at Girasoles in the heart of historic Watkinsville. José learned his trade at an early age from a French chef in California. He later moved on to work in several top-notch eateries until 1999, when he moved to Athens, Georgia and opened his first restaurant. While there, José met his future partner Marta Whigham and, in 2005, the duo opened Girasoles to rave reviews. Guests of the popular eatery are always warmly welcomed by one or both of the owners and then treated to an extraordinary meal, highlighted by perfectly prepared cuisine and exemplary service. Girasoles' broad menu offers diners everything from pheasant to fish, and José is happy to cook any dish to order. Instead of choosing an entrée, you can request Chef Jose's VIP treatment, and he will then surprise you with a succulent specialty of the house prepared just for you. Jose reinvents a Southern classic with his shrimp and grits. Sautéed chicken breast becomes the base for creative expression in Chicken Zambrano and Oaxaca Chicken. A popular dessert is the signature chocolate passion pie. In addition to serving fine cuisine, José and Marta offer a series of in-house cooking classes for budding chefs of all ages. Send your taste buds soaring with a visit to Girasoles, where you will discover magic in every bite.

24 Greensboro Highway, Suite A, Watkinsville GA
(706) 310-0410
www.girasolesrestaurant.com

Sia's

Since opening in 1998, several prestigious publications, including *Atlanta Magazine* and the *Hudspeth Report* have declared Sia's one of the metro Atlanta's top ten restaurants. The restaurant's color scheme is bright and warm, with a Mediterranean flavor. Warm hues of tangerine complement the cobalt blue accents and brushed chrome highlights that create the simple and sophisticated ambience. Sia's features innovative American cuisine with Southwestern and Asian influences. Executive Chef Bruce McQuain exemplifies creativity with signature dishes such as ginger-glazed organic salmon and caramelized jumbo sea scallops with wild mushrooms. Notable appetizers include lemon crab cream cheese fritters and the house-cured meats, terrine and sausage platter. Chef McQuain's warm liquid chocolate cake with white chocolate ice cream is legendary. Sia's serves only organic meats and takes the concept of freshness to a new level. Cheeses used in Sia's recipes are made fresh locally. Seafood is flown in daily from around the world. The wine list is varied and international. Sia's provides catering services off site, as well as private and corporate events at the restaurant's facilities. Owner Sia Moshk and all of his staff invite you to come experience Sia's exemplary food and service.

10305 Medlock Bridge Road, Duluth GA
(770) 497-9727
www.siasrestaurant.com

Ninja Steak & Sushi

When your meal is prepared right before your eyes, you can be sure the chef is skilled and the food is fresh. Such a philosophy of excellence has earned Ninja Steak & Sushi top marks from the local press. *Gwinnett Magazine* awarded it a Readers Choice "Best of" in 2004, 2005 and 2006. Brothers Edward and Steven Sun launched the restaurant in 1999 and now offer four locations: Lawrenceville, Hamilton Mill (Dacula), Cumming and Holcomb Bridge (Roswell). A specially trained hibachi chef turns a fine meal into performance art, while such sushi favorites as the Godzilla or dragon rolls promise prizewinning quality. Ninja features choice steak, fresh poultry and crisp vegetables. It makes its sauces and dressings onsite. The salmon and tuna are never frozen. Children love Ninja, especially on birthdays when the staff takes their picture, sings them a Japanese birthday song and serves free Japanese fried ice cream. The Suns have been in

the restaurant business for 18 years and are skilled in all styles of Asian cuisine. Their décor is contemporary, with dramatic lighting that complements the dramatic cooking. The bar serves many types of beer, wine and cocktails, including cold and hot sake, Japanese beer and several martini varieties. For creative cuisine and a good time, come to Ninja Steak & Sushi.

2115 Hamilton Creek Parkway, Suite 106, Dacula GA
(770) 831-7131
www.ninjasteak.com

Iron Wok China Bistro

You know you are in the hands of masters at Iron Wok China Bistro, the creation of brothers Edward and Steven Sun. It didn't take diners long to discover the quality of the gourmet Chinese food. Iron Wok opened in 2004 and in 2005 the *Gwinnett Daily Post* named it Best in Gwinnett County. The modern interior glows with just the right amount of light, while an open kitchen design allows you to watch the chefs at work. The fusion-style low-carb dishes are deft demonstrations of Asian food styles. Dishes feature meat, chicken, seafood and vegetables. The chicken lettuce wrap is a popular starter. For a spicy main course, diners often select the Volcano Shrimp, while for spectacular presentation, try the glorious Seafood Tower in its clay pot. All meals are free of MSG and all sauces are freshly made. The restaurant also makes its four flavors of ice cream onsite: green tea, red bean, vanilla and rainbow. A deep-frying technique

puts a crunchy shell around the silky center of the ice cream for a delightful close to a meal. Not only does the full bar offer a select wine list, but the chefs make canny recommendations for food pairings. The food presentation and the friendly service are upscale, but reasonable prices and a kid's menu make families welcome. Spoil yourself with a visit to Iron Wok China Bistro.

3515 Braselton Highway E-1, Hamilton Mill, Dacula GA
(770) 831-6988
www.ironwokbistro.com

Winchester Woodfire Grill

In the heart of a Georgia boy lived the dream of a Wild West cowboy. As the boy grew into a man, he indulged his dream with visits to saloons and dining establishments in Colorado, New Mexico and Wyoming. Eventually, the grown-up R.L. Glosson and his wife, Rita, brought the cowboy dream to the Appalachians, where they run Winchester Woodfire Grill. The Glossons combed the countryside from Alabama to Arizona in a quest to assemble the most genuine artifacts for fitting out the restaurant. They knew that prints and reproductions were not adequate for the size and scope of their vision, so they filled the Winchester with original oil paintings, handcrafted saddles and chaps and a world-class collection of Winchester rifles like those held by the men who settled the West. The building pays tribute to Western history with hand-hewn timbers, beams and heart pine salvaged from long ruined saloons, hotels and restaurants. The Glossons chose the Winchester's employees from among Atlanta's most talented and dedicated restaurant professionals. The top chefs in the Southeast use their expertise to select the finest hand-cut steaks and freshest seafood found in these parts. The entire staff dedicates itself to creating beautiful, unique and delicious dishes served in an atmosphere of relaxed Western refinement. Come enjoy dinner by the Winchester Woodfire Grill's hand-built fireplace or try a cocktail in the saloon. But remember, no spurs on the bar.

110 Mount Vista Boulevard, Canton GA
(770) 345-8000
www.winchestergrill.com

UMI Japanese Steak House & Sushi Bar

Famed for its 35 different *maki* sushi (sushi rolls), UMI Japanese Steak House & Sushi Bar will satisfy your craving for Japanese cuisine. Owner Andy Lin trained as a sushi chef at his family's restaurant before coming to Henry County in 1998. Among the 35 varieties of sushi rolls are shrimp and salmon, along with less common varieties such as the bagel roll, which comes with smoked salmon and cream cheese, or the Green Salad, which features lettuce and crab topped with shrimp. Andy's shrimp tempura is popular, partly due to his family's secret recipe for tempura sauce. Tempura vegetables that accompany the shrimp include sweet potatoes, onion rings, zucchini and mushrooms. With its 12 sizzling hibachi grills, UMI is the biggest hibachi restaurant in the area. Guests can watch as UMI's friendly, expert staff prepares succulent steaks and other favorites. Seafood lovers will delight in the range of fresh-grilled options, including calamari, lobster, shrimp and scallops. A children's menu features smaller portions for little ones. Top off your meal with some Japanese green tea ice cream. You'll find a rich selection of cocktails at the bar, as well as saki, Japanese beer and plum wine. For excellent Japanese steak, sushi rolls and seafood, come to UMI Japanese Steak House & Sushi Bar.

550 Eagles Landing Parkway, Stockbridge GA (770) 389-6999

D. Morgan's

A beautifully renovated old furniture warehouse is the site for the new American cuisine of D. Morgan's Restaurant & Wine Bar. Chef Derek Morgan takes seasonal ingredients from local organic farmers and turns them into something quite extraordinary. "The challenge is not to overwork a dish," he says. "Either in flavor or presentation, you have to know when to step away." Derek describes his culinary style as grand simplicity—creating complex flavors using a few simple key ingredients. You might begin your evening with lobster bisque with porcini essence and chives. Alternatively, try the Asian pear salad with spiced pecans and Maytag bleu cheese. Ginger-glazed monkfish, Colorado rack of lamb and duck cassoulet with white beans and andouille are just a few of the outstanding entrées, all presented in the clear, simple fashion that is Derek's trademark. Wines for every dish, mood and occasion complement the dining experience. The wine cellar at D. Morgan's provides a space for private parties. A Cartersville native, Derek brings a West Coast sensibility to his craft. Derek has worked in famous and trendy Los Angeles and Phoenix kitchens. He is proud to return to Cartersville at a time when his town is transforming itself into a destination for entertainment, boutique shopping and fine dining. For sophisticated dining away from the big city, come to D. Morgan's.

28 W Main Street, Cartersville GA (770) 383-3535 *www.dmorgans.com*

Andy's BBQ

Andy's BBQ combines local history with the Holder family's secret recipes to create a delightfully messy dining experience. Owners Andy and Diane Holder opened the restaurant seven years ago. They framed their building with logs milled on the family farm and moved a 100-year-old cotton mill house to the site to serve as the main dining room. Once inside, you can read up on local history from the old newspaper articles that plaster the walls. Andy and Diane honor family members by using many of their timeless recipes, for example Poppa Royal's barbecue sauce. The recipe for Grandma Langford's Brunswick stew is so closely guarded that even Diane doesn't know the secret ingredient. Diane knows every last pinch of seasoning in the beans, though, because they are one of the signature dishes she has enjoyed perfecting over time. Andy's smoked wings and ribs are sure to please any barbecue lover, and Andy says his method of eliminating grease reduces heartburn and cholesterol. The rustic restaurant's great service and food make it a fun place for a family get-together or other special occasion, and the banquet room accommodates up to 130 diners, with a total seating capacity of 250. Come on down to Andy's BBQ and enjoy some down-home dinners—from the Holder family to your family.

100 Friendship Road, Eatonton GA
(706) 485-5802

Armaan—American-Asian Fusion Restaurant & Lounge

Armaan, located at the corner of old Norcross and Breckenridge in the heart of Gwinnett, is a contemporary restaurant that promises a stimulating and unique experience. Armaan's cuisine is inventive yet approachable. The menu is a combination of American cuisine with a splash of Asian flavors, sure to satisfy all curious taste buds. Enjoy the lobster tail your way—fried, broiled or tandoori—or the signature burger with creamy goat cheese and shitake mushrooms. Armaan boasts a sleek and chic décor on two levels. The upstairs lounge offers a fabulous blend of mixed cocktails. Choose from an array of 50 different exotic wines. Deciding between the pamatini (pomegranate martini) and the mango Margarita will make you into a regular. There's live music and belly dancing on featured evenings. Armaan dazzles one and all with a glass waterfall that trickles from the upstairs lounge. Armaan has semi-private dining for groups up to 35, and is perfect for intimate dinners, engagement parties and corporate meetings. Surround yourself with beautiful people, fabulous atmosphere and the soothing sound of jazz music in the background while you enjoy exquisite food and great ambience at Armaan.

3064 Old Norcross Road, Duluth GA
770-923-2323 or (888) 7ARMAAN (727-6226)
www.thearmaan.com

Firefly Café

At Firefly Café, head chef and owner Sharon Stinogel gives simple foods a creative twist, in a style she calls American eclectic. Since opening five years ago, the restaurant has not only become a staple in Savannah's trendy historic district but has received generous national praise as well. *Southern Living* and *The New York Times* featured the restaurant in 2007. Local patrons are so pleased with Sharon's style that they aren't shy to eat there more than once in a day. In addition to daily breakfast, Firefly serves a weekend brunch that *Savannah Magazine* readers voted Best Brunch in 2006. Those who like a custom feast enjoy the My Way omelettes at brunch, while others swear by the Bay Street hash or banana nut French toast. At lunch and dinner, shrimp is one of Savannah's favorite ingredients, adding a regional kick of flavor to salads, showing up sweet in Burmese coconut shrimp pasta or spicy as Caribbean shrimp with habañero peppers. Vegetarian and vegan options such as pastas, sandwiches and salads are also artfully prepared. Firefly offers indoor and outdoor dining in a cheery ambience. For food as fun as it is healthful, visit Firefly Café.

321 Habersham Street, Savannah GA
(912) 234-1971

Creekside Grill

Wilmington Island now has a celebrity in its midst. In 2006, *Coastal Living* magazine voted the Creekside Grill one of the 25 Best Seafood Dives in the country. The locals, of course, put their stamp of approval on the restaurant when it first opened in 2000. They have been gathering in its lovely outdoor areas ever since. Angela Thompson owns the restaurant and operates it with help from her son, Gray. It's a big job, because Creekside serves its coastal specialties for lunch and dinner seven days a week. The seared tuna tartare on a bed of crispy wontons

with a wasabi cream sauce is one of the most famous dishes. Another popular specialty is the crispy scored flounder, a whole, headless flounder flash-fried and served with an apricot shallot glaze. Angela buys wild shrimp from the local shrimp boats. Meat lovers enjoy hand-cut steaks and slow-roasted prime rib. The soups are fresh creations of the house. The salads put a lively spin on greens. Innovative desserts include the banana split ice cream pie. You can eat indoors, but the outdoor patio and deck areas offer landscaped ambience to as many as 100 diners. Live music picks up the pace four nights a week. The press loves Creekside, and rave reviews have appeared in *Island Living* and *Savannah Morning News*. Let coastal flavor rule your day with a visit to Creekside Grill.

216 Johnny Mercer Boulevard, Savannah GA
(912) 898-4161
www.creeksidegrill.net

Maison Bleu

When you step into Maison Bleu in historic downtown Watkinsville, you immediately sense you are in a bistro located somewhere in the French countryside. Your surroundings are designed to simulate an outdoor plaza. Anne Miller-Andersen and her daughter Alana Tamara Miller own Maison Bleu. Anne was trained as a chef in Chicago. Her eclectic menu comes from her travels as well as the many cities she has called home. Look for traditional French fare coupled with American style and hints of the Middle East, Asia and Australia. Anne is passionate

about cooking and is a true creative force in the kitchen, designing dishes that are as wonderful to behold as they are to eat. All the food is fresh, and Anne grows many of her own herbs. Soups, salads, dressings and desserts, including ice cream and sorbet, are made on the premises. The interior is designed to simulate an outdoor plaza with a two-story atrium dining room surrounded by an interior mezzanine for semi-private dining. A private dining room is also available. Maison Bleu is open for lunch and dinner. Customers come from throughout Oconee County for the dining experience, which earned the restaurant a *What's Hot* listing in *Restaurant News*. Make a reservation at Maison Bleu for your opportunity to experience a foreign and totally charming French restaurant.

2 S Main Street, Watkinsville GA
(706) 769-6480
www.maison-bleu.com

The Village Corner

The Friese family wants you to feel the *Gemütlichkeit* at the Village Corner, a bakery, tavern and German restaurant in historic Stone Mountain Village. *Gemütlichkeit* describes a feeling of ease and belonging that can persuade you to linger and enjoy the company, surroundings, food and drink. The Village Corner's Old World charm and authentic dishes will make you feel as if you have traveled to Germany. Sample the Wiener schnitzel served with fresh sautéed vegetables or sauerbraten, Bavarian *spätzle* noodles and red cabbage. The first thing you encounter when you walk into the Village Corner is the bakery, scented with the aroma of sugar icing and spices. Cookie choices include *Pfeffernüsse*, *Linzer* tartlettes and *Lebkuchen*. You'll find German breads, tortes and chocolate cake. The bakery creates many wedding cakes, and at Christmas you can learn to make a gingerbread house. Founders Hilde and Claus Friese continue to work here. Their son, Carl, the restaurant's executive chef, is a Johnson & Wales Culinary School graduate who has mastered the art of fine cuisine. A banquet room accommodates weddings, receptions and other special events. The tavern offers German beers, bottled and on tap, along with distinctive wines and spirits. The establishment first opened in 1974 as a wholesale bakery with a small lunchroom. As Hilde Friese's cooking became famous, the enterprise grew, moving three times over the years. For a bit of Europe without the plane fare, visit the Village Corner.

6655 James B. Rivers Drive, Stone Mountain GA
(770) 498-0329 *www.germanrestaurant.com www.germanbakery.com*

Zanzo Italian Café

With Tim Bates as the chef, the Bates family runs Zanzo Italian Café with a lively interest in serving the families of others. The minestrone soup is a popular starter. Tim's freshly made focaccia bread, which customers dip into herb-infused oil and Parmesan cheese, accompanies the entrées. Specialty sauces and dressings add zip to such favorite dishes as marinated and pan-fried calamari, Tuscan-style salmon and Italian beef tenderloin. Those who save room for dessert adore the silky tiramisu and the cheesecake of the day. It's easy to see why Zanzo has become well known through word of mouth in its six years of operation. It has recently opened a second location at the Orchard Golf and Country Club. Tim is a hands-on owner who manages his own kitchen and contributes to the community with meals for the needy. His wife, Joni, and mother Brenda take care of the books, while father Neil is the fix-it man. Tim trained under Italian chefs in Florida, then moved north to Atlanta to open Pasta Works. He continued further north, finally opening a Zanzo in Cleveland, then moving it to Clarkesville, where he has created a comfortable restaurant space with extra room for small and large private parties. An area in the back works well for dinner theater productions. Loosely translated, Zanzo means *run about,* and that is just what the Bates family does to keep its restaurant operating smoothly. For authentic Italian meals, visit Zanzo Italian Café.

1435 Washington Street, Clarkesville GA (706) 754-8922

Noodle

Bringing together the cuisines of Asia is a family tradition at Noodle. Lina Kuo and her siblings, Lili and Lenny, were inspired to open this restaurant, with its three distinctive locations, by their mother, Kuei Shou. Kuei was in the restaurant business all of her life and passed on her love of fine food and service to her children. The menu at Noodle reflects the family's Korean and Chinese roots with such all-time favorites as *jung bong* spicy seafood broth, an intoxicating mix of spices, thick noodles, shrimp, calamari, mussels and vegetables. Asian dishes range from Japanese udon noodle soup to Vietnamese cold noodle salad. The restaurant is renowned for Lenny's homemade sauces, which add a spicy kick to some of the dishes. The appetizers and entrées here are big enough to share, so you might want to split some pork dumplings and satay chicken with others in your party. You can enjoy a bottle of wine or a martini from the bar with your meal. Each restaurant has an individual style. The Decatur location was originally designed to appeal to college students with an organic, earthy décor. The Atlanta location offers a trendy, high-energy feel with black and red Asian artwork and illumination from fiber-optic projections. The College Park location has a cute, retro style and an outside patio area for dining in the spring and summer. When you are ready to sample the varied flavors of authentic Asian cuisine, try a Noodle restaurant near you.

**205 E Ponce De Leon Avenue, Decatur GA
(404) 378-8622
903 Peachtree Street, Suite A, Atlanta GA
(404) 685-3010
3693 Main Street, College Park GA
(404) 767-5154**
www.noodlehouse.net

Shucker's Seafood Bar & Grill

Good food and daily specials have a way of bringing people from all walks of life together. This is definitely the case at Shucker's Seafood Bar & Grill, where whole families mingle with folks in work clothes and businesspeople in suits. They come for the fresh seafood and steaks, including those dandy specials. Shucker's features all-you-can-eat catfish on Monday and Tuesday nights, all-you-can-eat crab legs on Wednesday nights, and a prime rib special on Friday and Saturday nights. Co-owner Mary Anderson goes on about the prime rib. "It's absolutely to die for," she says. "Everyone who's had it swears it's the best prime rib they've ever had." Mary tends to know exactly what her customers are thinking, because she and her husband, Gene, like to drop by each table to say hello and ask for feedback. She believes that this is another reason why her restaurant is so popular. "It makes the customer know they're important to us," she says. Customers take center stage in the bar on weeknights, when karaoke is the attraction. Scheduled performers entertain on the weekends. For a popular dining choice, join the happy crowd at Shucker's Seafood Bar & Grill.

883 Harmony Road, Eatonton GA
(706) 923-0443

The Village Porch Café

When Carterville wants lunch, it turns to the Village Porch Café for fresh and flavorful gourmet sandwiches, soups and salads. Just follow the workers, shoppers and tourists to a building on the town square that has housed restaurants since it was built it the early 1900s. Mike Phillips owns and manages the café. His experience in the business began with washing dishes at age 12 and progressed to eventually running a 225-seat restaurant. After stints managing and owning several restaurants and a partnership in a construction company, Mike returned to Cartersville in 1997 and established the Village Porch Café in 2003 with his wife and co-owner, Dorothy Phillips. The delicious assortment of sandwiches includes a chicken salad embellished with grapes, celery, onions and pecans. The Village Porch also makes what many customers insist is the best Reuben in the South. For a special treat, try the Caribbean Twist, a

mix of Jamaican jerk chicken, *pico de gallo*, avocado cream sauce and melted pepper jack cheese served on a hoagie roll. The restaurant makes a hearty soup each day, such as the popular white bean chicken chili. Crunchy salads, spicy quesadillas and enticing ice cream specialties complete the menu. Try lunch Tuesday through Saturday (breakfast is also served on Saturday) at the Village Porch Café.

25 N Wall Street, Cartersville GA
(770) 386-3100

Red Sky Café & Coffeehouse

Offering favorite old-fashioned Southern foods with a modern twist plus a full array of coffee drinks, Red Sky Café & Coffeehouse keeps customers coming back for more. It's not unusual to see standing room only and customers lined up out the door for lunch at this Buford restaurant. Red Sky has soups and sandwiches, including the restaurant's famous roasted pimento cheese sandwich with toasted pecans, jalapeños and a side of strawberry preserves. Comfort foods are livened up with a bit of feta here, a touch of basil there. Dinner is served Tuesday through Saturday. Although lunch is Red Sky's forte, breakfast is also popular. The aroma of fresh, warm biscuits greets passers-by, inviting them to come in and enjoy the many biscuit dishes, which include the classic biscuit and gravy, the salmon biscuit and a country ham biscuit. You'll also

find omelettes and French toast. The restaurant gets its name from the beautiful murals on the walls that depict the evening sky in Georgia in all its red, purple and blue glory. Owner Pam Chandler has been involved in the restaurant business for many years and bought Red Sky from Cathy Holderfield and Lynn Tankersley in May 2007. Pam brings her experience in providing friendly service to the Red Sky every day. For a heavenly meal and coffee, come to Red Sky Café & Coffeehouse.

2033 Buford Highway, Buford GA
(770) 614-0031

Dominick's

Mark D'Angelo and Monte Jungman are New Yorkers who, in 1994, brought their Italian traditions and menu to Norcross and, recently, to the Lawrenceville square. Everything at Dominick's is made in-house, which means you are going to love the sausage, meatballs and sauces just as much as the fresh bread and desserts. Among many fine appetizers, regulars choose the *spedini* bread, a loaf of seeded Italian bread stuffed with mozzarella, wrapped in prosciutto and baked in garlic and butter. Some of the most popular entrées include the eggplant parmigiana and chicken *scarapiello*, which combines chicken with sausage, rosemary, garlic and peppers. No Italian meal would be complete without dessert, which means you must save room for the cannoli, or at least order one to-go. With the motto Little Italy, Lotta Food, a to-go box is almost inevitable. Dominick's offers a full bar and a generous, reasonably priced wine list. You'll find the same great menu and private dining rooms for special events at both locations. Catering is available. Dominick's has received the Zagat Survey's Award of Distinction every year since 2000 and the Award of Excellence in 2002 and 2003. Like a true Italian, Dominick's wants to do more than satisfy you. It wants you to become a member of the family. The conviviality and family style dining at the monthly wine dinner helps accomplish this goal. Bring your appetite to Dominick's and, as the Italians say, *mangia,* or eat up.

95 S Peachtree Street, Norcross GA
(770) 449-1611
197 W Crogan Street, Lawrenceville GA
(770) 277-8477
www.dominickslittleitaly.com

Grapes & Hops Bar & Bistro

Knowing what wine to pair with your meal is a cinch at Grapes & Hops Bar & Bistro, where a set of dots on the menu point you to the most appropriate wines for your meal. If you choose Chef Timmy Lee's famous crab and lobster bisque, a soup that places a lobster garnish over blue crab meat in a sherry coconut cream, you will want to pair it with a medium or full-bodied white wine, according to the dot system on the menu. This Flowery Branch restaurant, located near the Falcons' training camp, was opened in 2004 and has been owned by Michelle Schreck and Bernd Koerner since 2005. Michelle is the wine professional who pairs the wines with items on the seasonal menus of the chef. Michelle belongs to the Wine and Spirits Education Trust, has taught classes in wine and has judged wine tasting events. She offers 60 wines by the glass at Grapes & Hops. Timmy is an inventive chef, trained at the Art Institute of Atlanta. He brings international influences to the American food served at the bistro, which includes many seafood and beef selections, including a superior filet mignon served with burgundy-braised wild mushrooms. You can enjoy wild game, such as venison, pheasant, ostrich and duck. Grapes & Hops is a beautiful place to eat, with fine linens on the tables and the warmth of brick walls. It holds monthly wine tastings, special champagne tastings, wine dinners and wine classes. You'll find live music on the patio in the summer and a pianist on the weekend. Michelle and Bernd would like to welcome you to experience the difference in the pleasant atmosphere of Grapes & Hops Bar & Bistro.

4856 Hog Mountain Road, Flowery Branch GA
(770) 965-9145 *www.grapesandhopsbarandbistro.com*

Home Sweet Georgia

Located on Gainesville's historic square, Home Sweet Georgia is an official visitor center of the Gainesville Convention & Visitors Bureau as well as a gift shop and a colorful café serving feel-good food. Owner Kathy Vitti offers an array of locally-made gifts celebrating Georgia and the South and serves up down-home cooking for breakfast, lunch and brunch. Regulars come as early as 7 am for the fresh-roasted coffee and pastries, including peaches and cream strudels and a chocolate chunk muffin that sells out every day. *Good Housekeeping* has made these muffins even more famous, so make sure to snag one before they're gone. Lunch features hot and cold croissant sandwiches and the signature Southern Hot Plate. The chicken salad, locally made by a 50-year-old neighborhood grocer, is also popular—Gainesville has been called the chicken capital of the world, so chicken is almost as big a deal as peaches. Visitors can sit outside or inside the charmingly decorated café or grab an ice cream or smoothie to-go and browse the gift shop. You'll find Georgia peach jelly beans, white chocolate bark with peaches and local pecans and peanuts seasoned in a variety of ways. Gourmet kudzu and moonshine jellies go well with pancake and grits mixes. The locally roasted St. Ives coffee comes in 100 different varieties. You'll also find t-shirts, candles and bath products. Home Sweet Georgia specializes in made-to-order gift baskets that you can send home or to your loved one, for a taste of the Peach State and of the South. Visit Home Sweet Georgia and start your tour of Gainesville at the source.

110 Washington Street NW, Gainesville GA
(770) 534-7151
www.homesweetga.com

The Oar House

Diners looking for a great view and a delicious dinner will be deeply satisfied by all aspects of lunch or dinner at the Oar House in Dahlonega. Two decks overlook the Chestatee River, offering peaceful views from almost every seat in the house. Everything on the menu, even the pickles in the sandwiches, is fresh and flavorful. All the meats are cut in-house, and you won't find any artificial colors or flavors. What you will find is a distinctive menu featuring such favorites as prime rib with horseradish cream sauce and crab cakes topped with lemon-caper sauce and grilled asparagus. Pair the Oar House reserve filet mignon with a Kendall Jackson Pinot Noir, or consider a Saintsbury Chardonnay with your penne pasta. The Oar House overflows with suggestions for pairing fine food with fine wine and offers monthly wine tastings to refine your knowledge and broaden your palate. All the desserts are made fresh every day by the owner. The restaurant features live music on Friday and Saturday nights and closes Sundays for a day of rest and prayer. Its riverfront beauty and spacious veranda are well suited to special occasions, and the Oar House regularly caters events for up to 150 guests. For fresh food in a calm, beautiful environment, come to the Oar House.

3072 E Highway 52, Dahlonega GA
(706) 864-9938
www.theoarhouse.com

Family Tradition Restaurant

Family traditions seem to revolve around food, from backyard cookouts to mom's Tuesday night meatloaf, and for generations, families have gathered around a table to share a meal and share their lives. At Family Tradition Restaurant, father and son team Jim and Matt Dixon honor and accommodate these treasured times. Since 1998, when they opened their first location, Jim and Matt have been dedicated to providing a warm and welcoming eatery that offers great food and fair prices. The duo has used only word-of-mouth advertising since the beginning and has built a faithful customer base by providing exceptional service and fresh, family style cuisine. Jim and Matt believe that General Manager Waylon Walls and his personable staff have contributed greatly to the restaurant's success. In 2004, the Dixons opened their second location, which offers a larger seating capacity while still providing the same great food and friendly service. Family Tradition Restaurant specializes in home style cooking and features popular favorites, such as succulent fried chicken, tender catfish and hearty country breakfasts that will really stick with you. The restaurant also offers a delicious assortment of sandwiches and burgers, along with homemade soups and crisp salads. Family Tradition Restaurant offers a catering menu that is perfect for special occasions and is destined to make your next event the talk of the town. Create lasting mealtime memories with your family at Family Tradition Restaurant.

7830 Hickory Flat Highway, Woodstock GA
(770) 345-7117
4379 Town Lake Parkway, Woodstock GA
(770) 852-2885
www.familytradition.net

El Torero Mexican Restaurant

The recipes of Mexico are as vibrant and rich as the nation's history and culture. You can savor them all at El Torero Mexican Restaurant, where founder Manuel Magana has cleverly integrated his exceptional Mexican cuisine into the Chamblee repertoire of favorites. Manuel opened his original restaurant in 1981 and has since expanded to nine locations, six in Metro Atlanta and three in Tennessee. Check El Torero's website below for the location closest to you. El Torero uses only the freshest quality ingredients in preparing its dishes. Popular dishes include the taco *de carne asada*, made with prime Angus beef, tomatoes and rich creamy guacamole, as well as the perfectly seasoned and stuffed burritos, deep-fried chimichangas and tamales that taste like comfort wrapped in love. The restaurant's recipes come from Manuel's family collection in the Mexican state of Jalisco—Manuel was born and raised there before coming to the United States. All the of the family-friendly El Torero locations are non-smoking and feature gracious, warm staff members who are dedicated to making your dining experience perfect. When hunger pangs strike, head straight for the great plates that await at El Torero Mexican Restaurant.

5575 Peachtree Industrial Boulevard, Chamblee GA

(770) 451-5420 *www.eltorero.net*

Lil' River Grill

Lil' River Grill offers patrons an Old World dining experience in an upscale, yet casual atmosphere, highlighted by live music and superb service. This popular Lawrenceville eatery is owned by brothers Todd and Bob Johnson and by Michael Williams. It is located in the historic Rhodes Jordan Building, constructed in 1908. The Lil' River Grill features an elegant dining room, relaxing patio and the lively Lil' River Tavern where you can enjoy a quiet drink or a full meal. The second floor, which overlooks Lawrenceville Square and the historic Gwinnett County Courthouse, is reserved for private occasions and is an ideal place to host banquets, corporate dinners, bridal rehearsal suppers and other important events. The menu offers a choice selection of savory concoctions created by Executive Chef Patrick Knight, who boasts an impressive culinary career. He is assisted by his sous chef, Art Raymond, and their talented kitchen staff. The cuisine is American with French and Southwest influences. Every dish is perfectly prepared using the finest quality ingredients, including prime Angus beef. Each staff member is delighted to help you in every way, from offering entrée suggestions to suggesting wine pairings from the distinguished wine list. Savor an exceptional dining experience at the Lil' River Grill.

179 E Crogan Street, Lawrenceville GA
(770) 339-0689
www.lilrivergrill.com

Photo by Vicki Hunt

Mittie's Café & Tea Room of Alpharetta

Mittie's Café & Tea Room of Alpharetta is located in a charming brick cottage in the heart of historic downtown. The café's name pays homage to Mittie Bulloch, the daughter of Civil War veteran General Bullock and the mother of Theodore Roosevelt. Many of the restaurant's recipes are heritage legacies, passed down from eminent Southern kitchens, such as those of the Carter, Bullock and Roosevelt families, to Mittie's own delectable menu. Local farmer's markets provide Mittie's with the freshest ingredients. Breakfast dishes are served all day. The lunch menu ranges from hearty sandwiches, soups and garden-fresh salads to indulgent quiches and crepes, all of which are homemade daily. The signature meal is chicken salad and lobster bisque, both of which have become local favorites. High tea, low tea and Teddy Bear Tea for the youngsters are served any time of day and include an assortment of menu items and special extras. The café has been recognized by area publications for its culinary excellence and gracious atmosphere. The smell of freshly baked scones often greets customers at the door. Elegant local artwork from the Roswell Photographic Society and other community artists decorates the dining room. The restaurant is family owned and operated, making it a perfect environment to host baby or bridal showers, birthdays or get-togethers. Mittie's Café & Tea Room is a charming, historical restaurant that will fill your needs and your stomach.

62 N Main Street, Alpharetta GA
(770) 772-0850
www.northfultonshops.com/mittiescafe

Kani House

It is true that people don't usually think of Georgia when they think of great Japanese cuisine, but perhaps they should think again. In 1999, Mr. and Mrs. Young Park opened their first restaurant, Kani Japanese Steakhouse and Sushi, serving up traditional Japanese food and a great show in Woodstock. Two additional branches have since opened, with another opening soon in Cumming. Individual chefs prepare your meal tableside while you watch, using only the freshest ingredients. The method at Kani House is teppanyaki, a traditional style of Japanese cooking. *Teppan* means iron plate or steel sheet and *yaki* is to stir quickly or stir-fry. What this word doesn't tell you is the incredible skill and dexterity displayed by the Kani House chefs. The blurring hands of the teppanyaki chefs, as they slice, dice, whirl, stir and season succulent meats and vegetables, dazzle patrons. Sushi lovers will adore the fresh and extensive selection of delicious options, such as tataki, kani, tai, or sashimi rolls. The menu also includes steaming crab and tender juicy steaks. This family-owned and operated restaurant is well known not only for terrific food, but also for friendly, fantastic service. Many of their customers end up returning again and again. Instead of being regulars, they become more like fond relatives. Whether you are in the area for a quick business trip or are searching for a new family favorite, enjoy a fresh flavorful meal at Kani Japanese Steakhouse and Sushi.

3208 Buford Drive, Buford GA
(770) 271-5272
2455 Towne Lake Parkway, Woodstock GA
(770) 592-5264
10820 Abbotts Bridge Road, Duluth GA
(770) 495-7989
www.kanihouse.com

Historic Glen-Ella Springs Country Inn

The Historic Glen-Ella Springs Country Inn offers an idyllic retreat at the southernmost tip of the Blue Ridge Mountains. The inn is more than a place to stay—the award-winning dining room is open to the public seven nights a week for American and Continental fare with a Southern touch. Constructed in 1875 as part of Glen and Ella Davidson's working farm, the home was expanded in 1890 and again in 1905 to take in paying guests. From the early 1900s until the 1920s, the house often served as a place for wealthy coastal Georgia families to escape the threat of yellow fever during the summer. The inn ceased operations in the 1920s and passed through several ownerships before Bobby and Barrie Aycock began a year-long restoration of the property in 1986. The Aycocks were delighted to find that the home's features remained intact, including original heart pine floors, walls and ceilings. Electricity and bathrooms were added, and today the inn proudly offers 16 guest rooms furnished with antiques and locally made furniture. Extensive herb and perennial gardens, meadows and a large swimming pool grace the 18-acre grounds. Guests enjoy bountiful breakfast buffets. Outdoor activities are close at hand, including world-class trout fishing and boating on nearby lakes and rivers. Whether you're planning a business meeting, searching for a romantic wedding site or just looking for a relaxing getaway, make plans to visit the Historic Glen-Ella Springs Country Inn.

1789 Bear Gap Road, Clarkesville GA
(706) 754-7295 or (877) 456-7528
www.glenella.com

Paco's

Paco's serves traditional Mexican cuisine with a twist. The restaurant offers food from the secret recipes of traditional Mexican families. In addition to a comprehensive menu of dishes and combinations, Paco's prepares a fresh lunch buffet seven days a week, perfect for business professionals and others with big appetites and limited time. Of course, the chips and salsa are homemade and served throughout the meal. The food is always reasonably priced and well presented. Paco's serves wine, beer, Margaritas and other alcoholic and non-alcoholic beverages. Chef and owner Poli Castro arrived in the United States from Mexico at age 12. One of five children, he has been in the family restaurant business since 1984. Eight years ago, Poli opened Paco's, eight miles out of Atlanta and within walking distance of the Marble House Barnes Amphitheatre. The restaurant has since become a neighborhood and family favorite, with food and flavors that draw customers from out of town to enjoy a meal. As a community-minded business owner, Poli provides Paco's food at many civic, cultural and community events. The restaurant also caters receptions, parties and other gatherings with its authentic cuisine. If you're like most customers, Paco's will become one of your favorite places to dine. Spice up your life with a meal and a good time at Paco's.

5015 Floyd Road SW, Suite 100, Mableton GA (770) 819-4444

Delkwood Grill

Enjoy delicious food and entertaining karaoke at Delkwood Grill, a pizza restaurant that's the most popular sports bar in Marietta. From hot cheesy pizza to juicy mouthwatering steaks, Delkwood Grill offers something for every palate. Matt "Bimbo" Chutich and his wife, Betsy, make sure that someone from the Chutich family is always on hand to offer a heartfelt greeting to customers. The grill first opened in 1988 under the name Bimbo's Saloon & Eatery and has since become a dining tradition for many area families. Matt began his career as a restaurateur in 1959, when he opened his first pizza parlor in Virginia, Minnesota. Since that time, Matt, Betsy and their children, Dawn and Paul, have owned more than 35 bars and restaurants across seven states. The hallmark of the Delkwood Grill is its relaxed, welcoming atmosphere. It's an inviting place to gather with friends and family for a delicious meal from a diverse menu that offers award-winning chili and fresh salads, as well as hearty sandwiches and burgers. Try Delkwood's famous Yankee pot roast, made from an old family recipe, and the Chicago-style pizza with a thin, crispy crust. Delkwood offers a choice array of libations at a four-sided bar, as well as more than 25 televisions, so you never have to miss the big game. Those who prefer to dine al fresco will appreciate the large outdoor patio with its cozy seating and lovely views. Treat your family to a dining tradition with a visit to Delkwood Grill.

2769 Delk Road, Marietta GA
(866) 797-8747
www.delkwoodgrill.net

The Cabin Grille

Bill and Amy Taylor want your experience of the North Georgia mountains to include superior food preparation and the charms of a mountain lodge setting. In 2004, the couple opened the Cabin Grille in Blue Ridge. Its barbecue was soon recognized as one of the best in the tri-state area of Georgia, North Carolina and Tennessee. Other specialties include a signature smoked prime rib and a pecan-crusted rainbow trout. Bill, a graduate of the Culinary Institute of Atlanta, was destined for a career in cooking from the age of six, when he put together his first recipe from a *Highlights* magazine for children. He wasn't actually planning to open his own restaurant until he decided to develop a highway location in the mountains he had come to love during summer camping trips. The Taylors have created the kind of restaurant that lets you truly celebrate your escape from the city. You'll love the locally grown foods and innovative preparation, not to mention the white-cedar-log building with oversized river rock fireplaces and wildlife décor. Catering services and spacious party rooms promise memorable gatherings. Enjoy your aged steak or mountain raised chicken at the Cabin Grille, far from the hustle and bustle of the city.

5771 Appalachian Highway, Blue Ridge GA
(706) 632-3999
www.thecabingrille.com

The Silver Skillet Restaurant

Few diners from the 1950s still hold onto the diner tradition, but the Silver Skillet Restaurant is an exception. The Silver Skillet, with a 50-year history in Atlanta's midtown, is one block from Georgia Tech. Teresa Breckenridge took over the restaurant from her parents in 1988. She kept the period look and many of the favorite dishes. These include country ham with redeye gravy and fresh biscuits for breakfast, baked meatloaf or a hot roast beef sandwich for lunch and the famous lemon icebox pie for dessert. Teresa offers fresh salads, cold plates, sandwiches and burgers. She is known for her à la carte vegetable plates, which allow customers to make a meal of such vegetables as collard greens, black-eyed peas, yam soufflé and squash casserole. The vintage décor has made the Silver Skillet a popular choice for movies, videos and print advertisements. Many celebrities have enjoyed its Southern comfort food. Teresa is a celebrity in her own right, with guest appearances on NBC's *Today Show* and ABC's *Good Morning America*. Breakfast is served all day every day, and lunch is available Monday through Friday. For friendly waitresses, comfortable surroundings and food that could have come right from a Southern mom's kitchen, visit the Silver Skillet.

200 14th Street NW, Atlanta GA
(404) 874-1388
www.thesilverskillet.com

Willingham's Kitchen

Nestled in an unassuming shopping center in McDonough, just a dozen or so miles from Atlanta, sits a restaurant that, according to locals, has the finest country cooking and soul food in the country. Well-traveled visitors call it the best in the state. Willingham's Kitchen has built a sterling reputation for quality meals. It's a combination of time-honored family recipes, fresh ingredients and a pinch of love in each entrée that keeps Willingham's customers coming back again and again. Willingham's Kitchen is a family thing, with owners Barbara and Tony, along with their two sons, Justin and Anthony, making up most of the staff. Perhaps that's why when we visited the Henry County eatery, we felt so at home. And while the staff is friendly and the atmosphere pleasant, it's the food that's the star at Willingham's Kitchen. Only fresh (yes, fresh) Georgia-grown vegetables are used and each meal is prepared from scratch. "Even though it's a great deal more work to prepare food fresh daily, we believe it's worth it," says Tony. So, too, do their customers. Whether you choose the smothered pork chops, the authentic fried catfish or the country-fried steak, you'll feel like it is Sunday dinner at grandma's house. The choice of vegetables and sides is enormous. You can try macaroni and cheese and collard greens today, and then return tomorrow for coleslaw, creamed potatoes or yams. For an authentic Southern lunch or dinner, come to Willingham's Kitchen. You'll be glad you took the extra few minutes to get there.

2016 Highway 42 N, McDonough GA
(678) 432-7440
www.willinghamskitchen.net

Photos by J.D. Graphics

O.B.'s Bar BQ

When you're looking for melt-in-your-mouth barbecued meat and plenty of it, you'll want to stop in at O.B.'s real pit barbecue. Owners Steve and Tammi Duncan serve up friendly Southern hospitality that makes you feel like you're one of the family. Dedicated customers from all around the region flock to O.B.'s to enjoy the consistently terrific hickory-smoked specialties that have made the restaurant famous. Memphis-style ribs, pork and chicken are cooked to perfection in the four barbecue pits on site. The restaurant offers several combination platters for those who want a taste of several dishes. Farm-raised catfish and hand-breaded deep-fried jumbo shrimp are other tempting choices. O.B.'s offers char-grilled T-bones and rib eyes as well. All of the side dishes are freshly made from scratch each day. The award-winning Brunswick stew turns many a first time visitor into a regular customer. Beer and wine are also available. The restaurant is housed in an authentic log cabin, with a central stacked stone fireplace. Outside, you'll find the four barbecue pits, presided over by O.B.'s barbecue pit master of 16 years. O.B.'s also offers full catering services for off-site private events. It's no wonder that its customers consider O.B.'s the best barbecue restaurant in the Southeast. Steve and Tammi go the extra mile to make sure your visit is a happy and delicious experience. They hope you'll come and join them soon.

725 Industrial Boulevard, McDonough GA
(770) 954-1234 or (678) 432-6002
www.realpagessites.com/obsbarbq

Redz

Located in the heart of McDonough's historic town square, Redz is an elegant restaurant that embodies Southern charm. The 1914 French pressed-tin ceiling, lovely Italian-style wall frescoes and live music create a romantic and intimate atmosphere that makes this a perfect spot to celebrate any special occasion. Head Chef Michael White deftly combines French-style cooking with a fine selection of steaks and seafood, all freshly prepared. Some of Redz' outstanding entrees are the juniper-crusted New Zealand rack of spring lamb and caramelized salmon. Steak choices include generous portions of natural Angus beef. The wine list is well-rounded and extensive. Private dining rooms accommodate larger parties, seating up to 500 guests, making Redz a good choice for banquets, wedding rehearsal dinners or any other private event. In summer, enjoy the rooftop patio room overlooking the beautiful town square. Owner Quinn O'Neill is a passionate, lifelong restaurateur, with a charismatic and hospitable personality. He makes a point of personally visiting each table to be sure his guests are pleased with their dining experience. One of his waiters, Christopher, is a talented singer, beguiling customers with his delightful opera tenor voice. Quinn and all of his talented staff hope you'll join them soon for an unforgettable dining experience at Redz.

32 Macon Street, McDonough GA
(770) 914-5723
www.redzrestaurant.com

Maritza & Frank's

The entire Tobias family plays a part in making Maritza & Frank's Restaurant a pleasant place to enjoy Southern comfort food. The Southern hospitality runs deep here, too—all the way south to Ecuador, where Maritza Tobias grew up. Maritza lived in New York City before coming to Atlanta, a city that immediately captured her heart. She met her husband Frank, an Atlanta native, while working in an area restaurant, and the pair set their sights on becoming restaurant owners, opening Maritza & Frank's in 2002. Their children, Jocelyn and Gustavo, help out here, too. Breakfast options are hearty and include steaks, three-egg omelettes and several biscuit specials. Choices for French toast and pancakes are plentiful. You can start lunch or dinner with fried green tomatoes, onion rings or chicken tenders, then choose everything from sandwiches and salads to barbecue, steaks or seafood served with a nice assortment of vegetables. You can't go wrong with the fried chicken livers, and the locals swear by the meat loaf, the turkey and dressing, and the beans and greens. Every Southerner understands the importance of a good dessert, and Maritza and Frank's will not disappoint. The dessert of the day could prove to be blueberry or blackberry pie, peach cobbler or rice pudding. For a dining experience that will make you feel like extended family, comforted by foods as good as anything you would find at home, come to Maritza and Frank's.

637 N Central Avenue, Hapeville GA
(404) 559-6110

Kafe Kelly's

In historic Hapeville, what was once a gas station now offers a different sort of fill-up—with food and engaging entertainment. Kafe Kelly's opened its doors a year ago and has already become a comfortable gathering place for a local crowd. Owners Michael and Arnita Kelly are proud of their restaurant's popularity. They're also proud of their building's past and decorate with antique memorabilia. Food choices delight every member of the family. Kids dine on such favorites as grilled cheese and hot dogs, while adults choose from an array of temptations, including smoked turkey legs, a signature hamburger and Caesar salad. The buffalo wings with the volcano sauce option are not for the faint of heart, but rest assured, Kafe Kelly's offers refreshing beverages from its full-service bar to cool things down. The addition of a pit barbecue

promises some smokin' good menu additions. Give into the temptation to indulge in key lime pie, a rich chocolate layer cake or one of four flavors of cheesecake while enjoying a night of poetry, comedy or karaoke. Weekend parties include dancing and much merriment. A cozy covered patio, equipped with ceiling fans, provides a cool and restful hangout. Patrons in a hurry can call ahead to place an order. Kafe Kelly's also offers catering services. Gather together with friends or make new ones with a visit to Kafe Kelly's.

3259 Dogwood Drive, Hapeville GA
(404) 766-1479
www.kafekellys.com

Michon's Smoked Meats & Seafood Restaurant

After 13 years in St. Louis, Michon's Smoked Meats & Seafood Restaurant moved to the Atlanta area in 2003 to the delight of owners Al, Gaye and Michon Wilson and their many fans. The Wilsons made the move with the help of one of the original St. Louis chefs, the late Lafayette Turner, and they continue to feature smoked wings and ribs made with the restaurant's own seasoning mix and slow cooking methods. The restaurant also offers tantalizing seafood, ranging from Alaskan king crab legs to blackened catfish, and a dizzying array of house-made side dishes, including yams, baked beans and collard greens. Dessert is worth your attention. Consider the family's fourth-generation recipe for pound cake or such delights as red velvet cake,

apple crumb cobbler and the decadent white chocolate raspberry bread pudding. In the spirit of Southern hospitality at its finest, the Wilsons embrace all customers, locals and visitors alike, as friends and want them to linger, whether cheering at Monday night football or relaxing to the sweet sounds of live jazz. Michon's is close to the Atlanta Hartsfield-Jackson International Airport, putting new arrivals just moments from a refreshing experience. For those who can't come by regularly, Michon's will ship their succulent smoked wings anywhere. Michon's and skilled catering staff are happy to accommodate banquet or catering requests for anything from a wedding reception to a tailgate party. Come to Michon's Smoked Meats & Seafood Restaurant, where the taste speaks for itself.

811 Virginia Avenue, Hapeville GA
(404) 766-7770
www.michons.com

The Sycamore Grill

The Sycamore Grill's captivating setting, with a breathtaking view of Stone Mountain, is the first thing a visitor notices. This fine dining establishment opened in 1998 in a Southern mansion that dates back to 1836. A 150-year-old sycamore tree in the yard gives the grill its name. It was just a sprout during the Civil War, when General William Tecumseh Sherman spared the home. You can enjoy the ambience sitting at a table with a crisp white tablecloth while sipping one of 40 wines available by the glass. *Atlanta Magazine* named the filet mignon the best in Atlanta. The signature blackberry chicken salad is another favorite. Among the famed desserts are the angel food pound cake, the key lime pie and the Georgia peach cobbler. A Sunday champagne brunch offers dozens of buffet choices. Diners can thank the owners, Executive Chef Paula Sims Ballard, General Manager Enid Wilson Britton, Anna Sims and Maria Brown, for the quality and consistency of the inspiring dishes. They consider the grill their shared passion. The Creole/Cajun influence in some dishes hints at Paula's New Orleans background, when she watched her grandmother prepare all the local favorite dishes. The restaurant offers on and off-site catering, cooking classes, monthly wine tastings and summer jazz on the patio. An online retail store carries gourmet desserts, cookbooks and specialty gifts. With six dining rooms, the grill can accommodate everything from an intimate dinner to a large event. Let them charm you at the Sycamore Grill.

5329 Mimosa Drive, Stone Mountain GA
(770) 465-6789
www.sycamoregrill.com

Soho South Café

Soho South Café just might be Savannah's most popular lunch spot, according to a feature story in *Better Homes and Gardens* magazine. Many regulars come strictly for the tomato basil bisque, which has earned fame far beyond the city limits. Another specialty is the ham, brie and green apple sandwich on a baguette. Recently, the restaurant added dinner to its lunch and Sunday brunch offerings, with freshly caught seafood and daily pasta specials headlining the menu. The café's wine list reads like a global tour. Bonnie Retsas, proprietor and chef, takes cooking very seriously and turns food into art at her upscale version of a diner. After 25 years in New York City, where she worked and attended culinary school, Bonnie returned to Savannah in 1997 and turned a former Kieser auto dealership into a restaurant. The bistro offers a casual, quirky surrounding with bold colors and adventurous art on the walls. A gift store invites browsing. In many ways, the restaurant is anything but serious and mimics the feeling you might have upon entering a Soho loft, what *Better Homes and Gardens* calls a "laid-back, slightly cheeky attitude." Put a little attitude into your next meal out at Soho South Café.

12 W Liberty Street, Savannah GA
(912) 233-1633
www.sohosouthcafe.com

Vic's on the River

Vic's on the River offers up traditional Southern charm in an historic building, once home to an 1870s cotton warehouse, that overlooks the beautiful Savannah River. The cuisine is contemporary Southern, featuring fresh seafood, Angus beef and prime rib entrées. Signature courses include pan-roasted black grouper, cedar-plank-roasted wild salmon and a surf n' turf platter of Angus filet and poached lobster. The roasted tomato and basil bisque and the sweet Vidalia onion soups are exceptional, as are the fried green tomato appetizers. The wine list is well-rounded, and includes unusual selections from New Zealand, South Africa and Argentina, along with many choices from France and the Napa-Sonoma region. Try the coffee chocolate martini for a unique after-dinner drink. The restaurant's bar and wine cabinet are made of the original 1860s pinewood, set off nicely by the wood plank flooring. Be sure to see the hand-drawn map on display in the main dining room, detailing General Sherman's march through Georgia to the sea during the Civil War. Vic's on the River offers private dining rooms for large parties and events. The Stoddard Room seats up to 165 guests. Dr. Irving Victor and Bill Hall, co-owners, cordially invite you to enjoy an evening of contemporary fine dining at Vic's on the River.

26 E Bay Street, Savannah GA
(912) 721-1000
www.vicsontheriver.com

Rib Ranch

The menu at the Rib Ranch in Marietta states that their smoked beef ribs are almost the size of Texas. That's a good indication of the kind of barbecue found at this restaurant. Texas barbecue is noted for its rubbed-on seasonings and big Western flavor. The owners make sure the side dishes are as pleasing as the beef. The Rib Ranch was first opened by Cindy Newman, but is now operated by her younger sister Barbara, David Newman and former attorney Ed Sullivan. When the restaurant was struck by lightening and burned to the ground in 1996, Ed and Barbara rebuilt the place with a full-blown Texas tenacity. The new facility was bigger and featured more updated equipment. The project spurred Ed to give up his law practice and contribute his grit and passion to the business of barbecue, fulltime. The Texas decor within the restaurant includes Texas license plates and Texas banners mounted on the wall. The atmosphere is big fun, but barbecue reigns supreme as the star attraction. The pork barbecue, a Southern favorite, won the Taste of Marietta cookoff three years running. The restaurant has been featured on a national cable channel, Turner South, as a Blue Ribbon winner for barbecue in the South. For six years, Rib Ranch has been Zagat rated, and AOL subscribers have voted them the best barbecue in metro Atlanta. With this kind of backing by patrons and critics, you can't go wrong.

2063 Canton Highway, Marietta GA
(770) 422-5755
www.theribranch.com

Stefan's Off the Square Restaurant

The cuisine has a subtle set of flavors that pervade the senses while reminding us that food is more than a necessity—it is a comfort, an art form and for some, a way of life. Stefan's Off the Square Restaurant, owned by Slovakia natives, Stefan and Ivana Bencik, offers patrons an authentic taste of the Old World by serving up an array of divinely prepared traditional dishes that are all made-from-scratch by Chef Stefan. Celebrated menu items include sauerkraut soup, made with slow-cooked pieces of smoked and fresh pork. Other favorites are the beef Wellington, Angus rib eye steak and Mahogany Roasted Duck served with Euro-style dumplings and sauerkraut or red cabbage. The menu has tons of seafood choices. Be sure to try Becherovka, a delicious herbal infused Czech liquor that tastes of clove, licorice and just a faint hint of mint. Not only is it delicious, it is also an excellent digestive. The Benciks first fell in love with Georgia while on vacation and soon decided to stay and open a restaurant. Today, their fantastic food and hospitality rivals even the most gracious of Southern hostesses. From the richly paneled walls to the native Slovakian memorabilia and costumes, Stefan's Off the Square provides an authentic Eastern European and American dining experience unlike any other, and the Benciks are waiting to share it all with you.

164 Roswell Street, Marietta GA
(770) 792-4443
www.stefansoffthesquare.com

The Seasons Bistro

If there were a beauty contest for restaurants, the Seasons Bistro would be a serious contender. Its cultural fusion cuisine is presented with artistic flair, and every detail of the dining area has been arranged with an eye for color and design. The exposed brick and hardwood floors of this old building, which once housed McDonough's Buggy Works, have never looked so good. Owner Lynn Loggins attends to the décor, which features lots of local art. She also puts together the menu with Tin Pham, her brother-in-law and the executive chef. They describe the food as American with strokes of Vietnamese, Thai and French. As the name of the restaurant implies, the menu changes throughout the year to emphasize freshness and seasonal favorites. Popular dishes have included vichyssoise, rosemary roasted pork tenderloin with blueberry sauce, and calamari with red pepper aioli (garlic mayonnaise). It's hard to pass on dessert when such temptations as crème brûlée and peach cobbler are being offered. Linger over a glass of wine on the weekends and fall under the seductive spell of the soft music provided by local musicians. In 2006, *Main Street McDonough* named the Seasons Bistro the best business of the year. Located just off the downtown square, the restaurant is open for lunch and dinner. Come enjoy the Seasons Bistro, where every season is a new experience.

41 Griffin Street, McDonough GA (770) 288-2544 *www.theseasonsbistro.com*

Van Gogh's

Van Gogh's owners, Michele and Chris Sedgwick, know how to create restaurants that excel as culinary masterpieces. Their flagship restaurant joins an intimate atmosphere, fresh American cuisine and extraordinary wines, liquors and liqueurs together for a dining experience that promises sheer artistry. Begin your meal by choosing from a palette of appetizers, including some of the world's fine cheeses, steamed mussels or crab cakes served with sour apple slaw and citrus vanilla vinaigrette. Lunch and dinner entrées are highly creative and include oven-roasted rack of lamb, grilled fillet of beef and seared wild salmon, each accompanied by masterfully prepared vegetables and remarkable sauces. Several artists claim wine as the source of their inspiration, and Van Gogh's honors those artists with a wine cellar that contains more than 500 selections from great wine producing regions around the world. Van Gogh's bar gives you reasons to linger, thanks to a cozy fireplace setting and astounding choices, including more than 100 Scotches and a large selection of Ports and rare Cognacs. One of the dessert martinis can make a spectacular after-dinner finish to your repast. Van Gogh's earns accolades locally and nationally. It has spent seven consecutive years on Hudspeth's Top 10 list and is consistently rated as one of the top 20 restaurants in Georgia by the Zagat Survey. For dining that promises artistry and good taste, visit the masters at Van Gogh's.

70 W Crossville Road, Roswell GA (770) 993-1156
www.knowwheretogogh.com

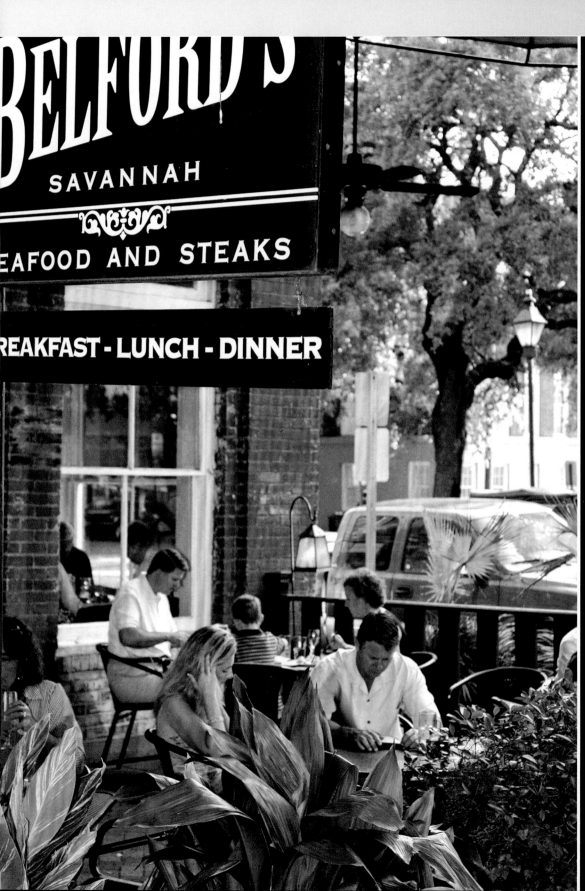

Belford's Savannah— Seafood & Steaks

Belford's Savannah—Seafood & Steaks offers dining excellence in the historic City Market area of downtown Savannah. The restaurant is located in a handsome old brick building, an example of the Italianate commercial style. The edifice, which was completed in 1902 for Savannah's Hebrew Congregation, received Historic Preservation status in 1985. Meanwhile, Belford's restaurant is making some history of its own. Since opening for business in 1997, it has won three awards in the annual Taste of Savannah event judged by *Southern Living Magazine.* Menu specialties include pan-seared jumbo lump crab cakes (winner of best menu item in 2001), and the Shrimp, Greens & Grits (best entrée in 2004). In this dish, the shrimp are prepared with apple-smoked bacon, green onions in Chardonnay butter sauce and served over grit cakes and collard greens for a full Southern twist. Belford's also features Cajun lobster ravioli tossed with shrimp and scallions (best entrée in 2006). The menu includes filet mignon, rib eye and New York strip steak, all of which are cut in-house from high-quality Choice beef. Even the side dishes are notable, such as the Savannah red rice that comes with a seasoned pork chop and the garlic mashed potatoes that are served with the lamb chops. Clint Eastwood, Kevin Spacey and Garrison Keillor are just a few of the celebrities who have dined in this restaurant. Make Belford's Savannah a part of your Savannah experience.

315 W St. Julian Street, Savannah GA (912) 233-2626
www.belfordssavannah.com

Busy Bee Café

The buzz is out about the Busy Bee Café, which has been busily serving up one scrumptious meal after another for more than 60 years. Lucy Jackson founded this popular eatery in 1947 and ran the operation until 1968. Current owner Tracy Gates inherited the charming diner from her father in 1987, five years after he purchased the restaurant, which by then was considered a community landmark. Tracy and her mother, Georgia, continue to offer the same down-home Southern hospitality and cuisine that has kept guests coming back for so long, including treats you'll want to sample again and again, such as Georgia peach cobbler, freshly-squeezed lemonade and the best little corn muffins east of the Mississippi. Busy Bee Café's top seller is fried chicken, described by patrons as *beelicious*. Also popular are tender pork chops and an array of sinfully delicious desserts, including key lime cake and banana pudding. Home of Southern cookin', the café serves a steady stream of people six days per week. It certainly lives up to its name by exuding a cheerful vibration that reminds visitors of a hive of happy bees going about their business and enjoying the finer things in life, including good friends and good food. Treat yourself to a honey of a meal with a trip to Atlanta's own Busy Bee Café.

810 Martin Luther King Jr. Drive SW, Atlanta GA
(404) 525-9212
www.thebusybeecafe.com

Zucca

Zucca is owned by a trio of friends, Tim Langell, Joe Romano and John Gibney. They met during their freshman year in a New York high school, and they have maintained their friendship for more than 25 years. Armed with a family friend's secret recipe, the triad opened Zucca Bar and Pizzeria and met with instant success. Even better, they have persuaded executive chef Danny Arturo to join their dream team. Chef Arturo specializes in authentic, home-cooked Italian menu favorites. Zucca serves thin-crust, New York-style specialty pizzas, such as white pie, chicken parmesan and pizza margherita. The menu includes flavorful calzones, salads, appetizers and pasta dishes, as well as fresh chicken, veal and seafood entrées that will keep you coming back until you have tried them all. Then you'll want to start all over again. Whether you are planning a large gathering of family and friends or just an intimate night out, Zucca's is the place to be. The owners invite you in because "NYC is so far away, and life's too short to eat bad pizza." Step into Zucca Bar and Pizzeria and soak up the energy these friends have created.

2860 Atlanta Road, Smyrna GA
(770) 803-9990 *www.zuccaonline.com*

Vintage Tavern

The Vintage Tavern is connected by a hallway to Zucca Bar and Pizzeria. Both Vintage and Zucca are owned by the same three charmers and shares the same chef extraordinaire. But while the Zucca side is a taste of the modern, Vintage Tavern contains elements of the past. The bar was originally located at the old Manuel's Tavern on Atlanta's Memorial Drive. For nearly a century, this vintage bar was the center of good times. In a spirit of tradition that has been going strong since 1910, patrons continue to line the historic bar. The floorboards of the Vintage Tavern also hail from one of Smyrna's oldest homes, which dates back to the 1800s. These classic pieces of history provide the foundation for the Vintage Experience. The dynamic trio of owners strives to continue a tradition of outstanding service, satisfying food and good times. They extend their hope that you will enjoy your own Vintage Experience. In the immortal words of Samuel Johnson, "There is nothing which has yet been contrived by man by which so much happiness is produced as by a good tavern." Visit the Vintage Tavern and see what old Sam was talking about.

2860 Atlanta Road, Smyrna GA
(770) 803-9793
www.vintagetavern.com

Padriac's

When you think of Ireland, the city of Atlanta may not immediately come to mind. However, the many regulars at Padriac's, known unofficially as the Pad, are well aware that you don't have to go all the way to Dublin to get a little Irish flair with your meal. Padriac's has a neighborhood feel, with 39 beers on draught and good food that borrows from many well-loved cuisines. It's also on the cutting edge of the regional live music scene, with some of the best local acts performing on Wednesdays and Saturdays. Owners Joe Freer, Greg Wakeham and Ernie Franchell do all they can to provide a genuine casual atmosphere. Fun is the goal and guiding force behind Padriac's, with trivia contests and other fun that will make you want to stay until the wee hours of the morning. The food is varied and outstanding, with such offerings as jumbo lump crab, Moroccan lamb loin and jerk marinated chicken breast. You can also find burgers, portabella sandwiches and lobster nachos, to touch just the surface of the possibilities. Drop by the Pad sometime soon to see why customers echo the slogan: A day without stopping by Padriac's isn't a full and right day.

2460 Cumberland Parkway, Atlanta GA
(770) 433-2398
www.padriacs.com

The Blue Willow Inn

Writer and humorist Lewis Grizzard used to rave about the Blue Willow Inn, and he is hardly alone. A dozen media outlets, from *USA Today* to CNN, have done the same. *Southern Living* calls it the best small-town restaurant in the South. The Blue Willow is located in a Greek Revival mansion built in 1917. In its many years as a family home, it was visited by greats such as Margaret Mitchell, author of *Gone with the Wind*. Guests today say the experience is like a visit to grandma's house. Southern hospitality ensures you'll ask for seconds, and it works: 4,500 to 5,000 people flock here weekly to partake in authentic Southern dishes such as fried green tomatoes and the signature To Die For Southern Fried Chicken. The restaurant offers eight exquisitely appointed dining rooms. Between helpings or before dessert, be sure to explore Blue Willow's exquisitely maintained gardens. Stop at the gift shop, linger by the foot bridge and pond or stroll through the nearby Blue Willow Village, where you'll find a turn-of-the-century cluster of cottage shops, a 1950s-style soda fountain, an antique shop and a museum. Louis and Billie Van Dyke opened the old mansion as a restaurant in 1991 after extensive renovations. The Van Dykes beckon you to slow down and enjoy a relaxed pace of life, filled with Southern hospitality and the good food at the Blue Willow Inn, just off I-20 at exit 98.

294 N Cherokee Road (Georgia Highway 11), Social Circle GA
(770) 464-2131 or (800) 552-8813
www.bluewillowinn.com

Brookwood Grill

The enchanting community of Roswell, on the banks of the famed Chattahoochee River, offers visitors a bounty of festivals and historic attractions along with world-class cuisine. A favorite among locals, the Brookwood Grill provides personalized service and a menu that blends harmoniously with the restaurant's casual and welcoming feel. Owner Pierre Panos opened Brookwood Grill in 1991, and with the assistance of managing partner Matthew Fairley, created what has now become a Roswell tradition. Brookwood Grill uses only fresh, quality ingredients that are carefully prepared to exceed your culinary expectations. The menu features internationally inspired dishes, including lobster and smoked Gouda ravioli, Asian chicken salad and hickory-grilled rib eye steaks. The Brookwood Room, ideal for groups of up to 40, is the perfect place to host private or corporate events such as birthday celebrations, showers and business lunches. The Brookwood team is always on hand to help you plan and organize your event so that you and your guests can sit back and enjoy great company and delicious food. Brookwood Grill's catering service brings the restaurant's excellent fare to you for larger events, such as weddings, graduation parties and corporate picnics. Treat yourself and your guests to something special with a visit to Brookwood Grill.

880 Holcomb Bridge Road, Roswell GA
(770) 587-0102 *www.brookwoodgrill.com*

Blackstone—
Steaks, Seafood & Spirits

Warm and inviting with intimate lighting and upscale dining, Blackstone Restaurant has the ingredients for a perfect dining experience. Blackstone opened its doors in 1999 and is a place where guests continue to enjoy the highest quality steaks and seafood and have a great time in the process. Blackstone features private banquet rooms, as well as patio dining and a full bar that attracts friendly, warm and vivacious people. The restaurant offers live musical entertainment and an award-winning wine list that features 120 different bottles, with more that 30 available by the glass. Blackstone is the ideal place to celebrate special occasions, meet with colleagues or host a private event. The menu offers savory dishes including such starters as steak tartar and tuna, steamed mussels and many others. Entrées that will delight your taste buds include veal meatloaf, Blackstone shrimp and pasta pan roast chicken breast, New York strips served with lobster, London broil and other delicious choices. Blackstone is frequented by numerous Atlanta personalities, celebrities and political leaders who enjoy the personable and distinctive service, as well as the fine cuisine. Make reservations today by phone or online. Blackstone Restaurant promises a satisfying dining experience.

4686 S Atlanta Road, Vinings GA
(404) 794-6100
www.blackstoneatlanta.com

Nirvana Café & Grille

Best described as creative American cuisine, the menu items at Nirvana are pure paradise. Nirvana is famous for adding creativity to its dishes with a true passion for delivering fresh and flavorful meals for dinner, lunch and weekend brunch. At lunch, enjoy gourmet sandwiches, bodacious burgers and sensational salads and soups. At dinner, try one of Nirvana's signature entrées, such as the barbecue-cheddar meatloaf or the Gorgonzola-encrusted steak. Brunch, served Saturday and Sunday, features smoked salmon Benedict in a caper-hollandaise sauce or French toast with fresh challah bread dipped in cinnamon, toasted almonds and garnished with caramelized bananas. Save room for the freshly made crème brûlée or the award-winning homemade Chocolate Nirvana Ice Cream—so unique they trademarked the name. The atmosphere is casual and comfortable with friendly service. Nirvana also offers catering and take-out options, a special events facility for private parties or meetings and creative cooking classes for adults and kids. Equally important to the Nirvana team is giving back to the community through a variety of programs designed to empower youth to tap into their full potential. Both Nirvana locations are delighting diners with heavenly fare seven days a week.

**5192 McGinnis Ferry Road, Alpharetta GA
(678-893-9000)
10930 Crabapple Road, Roswell GA
(678-277-2626)**
www.eatnirvana.com

The Crimson Moon Café

At The Crimson Moon Café, the creative spirit shines and inspiration abounds. The specialty organic coffee promotes conversation, and the custom omelettes, pizzas, eclectic sandwiches and delicious entrées bring smiles. Owner Dana Marie LaChance has designed a gathering place that celebrates Southern cuisine with a menu six pages long. The café has also become one of the South's most intimate music venues, hosting some of the nation's finest performing artists and songwriters of all genres. The Crimson Moon Café is located in the circa 1858 Parker-Nix Storehouse, listed on the National Register of Historic Places and the second-oldest building on Dahlonega Square. LaChance purchased the historic building following a successful career in the outfitting industry. In 2001, she opened The Crimson Moon as a gallery of eclectic art by local artisans. The gallery soon evolved into a café with build-a-bagel sandwiches, homemade soups and salads, plus live music on the weekends. LaChance, a songwriter and poet herself, now blends all her entrepreneurial and creative talents into a purpose-filled music venue that draws people from all over. If you enjoy a smoke-free atmosphere that supports creativity, with gourmet food, great coffee and select alcoholic beverages, then make The Crimson Moon Café your place to go in Dahlonega.

24 N Park Street, Suite A, Dahlonega GA
(706) 864-3982

The Pecan

When Tony Morrow was a student at Tuskegee Institute in Alabama years ago, pecan trees were so abundant he used to stuff his pockets with the nuts and send them home to his mother so she could bake him German chocolate cakes and pecan pies. He loved those pecans so much that when he started his own restaurant in College Park, it was only natural he'd name it The Pecan. Tony's upscale, fine-dining establishment features Southern cuisine with a twist. You'll find things like pecan cornbread, Italian collard greens with a bruschetta topping of diced tomatoes tossed in balsamic and parmesan, and oven-roasted buttermilk pecan chicken. The menu is creative and far-ranging, with such dishes as curry carrot ginger soup with lump crab, shiitake burgers with roasted peppers and Tybee Island crab cakes. Everything at The Pecan is made from scratch, including the breads and ice cream. The Pecan is open for lunch and dinner, with a Sunday brunch that features traditional Southern favorites such as waffles, pancakes, quiche and pancakes, along with creative specialties such as Atlanta fried lobster tails and pepper-crusted New Zealand lamb chops. Southern cuisine has deep roots. Tony has taken those roots and grown a culinary garden that blossoms beyond even the goodness of those pecan trees he remembers so fondly. Make it a point to sample the delicious and inventive offerings at The Pecan on your next trip to College Park.

3725 Main Street, College Park GA
(404) 762-8444 *www.thepecanonline.com*

Agave Restaurant

Southwest flair meets five-star service at Atlanta's eclectic Agave Restaurant. Jack Sobel, founder of Agave, has created a warm and friendly atmosphere that centers on incredible foods, an international wine list and a top-notch tequila bar. Sobel, having grown up in the hospitality industry, knows exactly what patrons want when they go out for a meal. His warm personality and hands-on approach to running the restaurant has made Agave the success it is today. Sobel's love of Southwest cooking began while he was living in New Mexico, the Land of Enchantment. He now blends his own exclusive style with the spicy and intoxicating flavors of the Southwest to create amazing dishes that will satisfy the pickiest of palates. Begin your meal with guajillo mussels, steamed in Agave's signature red chili citrus wine broth, or the traditional New Mexico hatch green chili stew, with hatch green chilies and tenderloin beef strips. Follow your appetizer with one of the succulent entrées such as the Diablo Crawfish Pasta in a spicy chili cream sauce or the Niman Ranch pork chops with ancho chili barbecue glaze. Agave Restaurant is named for the famed blue agave plant that gives its flavor to tequila. Indeed, the restaurant features an extensive tequila bar (and truly fabulous Margaritas). Sobel also stocks a choice selection of wines from around the world. Sobel and his exemplary staff look forward to sharing the flavors and scents of the Southwest with you at Agave Restaurant.

242 Boulevard SE, Atlanta GA
(404) 588-0006
www.agaverestaurant.com

Café Michel

Café Michel is a living tribute to two great cooks who have passed on their heritage, Michel Sola and Amir Askarian. These dedicated culinary artisans made the café one of Smyrna's most treasured community assets. Café Michel was started by Michel Sola, a Frenchman from Savoie who was a recognized master of the culinary arts. Michel passed the torch to Amir and Melanie Askarian in 1998, but not before staying long enough to teach them his most cherished secrets. Michel died not long after he left, inspiring Amir and Melanie to honor his traditions and raise the bar at Café Michel. During their eight years as owners, Amir and Melanie established a reputation for first-rate Continental cuisine that features touches of Italy, France and America. Along the way, the couple earned the city of Smyrna's Spice of Life award and were also honored for Best Entrée. Open for breakfast, lunch and dinner, with catering options and space for private parties, Café Michel is a busy place loved by both visitors and locals. Now Amir has passed away as well, and Melanie and her devoted staff carry on, continuing to astound customers with their signature dishes. The next time you are in or near Smyrna, be sure to sample the culinary excellence of Café Michel.

2860 Atlanta Road, Suite C, Smyrna GA   (770) 384-0032
www.cafemichel.com

Shopping
& Antiques

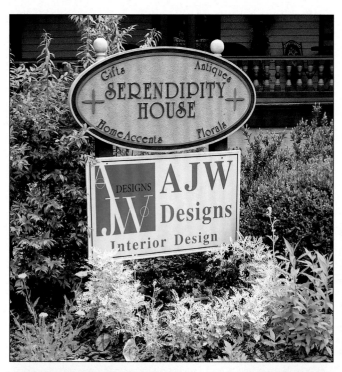

Serendipity House

Entering Serendipity House feels like stepping into the home of a good friend who happens to run a shop full of gifts and home décor. More than 10 years ago, owner Darlene Knight envisioned running her own boutique within a home-like setting rather than a traditional storefront. In 1995, Darlene purchased the 1879 Queen Anne Victorian she saw on the Acworth Historic Tour and renovated nearly all of its 11 rooms, filling each one with gifts, collectibles and home décor that would be appropriate for the room. The nursery holds gifts for babies and children, while the Victorian kitchen stocks gourmet foods and items for entertaining your guests. Interior design services, dining sets and tableware await you in the dining room. Look for a floral room, full of silk bouquets and arrangements, and a candle room with a selection of heavenly scents. The unique layout of the store and its furnishings invites you to spend time browsing, and because new items are continually stocked, you never know what you might find. The helpful employees at Serendipity House are happy to help you choose a gift for anyone on your list, living up to their motto, We Don't Just Have Customers, We Have Friends and Family. Stop by Serendipity House in downtown Acworth, where the Southern hospitality is as expansive as the selection of gifts and home décor.

4965 N Main Street, Acworth GA
(770) 966-1301
www.serendipityhouse.biz

Classic Expressions

Owners Tammy Williams and Bethany Henson use their backgrounds in crafts and other creative fields every day at Classic Expressions. Theirs is a multifaceted business combining a retail shop with such personalized services as event planning and interior design. The warm, inviting shop offers fine gifts and home accents, such as candles, bath and body products and jewelry. Treats for the kitchen include gourmet cookies and coffees. At times, Tammy and Bethany showcase artists and painters, as well as craftspeople who make purses and beaded items. They put their creative energies to work for customers with specific gift needs. For example, they love creating gift baskets. Just give them a theme, anything from baby to Italy, and they will assemble a beautiful and bountiful basket tailored to the request. Over the course of their 13-year friendship, Tammy and Bethany have planned and decorated scores of receptions and parties. Let them bring holiday brightness and cheer to your home, office or business with their Christmas decorating. When you need a creative solution to a gift or decorating need, consider Classic Expressions.

**780 Mayfield Road, Suite 102,
Alpharetta GA
(678) 319-0040**
*www.northfultonshops.com/
classicexpressions*

Mark of the Potter

Mark of the Potter started in 1969 in an old mill on the banks of the Soque River in the mountains of Northeast Georgia. Generations of visitors, young and old, continue to return each year to see what's new as well as to feed the enormous trout that congregate at the base of the shoals. Mark of the Potter has a staff of four potters and supports more than 25 regional potters as well. To compliment their work, there's a wide selection of metal, glass, jams and jellies, T-shirts and local books. Watching a potter work at the wheel remains a part of the Mark of the Potter experience. Many of the mugs, pitchers and vases produced here are coveted by the most discriminating collectors. Among the display shelves full of decorative and functional pieces, you are bound to find something that you will cherish for many years. The shop is open seven days a week, except Christmas Day. Experience the timeless art of pottery on a memorable excursion to Mark of the Potter.

9982 State Highway 197 N, Clarkesville GA
(706) 947-3440
www.markofthepotter.com

Blue Ridge Adventure Wear

Blue Ridge Adventure Wear can clothe you for such local sports as hiking, fishing, rafting, biking or horseback riding. Whether you are looking for hiking boots or sandals, the shop carries the lines most prized by recreationists, including Merrell, Keen and Born. The shop is easy to find, because it's right in the middle of town. It's loaded with popular clothing lines, such as Life is Good, Woolrich and Royal Robbins and also carries sit-on-top kayaks and many gifts that reflect a mountain theme. Look for locally made jams and jellies, baskets and kitchen signs, as well as bear figurines, stuffed animals and artwork. After 25 years as a lighting expert for Disney World, Todd Nichols went looking for a small town life along with his wife, Patty. Blue Ridge, located in the foothills of the Blue Ridge Mountains, had everything they sought. In 2003, the couple purchased a gift store, the Little Shop. In late 2006, they also bought Blue Ridge Adventure Wear. Once Todd and Patty pick a project, their focus is firm and their energy, boundless. The couple started improvements immediately, including greater square footage, a new storefront and a new wooden floor. Not only did they fall in love with Blue Ridge, but in a few short years, Blue Ridge fell in love with them. In 2004, Todd treated residents to the kind of fantasy Christmas light show you would expect at Magic Kingdom. Before venturing into the mountains or out to your back deck, slip into some sporty apparel from Blue Ridge Adventure Wear.

662 E Main Street, Blue Ridge GA
(706) 632-3991

The Little Shop

Run by Patty and Todd Nichols, The Little Shop offers Hallmark cards, seasonal gifts and items that express friendship, inspiration and the charms of the area. You can expect helpful service and complimentary gift-wrapping presented with loving attention by The Little Shop staff. When Patty and Todd prepared to leave their Walt Disney World careers for a new lifestyle, they found the life they wanted in Blue Ridge. After visiting the area for the first time in 2001, they immediately purchased a weekend retreat, only to be enticed to become full-time residents in 2003. It was at this time that they shed their corporate careers and purchased The Little Shop, a fixture in downtown Blue Ridge since the 1930s. Longtime residents still come in and talk about the purchases their parents and grandparents made here when they were children. Kelly Carter came to work for the couple in 2003, bringing a vibrant personality and a knack for making thoughtful card and gift selections. Part of the charm that attracted the Patty and Todd to Blue Ridge is the friendly community, and Patty always seeks employees with out-going personalities, adding to the small-town charm of the shop. The employees extend warmth and community pride to customers at The Little Shop as well as at the Nichols' second store, Blue Ridge Adventure Wear, located just down the street. Enjoy shopping for special gifts where the motto is: The Little Shop with a Big Heart.

781 E Main Street, Blue Ridge GA
(706) 632-3603

Out of the Blue

Step through the portico into a paradise of gourmet food and wine nestled in warm Tuscan colors and an even warmer proprietor. Let Sarah Auman, owner of Out of the Blue, introduce you to top food and wine from around the world, lovely French table linens and hand-painted ceramics from Italy, all of which are functional, beautiful and fit your lifestyle. With such a sophisticated inventory, you might think you are in New York or San Francisco until Sarah opens the refrigerator and offers you a generous sample of local goat's cheese, home-made bread or organic produce. Out of the Blue has a firm commitment to all-natural or organic products. "This is Blue Ridge," says Auman. "The Out of the Blue experience is all about visiting—being in the kitchen of your best friend's home, who also just happens to be an expert at entertaining excellence." Want to plan an evening of fabulous food with a perfect wine pairing? Sarah can match it to your individual taste—just ask the regulars of this destination shop. Sarah remembers favorite wines her clients bought months ago, and from such an outstanding and diverse collection, that is amazing. "Everything in Out of the Blue is fabulous," says Hans Rueffert, an award-winning professional chef. "They have removed any opportunity to make a mistake with all top quality products." Whether it is one of the popular cooking classes or just a weekend tasting, a visit to Out of the Blue is a must whenever you visit Blue Ridge.

647 E Main Street, Blue Ridge GA
(706) 258-2750
www.outofzbleu.com

Photos by John Anderson

Antiques & Interiors of Sandy Springs

Joan Leonard is retired, but her family continues to rely on her creativity and knowledge of antiques to run Antiques & Interiors of Sandy Springs. Joan and her daughter Rhonda Wigington took over the former Lakewood Antiques Gallery in 2005. Rhonda handles day-to-day operations. Her brother Gregg Leonard, the shop's CEO and an Atlanta homebuilder, revamped the shop. He added walls, lighting and paint to create a showcase for 85 high-end antiques dealers. "It was my mother's love for this place that got me involved in the antiques business," says Gregg, who appreciates his sister's managerial skills and his mother's creative design talents. The 33,000-square-foot store is filled with a huge variety of antique furniture, fine art, accessories and more. The hand-knotted Oriental rug display is quite impressive. The Leonards and their 80-plus dealers maintain a delightful atmosphere for the customers, with everything from tea, coffee and sweets to the one-of-a-kind treasures at every turn. Joan and Rhonda believe in serving the community as well. They sponsor the Juvenile Diabetes Foundation and frequently donate items for silent auctions in support of area charities. Let Joan and Rhonda's enthusiasm for antiques rub off on you. Pay a visit to Antiques & Interiors of Sandy Springs.

6336 Roswell Road, Sandy Springs GA
(404) 250-1057
www.aiss-online.com

Atlanta Arts and Antiques

Atlanta Art and Antiques offers a large variety of antique furniture, accessories, rugs and fine art at incredibly reasonable prices. Owners Darious and Jack Ebrams travel nationally and internationally to uncover the finest goods for their discriminating clientele. A large inventory allows them to offer merchandise at discounted prices, making Atlanta Art and Antique an exciting shopping experience. They are one of the oldest rug dealers in the Southeast, with loyal and satisfied customers since 1972. The more than 13,500-square-foot showroom expertly displays exquisite period furniture, delicate chinaware and a full selection of lighting and mirrors to match any décor. Hand knotted Persian, Chinese, Indian and Pakistani rugs delight the eye with intricately rich designs. On the walls, look for stunning tapestries evoking pastoral scenes and themes from days long past. Accessorize from classic to contemporary with hand-blown glassware, signature porcelain and fine ceramics. Ethnographic arts, oil paintings and sculptures provide the finishing touch. Convenient options for purchase of items, as well as fast and friendly service, are hallmarks of the store. Darious and Jack and their courteous staff look forward to assisting you with your decorating needs and dreams at Atlanta Arts and Antiques. For more information and new shipments, events and auctions, see the website.

3255 Peachtree Road, Atlanta GA (404) 264-1133 *www.aaaantique.com*

Southern Expression

Southern Expression, on Main Street in historic downtown Acworth, specializes in gifts with a personal touch. Cindy Hudgins, who owns the shop with her husband, Mike, can monogram almost anything available in the store, including tote bags, backpacks, clogs and much more. Cindy does her monogramming right in the store. The shop also provides personal printing and embroidery. Southern Expression carries personalized sterling silver jewelry, including mother's bracelets. Specialty gifts include personalized acrylics, ceramics, soaps and purses. One fascinating item is the Onesole shoe, a fashionable women's shoe with interchangeable tops. A whole section of the store is dedicated to stationary. Here you can find invitations for weddings, personalized note cards and thank-you notes for all occasions. Cindy has a great selection of invitations from Carlson Craft, Julie Azar and Tay Morgan. Whether it's Mother's Day, graduation, a new baby, a wedding or something else, Southern Expression has the gift that will always be remembered.

4857 N Main Street, Suite 200, Acworth GA
(770) 425-9537
www.southernexpression.com

Acworth Bookstore and Library

Acworth Bookstore and Library is located on the mezzanine level above Southern Expression. The old-style open architecture of the building makes shopping an adventure for men and women alike. Owner Guy Condra focuses on military history, especially books on the Civil War and World War II. Collectable models, prints and maps carry on the military theme. The inventory of books ranges well beyond war and other historical topics, however. The bookstore has cook books, self-help guides, books for children and art books. Volumes are available on gardening, railroads, autos and motorcycles. In addition to books and military memorabilia, Guy stocks puzzles and calendars. The shop even has Lodge cast iron cookware and Maurice barbecue sauces. Often, men go upstairs to the bookstore while their spouses shop downstairs or at other Main Street businesses. The men may still be browsing when the women are finished and ready to go. Visit Acworth Bookstore and Library, and you'll see how enthralling this shop can be

4857 Main Street #200, Acworth GA
(678) 300-7722

William Word Fine Antiques

For more than 45 years, William Word Fine Antiques has provided discriminating antiques buyers with one of the finest selections of 18th and 19th century English and Continental furniture to be found in the Atlanta area. Located on Atlanta's premier antique row, William Word Fine Antiques has more than 15,000 square feet of showroom space. Whether you are a beginning collector, seasoned buyer or design professional, Bill Word's knowledgeable staff will work with you to find the perfect piece for your needs. The shop has furniture in both rustic and formal styles. In addition, you'll find an enormous collection of porcelain and accessory items. Armoires, dining sets, desks and side tables are available in a variety of styles to suit your home's décor. You'll find outstanding tapestries, crystal chandeliers and mirrors, all hand-selected for superior quality and workmanship. Just one example of the shop's unusual items is the banjo barometer, so named for its resemblance to the musical instrument. Bill Word has criss-crossed Britain and France for more than three decades in search of different configurations and case styles of banjo barometers, which are as popular with collectors today as they were in the 18th and 19th centuries. Bill notes, "They make great accent pieces in large rooms, particularly in lieu of artwork." Bill and his staff hope you'll pay a visit to William Word Fine Antiques on your next trip to Atlanta.

707-709 Miami Circle, Atlanta GA
(404) 233-6890
www.williamwordantiques.com

Crew Outfitters

You don't have to be a commercial pilot or flight attendant to shop at Crew Outfitters. When you do, you can buy the same top-of-the-line luggage and accessories used by the professionals. If you travel, you know the importance of bags, kits and backpacks that are durable, versatile and comfortable. Crew Outfitters carries such luggage from its sister company, LuggageWorks. Swiss Army, Briggs & Riley and Travel Pro are other featured brands. You'll appreciate a pair of airport friendly shoes from Crew Outfitters the next time you need to walk from one end of the airport to the other to reach your gate. Model planes and other gifts appealing to the aviation buff are also available at the store. Customer service is faithful to Crew Outfitters' philosophy of always having the customers' best interest at heart. In fact, repeat customers often show their appreciation for the hardworking staff by bringing them back gifts from their travels. Although a Crew Outfitters location in the Atlanta Hartsfield-Jackson Airport is open only to airline and airport personnel, the Hapeville store welcomes everyone. Give yourself permission to land at Crew Outfitters the next time you are in the neighborhood.

3430 Lang Avenue, Hapeville GA (404) 766-6507
www.crewoutfitters.com

Photo by Charley Akers

Fräbel Glass Art Studio

For nearly 40 years, Hans Godo Fräbel has been the name people think of when they ponder superior glass artwork. Presidents, royalty and celebrities from around the world collect this master-craftsman's work, and Fräbel has often presented completed pieces to them personally. Now everyone can view the work of Fräbel and other master artists at the Fräbel Glass Art Studio in Atlanta. Fräbel, who originally lived in Jena and Mainz in Germany, founded the studio in 1967. He completed his training as a scientific glassblower at the legendary Jena Glaswerke and moved on to Georgia Tech where he began using molten glass to express his artistic vision. Later, he attained international recognition in the field of glass art when selected as the Absolut Vodka artist of the year, the first glass artist to be honored with the award. The Sculpture Gallery houses one of the planet's largest collections of fine flameworked sculpture. Traditionally, the gallery displays around 300 pieces at a time ranging from tiny, delicate flowers to major sculptures. The studio is also known for its stunning, custom designed state pieces such as a crystal palm tree presented to Queen Elizabeth II. Replicas of such pieces are displayed in a special section of the studio. Fräbel Studio shows visitors how the process works by allowing them to view the artists at their craft first-hand in the hot glass work and the annealing and mounting sections of the studio. Discover for yourself the whole new world that exists within each of these magnificent pieces—discover Fräbel Glass Art Studio.

689-695 Antone Street, Atlanta GA
(404) 351-9794 or (800) 843-1450
www.frabel.com

Divas and Dames Boutique

Ladies, get ready to get your glam on with a visit to Divas and Dames Boutique, where owners Shana and Jay Gould offer up a dazzling array of creative clothing and accessories that are, after the shop's motto, a little bit funky, a little bit trendy, but oh so chic. This spectacular shopper's paradise features a diverse collection of fashions, in sizes from zero to three extra large. Divas and Dames carries a choice selection of designer goods by such companies as Seven Jeans, Kenzie Shoes and Spanx Hoisery. Look for Brighton accessories, along with fun, fabulous jewelry, shoes and girly doodads that will delight divas of all ages. Shana adds stunning pieces created by local artisans, who craft original artwork and apparel that fits in beautifully with the shop's glamorous inventory. Let your little diva celebrate her next birthday or class party in style at Super Diva's, Shana's latest enterprise, located just upstairs from the boutique. The super friendly and welcoming staff at this charming enterprise magically transforms your darling and her pals into princesses, movie stars or models for a day, complete with gowns, accessories and makeover, as well as a photo shoot and a glamourous gift bag. Parents may bring refreshments, but don't be surprised if your special ladies are having too much fun to stop for cake. Add pizzazz to your day, your home and your wardrobe at Divas and Dames Boutique, where indulging your inner diva is always in style.

4809 S Main Street, Acworth GA
(678) 574-4777
www.acworth.net/divas.htm

Sandy Springs Galleries

In 1998, after 27 years in Sandy Springs, Eloise Pickard and her husband Jim moved their popular antiques business, Sandy Springs Galleries, to a country setting just outside Adairsville. Eloise has transformed the look and focus of the business over time, first specializing in antique furniture, then making use of ceiling space to add lighting fixtures and, finally, concentrating on antique lighting fixtures. Sandy Springs Galleries is a dream come true for shoppers trying to provide authentic lighting fixtures in period buildings as well as for those desiring additional depth and character in any indoor setting. Eloise refurbishes antique lighting fixtures and redesigns the fixtures to suit any number of eclectic environments. Restored and rewired pieces, including wall sconces and chandeliers, are displayed in a spacious showroom. Without the right lighting, even the finest antiques lose some of their appeal. Eloise has the artistic eye and antiques knowledge required to properly light your surroundings. Her work has been featured in such prominent publications as *Cottage Living*, *Southern Living*, *House Beautiful* and *Southern Accents* magazines. Next time you need extraordinary lighting or specialty fixtures, visit Sandy Springs Galleries, the largest supplier of antique lighting fixtures in the Southeast.

4645 Joe Frank Harris Parkway, Adairsville GA
(404) 252-3244 or (770) 386-3010
www.sandyspringsgalleries.com

The Bilt-House

Jan Bilthouse has a keen eye for what women want and has been providing it for more than 25 years, first at a chain of resort wear shops and, since 1993, at The Bilt-House, with locations in Buckhead and historic Roswell. Jan specializes in what she calls *carpool couture*, clothing for non-working moms, but working women also find fashionable choices at these unusual shops, where not only clothing, shoes and accessories are for sale but all the furniture, art, rugs and lamps as well. The second story of the Buckhead store is devoted to a young contemporary market where teens can shop while their moms are shopping the main level. Each year, more than 100 teenagers compete for eight spaces on the B-Hive teen board. These teens spend October to May assisting with buying for the junior department, serving local charities and modeling. Jan's products may turn over quickly, but her staff stays in place. Consider Buckhead Manager Christy Sothsavoth, who has been with The Bilt-House for 10 years. Both shops are located in older homes, where everything in the gardens is for sale, from birdbathsand planters to the very unusual yard art. There are stimulating surprises around every corner. Next time you need an outfit for yourself or just about any female in your life, visit The Bilt-House, where unique and fashionable items await you, your home and your garden.

511 E Paces Ferry Road, Atlanta GA
(404) 816-7702
1035 Canton Street, Roswell GA
(770) 552-8581
www.thebilt-house.com

Mountain Treasures

Capture the spirit of mountain living—timber-covered walls and the gentle gaze of the moose, deer and elk overhead invite you to slow down and enjoy your visit when you enter Mountain Treasures, in the North Georgia mountains. Discover furnishings from such respected companies as Old Hickory, Flat Rock, Marshfield, LaCrosse and Shadow Mountain. Find custom pieces from regional artists and one-of-a-kind antiques and decorative accessories ranging from metal and wood carvings to unique lighting, with styles that traverse time and space. What unites all of these offerings is the vision the owner, Dee Speer, shares with guests. Mountain Treasures is a place both intimate and welcoming, where families, couples and individuals will find the perfect fit for their lives and homes. Change the way you experience the mountains and make Mountain Treasures your destination for fulfilling dreams.

5711 Highway 52 E, Ellijay GA
(706) 635-5590
www.mountaintreasures.biz

Hastings Entertainment–Newnan

A leading multimedia entertainment retailer since 1968, Hastings Entertainment is dedicated to supplying small-town America with access to a vast collection of books, music, movies and games. In Newnan, according to store manager Heather, "Everyone still knows everyone else. It's kind of like Mayberry." The quiet, historic downtown has not yet been swallowed by Metro Atlanta. Hastings's all-entertainment focus encourages browsing and lingering and allows for a deep inventory that extends far beyond the mainstream. The inventory, in fact, fills 20,000 square feet. As Georgia's only Hastings, the store attracts customers from as far as Atlanta and Columbus looking for that specialized book, classic movie or back-listed CD. They stay to sample the inventory at CD listening stations and video game-playing stations, or in the book departments' quiet reading area, where the coffee is complimentary. Customers can rent as well as buy videos and games in the video department, which has earned a solid base of regulars. As a local entertainment nexus, the store is dedicated to promoting local artists, hosting book signings and concerts and offering local books and CDs on consignment. "These are the people who support our store," Heather explained, "so we want to support those who support us." Discover the local and international entertainment community at Hastings Entertainment.

54 Bullsboro Drive, Newnan GA
(678) 423-9444

Meg Pie Too

Meg Pie Too lies in the heart of historic downtown Cartersville in an 1800s building originally built to house a grocery store. Owner Patsy Jones' mantra of Everything You Want and Nothing You Need describes the witty, whimsical items that await discovery in this extraordinary shop. The eclectic combinations of colors, prints and patterns found on the walls, the floors and the painted furniture reveal Patsy's design talents and her credentials as a former art education teacher. Faux-finished pink and green walls, punched up with safari prints and artwork, show off everything from funky costume jewelry for teens and adults to such home décor items as hand-painted wine and martini glasses. Look for the Seda France candles, beautifully presented in toile gift boxes, and beauty and personal care items from Bella Il Fiore, both featured in *O, the Oprah Magazine*. Meg Pie Too offers Arthur Court silver designs for distinctive wedding and baby gifts as well as reasonably priced luggage to suit varying tastes. Expect to find lively artwork by Jules Burt, baby outfits by Little Giraffe and Manhattan Baby, and dolls and accessories by Groovy Girls. The coffee bar in the back room offers coffee, fresh pastries and desserts, so bring your lunch and socialize with friends or just relax and sample a bagel. For gifts that will make you smile, browse through the hip treasures at Meg Pie Too.

10 E Church Street, Cartersville GA
(770) 386-1231

Polka Dot Peach

When you want a whimsical gift, going to a shop with a fun name is a good start. Walking into Polka Dot Peach in Watkinsville will leave you feeling positively peachy as you browse through a shop that's as eclectic and fun-loving as they come. In fact, some say that entering Polka Dot Peach is like entering a Dr. Seuss book, with brilliant splashes of color ranging from neon pinks to lime greens everywhere, along with those ever-present polka dots. Since the store opened in 2004, owner Beth Porterfield has kept it amply stocked with some way-out finds that could bring on giddiness. The unusually designed lamps have been known to bring on fits of glee. Polka Dot Peach also stocks a wide variety of collectibles, including ornaments and figurines from Silvestri and Department 56. You'll also find napkins and paper products for your next party. Art lovers will delight in the shop's collection of work by local artists. You just can't be sure what kind of delightful oddity will surface at this weird and wonderful shop. Whether you are looking for a gift, an art object or some funky furnishings, for a warm, fuzzy feeling and plenty of surprises, come to Polka Dot Peach.

21 N Main Street, Watkinsville GA
(706) 310-9880

Hummingbird Embroidery & Gifts

Sandy Maynard, owner of Hummingbird Embroidery & Gifts, uses her embroidery ability to turn otherwise ordinary gifts into extraordinary ones. She can monogram a single set of towels or create a hundred shirts and hats with your company's logo or your school team's mascot. Sandy runs her creative gift shop with her daughter, Victoria Silvers, who handles much of the design and digitizing process. There is something heartfelt and personal about an embroidered blanket or bib for a baby or monogrammed bathrobes for newlyweds. Sandy takes requests for all sorts of specialty applications on everything from cloth to leather. She offers a baby registry and a big selection of Gund plush animals. In addition to embroidery, Hummingbird imprints everything from stationery to scrapbooks and Bibles. In the same spirit of personalization, the shop creates customized gift baskets. These baskets can feature products from Ellijay, regional items from North Georgia or goodies from throughout the state. Sandy's store is well-stocked with apparel, purses and linens. She's even prepared to handle quilting requests. During her career as a registered nurse, Sandy developed a machine embroidery hobby that became the basis for her business. She started with a machine for home use and today uses two elaborate commercial machines. Put some personality into your next gift with a visit to Hummingbird Embroidery & Gifts.

91 Highland Drive, Suite 106, East Ellijay GA
(706) 276-7726

Wrapsody in Blue

What do you name a gift store in Blue Ridge? If you are Michael Brunson and Jack Morton, you combine your love of music with the name of the town that captured your heart and call it Wrapsody in Blue, a store devoted to new furniture with timeless appeal as well as decorative accessories. The 3,000-square-foot store abounds with distinctive items, including original oil paintings, Italian dishware, Godinger crystal, Northern Lights Esque candles and serving pieces by Bea Triz Ball. You will find hostess gifts and such trendy items as Bootie Bags, along with sweets and Buckhead gourmet foods. Michael and Jack knew the Blue Ridge area from shopping trips over the years, but their love for this gateway to the mountains reached a new level in 2000, when they first took the Blue Ridge Scenic Train into the national forests and outdoor recreation sites. They decided to make themselves part of Blue Ridge, and so bought a home in 2002 and then opened Wrapsody in Blue. Michael is on the board of directors of the Blue Ridge Business Association and co-chair of Light Up Blue Ridge, a holiday event that residents and travelers await with anticipation. Jack, who also owns the award-winning Indulgence Salon in Atlanta, has emceed for the lighting event and for the Blue Ridge Arts Association Auction. Michael and Jack stay on top of trends in home décor with visits to the Atlanta Mart and other prestigious markets. Pick up distinctive gifts and a feeling for the Blue Ridge scene at Wrapsody in Blue.

771 E Main Street, Blue Ridge GA (706) 258-2700
www.wrapsodyinblueridge.com

Rattles & Rhymes

Maxine Guerrera and her husband, Joe, have decorated Rattles & Rhymes beautifully in baby colors and filled it with furniture that includes cribs, high chairs and rocking chairs. Along with strollers and car seats, the store carries gear and gifts such as comforters, framed pictures and plush toys. Maxine has steered clear of clothing, except for christening gowns. Maxine had been a shoe buyer for Federated Department Stores before branching out on her own. She almost decided to open a shoe store, until she noticed how many Athens parents were traveling long distances to locate furniture and accessories for their newborns and little ones up to the age of two. Fortunately for the parents and babies of Athens, Maxine decided to go with a baby store, and her guess paid off in a boom. She started in 2002 with a 2,000-square-foot space, expanded to 3,800 square feet and now fills a 6,000-square-foot shop. Maxine is prepared to add to the store as demand permits, but she is firmly planted with her family in Athens and harbors no franchising plans. Busy gift shoppers appreciate the baby registry and the online store. Parents with questions get the attention they require from Maxine's knowledgeable staff. Next time you need something for a baby, visit Rattles & Rhymes.

112 Athens W Parkway, Suite D, Athens GA
(706) 227-1008
www.rattlesandrhymes.com

Dearing Antiques

Indulge your passion for vintage furniture, fine antiques and collectible earthenware by browsing the selection at Dearing Antiques. In 1977, when the last of her four children began school, antique lover Gail Dearing considered the possibility that her desire to stay busy and her passion for antique American wicker could be combined into a thriving antiques business. Gail began by selling pieces out of her basement that she had picked up along New England's back roads. The business quickly grew, and, in 1984, she opened a small shop, Heirloom Wicker, with her friend Jeanne. The business continued to flourish, and today is known as Dearing Antiques, located in Atlanta's former warehouse district. The shop offers a diverse collection of French and English furniture along with an array of vintage American wicker. Gail carries a mesmerizing collection of majolica, a specialized type of earthenware originally created by the Minton Company of England. Gail operates the business with her daughters, Betsy Berry and Katie Newton, and welcomes all visitors, including children and pets. The family uses the shop's kitchen to turn out delicious cookies and baked goods for their customers to enjoy along with a cup of coffee or other beverage. You are sure to feel as if you are visiting with old friends each time you come. Find pieces of quality and style for your home with a visit to Dearing Antiques, an Atlanta tradition for more than 25 years.

670 Miami Circle, Atlanta GA
(404) 233-6333
www.dearingantiques.com

Brenda Evans Designs

Somebody forgot to tell Brenda Evans that the era of house calls is over, though you won't find any homeowners in her community volunteering to enlighten her. They enjoy being able to have someone from Brenda's design company come to their place with ideas that reflect the latest decorating trends. If you make a purchase, Brenda will either waive the fee for the house call or give you a discount on what you buy. She and her team are always visiting furniture markets and seminars to stay at the top of their field. They pass on the knowledge they acquire not only to homeowners but to local builders, who count on Brenda Evans Designs to know what is in style right now. The company's interiors have been featured in real estate brochures and local magazines. Visit the showroom to see all the furniture, home accessories and bedding that this business has on offer. "We carry a good product, with good warranties, that we can stand behind," says Brenda. "That makes all the difference." Brenda is also involved in community projects and joins Alex's Army in the fight to find a cure for cystic fibrosis. Whether you are decorating a room, an apartment or an entire home, consider picking up style tips from the experts at Brenda Evans Design, where the slogan is We Make House Calls.

2142 Tails Creek Road, Ellijay GA
(706) 635-7556

Christmas & More

When Helen's Christmas store closed in 2004, its passing presented a new opportunity for Judy Holloway, the owner of Classics, a collectibles and import shop in the same village. Judy seized the opportunity to build a new business and, with the help of Ola Masters, has created a distinctive shop filled with the holiday season's most cherished treasures. Here you'll find antique fixtures, Italian nativity sets and Spanish porcelain nativity scenes by Lladro. Ornaments of every description adorn the shop, from hand-painted ornaments made in Helen to hundreds of collectibles from names you'll recognize. Byers' Choice carolers, Delton dolls and Seraphim Classic angels are just a few of the items available to grace your home at the holidays. Expect to find stockings, lace mantel scarves and Advent towels to deck your halls and other rooms, as well as Christmas linens and fancy serving dishes for the Christmas table. Handcrafted dolls and toys will appeal to kids of all ages, and many of the imported and antique dolls have their own story to tell and serve as conversation pieces as well as decorations. From the sculpted snowmen and angels by North Carolina's Piney Woods Pottery to hand-painted Russian stacking dolls, every browser finds something appealing here. Stop in and say hello to Ola and her seven-foot Santa at Christmas & More, a store that celebrates Christmas year-round.

8580 N Main Street, Helen GA
(706) 878-1404

Classics

Founded 37 years ago, Classics was one of the first stores in the alpine village of Helen and continues to be a favorite spot to pick up imports, gifts and collectibles. Judy Holloway purchased the store in 1995. She had worked as store manager and knew the shop's potential. Every step through this shop is an experience in European flair. Well known for its wide variety of quality merchandise, Classics features such collectibles as Hummel figurines and Black Forest cuckoo clocks as well as treasured Steinbach nutcrackers. Exquisite Polish handblown glassware and Waterford crystal pieces create sparkling displays that capture your attention, as do the coveted Swarovski crystals that show a kaleidoscope of colors. The shop features the Manual Woodworkers and Weavers line of home décor, which includes tapestries, pillows, throws and wall hangings. You will also find plush Boyds Bears collectibles. German products abound, from music and videos to one-of-a-kind collectible beer steins of all sizes and descriptions. Collectors of exquisitely delicate Dresden china will be thrilled by the selection. Friendly and knowledgeable staff members are always glad to answer questions, so while you're there be sure to ask about the collectors' festivals held in September and October each year. When only the most classic gift will suffice, search for charming European gifts and collectibles at Classics.

8641 N Main Street, Helen GA
(706) 878-1411

Yonah Treasures

Yonah Treasures is a museum, art gallery and country store all in one. Yonah Treasures can outfit a mountain cabin, provide antiques for a living room and equip you with jewelry imported from Thailand. It even offers custom framing and restores old photographs. Yonah is the Cherokee word for bear, and Yonah Treasures carries bear items that run the gamut from napkin holders to welcome signs. The shop shows the work of more than 100 local artists, and displays an excellent collection of woodwork, stained glass and pottery. Much of the pottery comes from the famous Meaders family of Mossy Creek, subject of a PBS/Smithsonian documentary. Yonah Treasures has exhibited the work of many of Georgia's most famous artists. John Kollock captures the majesty of Northern Georgia in his watercolors and illustrations. *Farm Journal* magazine calls Jack DeLoney the Water Color Man, and he is indeed one of the top watercolorists of the South. Artist Judy Bynum George creates symphonies on canvas that depict flowers, mountains and trees. Emory and Judy Jones, Freda McAvoy and Kelvin Morgan opened Yonah Treasures in 2004. Visit their shop for the best in fine art, pottery and cabin accessories.

2047C Helen Highway, Cleveland GA
(706) 348-8236
www.yonahtreasures.com

My Sister's Gifts

Tucked in the rural community of Alpharetta, My Sister's Gifts is one of the top rated gift basket businesses in America. Owned by three sisters—Anna Garmon, Nina Carson and Jan Cunningham—My Sister's Gifts specializes in custom-designed gift baskets and gourmet foods. In 2001, the sisters restored the old Buice's Country Store, retaining the store's rustic character inside and barn-red exterior. They have recently moved the shop across the street. The sisters will help you create a custom gift basket, or you can simply give them a price range and they will do the rest. The sisters also have many specialty gift baskets available. They present most of their mixed treasures in woven wicker baskets, such as the popular Total Relaxation basket with its pampering assortment of lotions, perfumes and bath salts. For the Garden Lover basket, the sisters roll a hose into the shape of a basket and stuff it with a watering can, gloves and tools. Look for baskets named Heavenly Chocolate, Baby of Mine and the Coffee Connoisseur. The store sells many popular collectibles, such as the Willow Tree angels, the Prayer and Promises line and Snowflakes. Horses are a major theme in the surrounding region and get plenty of play in My Sister's Gifts, where cookies, mugs and T-shirts bear an equestrian theme. Pay the friendly sisters a visit, sample their rum cake or white chocolate pecan pound cake, and browse the gifts and collectibles at My Sister's Gifts.

980 Birmingham Road, Suite 604, Alpharetta GA
(770) 346-9692 or (877) 332-GIFT (4438)
www.mysistersgifts.com

Queen of Hearts Antiques & Interiors

Jim and Stacey Anderson both grew up with a passion for antiques, and as the owners of Queen of Hearts Antiques & Interiors, a premiere Atlanta antique resource, they are able to embrace this passion daily. The Andersons currently have three locations, in Alpharetta, Buford and Marietta, all of which are dedicated to providing first-rate service and top-quality antiques and collectibles. Queen of Hearts carries a vast selection of American and European furniture, as well as fine china, silver, glassware and jewelry from more than 500 different vendors. The malls also offer linens, stained glass, military memorabilia, coins, rugs and home décor. Queen of Hearts has been featured in many local and national publications, including *Southern Living*, *Atlanta Homes & Lifestyles* and *Good Housekeeping*, not to mention *Country Living* and *Country Living Gardener*. Additionally, Queen of Hearts is highly involved in the community, sponsoring local school sports teams, donating gift certificates to area schools to use for their silent auction fundraisers, and choosing local charities, such as North Fulton Community Charities, to help the less fortunate during the holidays. Whether you are looking to add to an existing collection or to find inspiring pieces of furniture and accessories to enhance your home, you can find it all at Queen of Hearts Antiques & Interiors.

700 N Main Street, Alpharetta GA (678) 297-7571
4125 Highway 20, Buford GA (678) 714-0643
2949 Canton Road, Marietta GA (678) 453-0600
www.queenofheartsantiques.com

Old Sautee Store

In business since 1872, the historic Old Sautee Store started life as a general store. Today, it retains much of its original flavor, acting as both an area museum and a place to purchase such goods as old-time candy, specialty foods and housewares. The store nestles into Georgia's Blue Ridge Mountains in the heart of charming Sautee-Nacoochee, a little village with a big name. You'll find such specialty foods as artisan cheeses, chocolates and preserves as well as toys, cookbooks and books with regional appeal. Name-brand outdoor apparel for men and women is always popular. It's also easy to find an unusual gift here, thanks to an assortment of handmade jewelry and traditional crafts, which feature some of the area's local talent. Outside, the store's aged golden wood is a graceful complement to an antique gas pump. In its spirit as well as its appearance, the Old Sautee Store looks back to times when customers would stop and stay to converse or simply watch the traffic go by. If you are a traveler on the historic Unicoi Turnpike, now Georgia Highway 17, you will be charmed by the experience awaiting you at the Old Sautee Store. Come on in to warm yourself by the fire or play a game of checkers on the broad front porch. You'll experience the true flavor of Appalachia and may get to hear the local legend of Sautee and Nacoochee.

2315 Highway 17, Sautee GA
(706) 878-2281 or (888) 463-9853
www.sauteestore.com

Karen's Gifts

Selecting and displaying new merchandise still motivates Karen Wilson, 12 years after her retail hobby turned into a thriving business. In the beginning, Karen needed only a small corner of her husband's pharmacy to sell the special pieces she had located. Later, her gifts became so popular that the merchandise spread and outgrew its designated space altogether. In 1999, Karen's Gifts and Carter's Pharmacy moved from its Cobb Drive South location to a larger and more modern site. Today, Karen's home accessories, baby items, shower gifts and other

special pieces take up 2,000 square feet of well-designed space. To complement the local art, candles, jewelry and furnishings that Karen secretly wants for herself, she displays collectibles from Waterford, Gail Pitman Pottery and Byer's Choice. Karen's Gifts offers a monogram service, not to mention free gift-wrapping. You will have to visit more than once to check out the one-of-a-kind items created by artisans and small shop owners in the Atlanta area and around the world. When you return, the store always looks different because Karen doesn't stop shopping and the inventory constantly changes. To pick up an item that you can't find anywhere else, visit Karen's Gifts, the home of beauty, creativity and surprises.

3988 Atlanta Road, Smyrna GA
(770) 435-9800
www.karensgiftsofatlanta.com

The Marsh Hen

A day in the tree-lined Redfern Village promises delightful shopping in the heart of St. Simons Island. The Marsh Hen has been calling this exclusive shopping area home since 1978, when Sarah Ellerbee and her late husband, Agnew, opened the gift shop, bringing a beachy atmosphere and whimsical offerings to customers. The store first opened as a kitchen and bath store and later expanded into gifts and home accessories not available anywhere else on the island. Sarah is sure "you will find something you are not looking for" in her shop, where hand-picked items reflect the mood and lifestyle of the island. The shop's name pays tribute to the marsh hen of the tidal marshlands, made famous by Georgia's poet laureate, Sidney Lanier, in a poem entitled "The Marshes of Glynn." Put some surprise into your shopping bag with a visit to the Marsh Hen.

214 Redfern Village, St. Simons Island GA
(912) 638-9845

Cast-On Cottage

Housed in a 1940s cottage in the charming historic section of Roswell, Cast-On Cottage is beloved by the knitting community. Visitors rave about the huge selection of yarns and accessories, fittingly described by one visitor as "everything and then some." They appreciate owner Betsy Laundon's know-how and friendly patience. From the shop's roomy walking space and attractive displays to the pleasing variety of music playing in the background, the atmosphere invites shoppers to relax and linger. "Customers can stroll from room to room," notes one guest, "and Betsy is available to answer questions without being the least bit intrusive." Betsy is an articulate spokesperson for the benefits of knitting and sees knitting as an art form, a therapy and a community building activity. "The process of manipulating the stitches on the needles has a rhythmic quality that is very soothing and therapeutic," Betsy says. "Knitters love to share the fun, the skills, the successes and failures. The big word is share." In this spirit of sharing, Betsy currently offers at least 11 classes weekly at her store, covering everything from the basic skills to advanced techniques. Whether you are already serious about knitting or need help getting started, you must visit Betsy at Cast-On Cottage.

1003 Canton Street, Roswell GA
(770) 998-3483
www.castoncottage.com

The Savannah Bulldog Cigar Company

John Patterson chose a Civil War era carriage house in the heart Savannah's historic district for the Savannah Bulldog Cigar Company, a shop that allows him to indulge his passion for fine cigars and conversation. In 1997, John left a 25-year career as a corporate attorney to open the store. John claims his store is part of a twelve-step program to help recovering lawyers become real people again. He sells 200 varieties of handmade cigars along with specialty cigarettes, exclusive pipe tobacco blends and pipes. The store has been voted Savannah's Best Cigar Store for nine years straight. Check out the beer steins, humidors and Franklin Mint collectible aircraft and cars. You'll find more chess sets in one place than anywhere else. It is also the only downtown store that sells music, including such rare treasures as Negro spirituals from the 1880s. John added music after his future wife, Elizabeth, with her English Bulldog Max, approached him about selling CDs. Elizabeth and John married in 2003. Another 2003 benchmark was the arrival of a second bulldog, Pinky. The bulldogs have inspired plenty of laughter and provided the name for the shop's own cigars, the Savannah Bulldogs. In 2003, *Conde Nast Traveler* called the store one of three Savannah gift stores "worth crossing the shady side of the street to look at." If you can't get to Savannah to see the selection, you can shop at the website. For the most fun, though, come in person to the Savannah Bulldog Cigar Company.

244 Bull Street, Savannah GA
(877) 728-2364 or (912) 232-2650
www.savannahbulldogs.com

The Whole Nine Yarns

Debi Light is a testament to the power of dreams. She had a great career, a wonderful family, a full life. But she also had a dream that wouldn't go away. Debi started knitting and crocheting when she was eight years old, and over the years her love of the fiber arts grew until she just had to do something about it. In 2005, she opened The Whole Nine Yarns, a yarn and fiber store in Woodstock that took off the moment she hung out her shingle. Debi offers an extensive array of raw materials for the fiber arts, with classes, knitting nights and events that cater to both beginners and accomplished artists. She carries books, patterns, kits, buttons, needles and anything else you'll need to complete your yarn projects. She hosts kids camps, birthday parties, bridal showers, spinning classes and charitable events throughout the year. If you love yarns, visit Debi at The Whole Nine Yarns or tap into her website. Birds of a feather, after all, should knit together.

105 E Main Street, Suite 126, Woodstock GA
(678) 494-5242
www.thewholenineyarns.com

Knitch

Yarn addicts rejoiced when Knitch opened its doors in the Virginia Highland neighborhood of Atlanta. They found the luxury yarn and knitting and spinning supplies they most desired. Owner Kim Nickels opened the quaint shop in the summer of 2006. Kim takes pride in supporting small businesses, so you will find products from artisan spinners here, including yarns by Material Whirled and Insubordiknit. The store is the only place in Atlanta where you'll find the Art yarns line, Suss Designs and Rowan yarns, plus lots of little surprises, including a five-ply hand-painted cashmere. Those looking for high-end products will delight in such luxury yarns as Tilli Tomas silk, which has crystals spun into it. There's plenty here for the beginning knitter, with expert help always available and a complete schedule of classes. Buyers of Be Sweet yarns will be pleased to know that profits from those sales go to benefit women in an area of South Africa that suffers 75 percent unemployment. The Ashford spinning wheels here could inspire you to spin your own yarn. The building, which started a century ago as a warehouse, has been converted into a clean, modern space. At the center is a long table where knitters sit down and visit as they work on their latest projects. For everything you need to keep yourself in stitches, visit Knitch.

1052 St. Charles Avenue, Atlanta GA
(404) 745-YARN (9276)
www.shopknitch.com

Broad Street Antique Mall

The dealers gathered at the Broad Street Antique Mall all share owner Sylvester Turner's fascination for historic items that tell a story and that astonish beholders with their craftsmanship. Discriminating shoppers find much in the 200 showcases to engage them, but the owner is especially proud of what customers won't find. The Broad Street Antique Mall is not the place to shop for reproductions, only for authentic antiques and vintage collectibles from credible dealers, many of whom have been at this location for 20 years. Syl Turner specializes in Black Americana, and the mall enjoys a strong reputation as a treasure trove of African American memorabilia, dating from the slavery period through the time of the Civil Rights movement. A slave's petition for freedom, old recruiting posters for Black regiments in the Army and autographed photographs of famous jazz musicians are typical of the items that Turner displays for sale on any given day. The mall features works of contemporary African American artists, including Jim McDowell, the only Black folk potter in America who creates face jugs from his ancestral traditions. Find merchandise with fascinating stories to tell at the Broad Street Antique Mall.

3550 Broad Street, Chamblee GA
(770) 458-6316
www.broadstreetantiquemall.com

Cottonwood Village

A treasure trove of quality antiques, Georgia folk pottery and art, as well as locally handmade goods and foods, is yours to enjoy at charming Cottonwood Village. Conveniently located near Gainesville, Dawsonville and Cumming, the village offers fascinating shops presenting an extensive array of goods and gifts to cherish. Cottonwood Village Antiques offers 5,000 square feet of fine furniture and art, collectible weapons and militaria, plus exquisite estate jewelry. Native American artifacts and Appalachian collectibles will appeal to the most discerning collector. Delicate porcelains, glassware and china grace the lace-covered tables. The Country Store features delicious Jill's Jams, Jellies and Relishes and Nora Mill stone-ground grains and homemade breads for that special meal. Pamper yourself with Greenstone's natural handmade herbal soaps and lotions crafted in Sautee-Nacoochee. Highly fragrant homemade soy candles delight the senses. The Gallery at Cottonwood Village exhibits nationally recognized and emerging artists. Oil and watercolor paintings by Georgia artists join pottery by local folk artisans. Owners Shawn and Heavenly Littleton bring knowledge, creativity and energy to their venture. They are always searching for quality art, firearms and antiques. Shawn spent six years as a nuclear engineer before following his passion for history and vintage weapons. Heavenly is an award-winning documentary filmmaker and a senior editor/producer at CNN, but she finds time to be a creative force in the growing village. Shawn and Heavenly warmly welcome you to come sit a spell and discover a day gone by at Cottonwood Village.

4300 Dawsonville Highway (53E), Gainesville GA
(770) 205-7800
www.cottonwoodvillage.net

Rust & Dust Antiques

When it's time to furnish a movie set, or make a commercial or a promotional music video, folks in the know turn to Rust & Dust Antiques, one of 21 antique shops on Chamblee's well-known Antique Row. Owner Shirley Maddox joins forces with some long-established dealers at the shop, which she opened in 1974. Jerry and Nansee Marglois of Way Back When have been with Shirley 20 years, while Pat Miller of the Muted Swan has a 27-year history with Rust & Dust. The shop offers fine art, vintage toys, furniture and sports equipment. You might find an old slot machine, a football helmet or a bamboo fishing pole. Movie companies rent scenery and props from the shop, and restaurants and other businesses find décor to match their themes. The shop is well-organized, so Shirley and her dealers can pull together necessary items on a moment's notice. They've supplied props for the movie *Fried Green Tomatoes* and the long-running television show *In the Heat of the Night*. Shirley does business from a 1940s building that once housed a drug store. You'll want to plan a full day to roam and shop on Antique Row. For non-traditional gifts, come to Rust & Dust Antiques. Its slogan is: Where the Unusual is the Usual.

5486-5492 Peachtree Road, Chamblee GA
(770) 458-1614
www.antiquerow.com/rustanddust.asp

Homestead House

A log cabin dating back to the 1700s on the Appalachian Mountain tourist trail makes a perfect place to shop for American country and primitive antiques. Leigh Johnston and her mother Gwendolyn Earle made their dreams come true when they started the business, Homestead House, inside the cabin. As impassioned spokespersons for the country and Early American style, they were eager to share their enthusiasm with customers, suggesting ways that they can bring a room or an entire home alive with tasteful blending of items from the store. Richness and warmth characterize the furnishings that they showcase. Handsome country reproductions complement the antiques, which include wing chairs, sofas and corner cabinets. The selection of pewter, rug hookings and original folk art is also particularly strong. Leigh has helped many people in the area coordinate a look for their home or vacation retreat. The hand-hewn cabin originally stood in Banks County and is known to have been the home of a federal agent to the Creek Indians. Leigh and her mother worked with local craftsmen whom lovingly reassembled it log by log in Clarkesville. Drop by to browse the beautiful merchandise and enjoy a cup of hot cider while you're admiring this remarkable structure.

511 Grant Street, Clarkesville GA
(706) 754-0789

Home Sweet Georgia

Located on Gainesville's historic square, Home Sweet Georgia is an official visitor center of the Gainesville Convention & Visitors Bureau as well as a gift shop and a colorful café serving feel-good food. Owner Kathy Vitti offers an array of locally-made gifts celebrating Georgia and the South and serves up down-home cooking for breakfast, lunch and brunch. Visitors can sit outside or inside the charmingly decorated café or grab an ice cream or smoothie to-go and browse the gift shop. You'll find Georgia peach jelly beans, white chocolate bark with peaches and local pecans and peanuts seasoned in a variety of ways. Gourmet kudzu and moonshine jellies go well with pancake and grits mixes. The locally roasted St. Ives coffee comes in 100 different varieties. You'll also find T-shirts, candles and bath products. Home Sweet Georgia specializes in made-to-order gift baskets that you can send home or to your loved one, for a taste of the Peach State and of the South. Regulars come into the café as early as 7 am for the fresh-roasted coffee and pastries, including peaches and cream strudels and a chocolate chunk muffin that sells out every day. *Good Housekeeping* has made these muffins even more famous, so make sure to snag one before they're gone. Lunch features hot and cold croissant sandwiches and the signature Southern Hot Plate. The chicken salad, locally made by a 50-year-old neighborhood grocer, is also popular—Gainesville has been called the chicken capital of the world, so chicken is almost as big a deal as peaches. Visit Home Sweet Georgia and start your tour of Gainesville at the source.

110 Washington Street, Gainesville GA
(770) 534-7151
www.homesweetga.com

Kennesaw Trains

The conversation and coffee are free at Kennesaw Trains, a haven for the model train enthusiast. Owner Kevin Mills isn't one to hide in the back room and let an assistant tend the shop. He says that he has learned a lot from older modelers in his store, knowledge that he especially enjoys passing on to the younger generation of train buffs. Kennesaw Trains specializes in HO, N, O and Lionel O-27 Scale trains. For the train modeler, spending a good part of an afternoon at Kennesaw Trains is even better than getting caught at a railroad crossing and watching all those cars roll by. In addition to a large selection of books, videos and magazines, you will find parts, accessories and tools. Kevin developed a love of trains while growing up in Nebraska along the Union Pacific rail line. After an early retirement from law enforcement in 2004, he jumped at the opportunity to learn the model train business from the previous owner of Kennesaw Trains. His shop is located in downtown Kennesaw across from the Southern Museum of Civil War & Locomotive History. For everything from the sale of model trains to information exchange, drop by Kennesaw Trains.

2844 S Main Street, Kennesaw GA
(770) 528-0990

Photo by Reinout van Rees

Casabella

Casabella is a destination worthy of a special trip. In Spanish or Italian, the name *casa bella* means beautiful home, and your beautiful home is the focus of this fresh and entertaining store. Casabella offers a large selection of Georgia gifts and furnishings, plus complimentary in-home design services, in-store floral design services and a popular bridal registry. Owner Ann VanDevelder is a hands-on owner who combines a strong artistic instinct with business savvy. After five years of selling her merchandise in a classy flea market, she opened her own store, where she displays her wares in attractive collage-style groupings that capture the imagination. Ann combines the vintage furnishings that she loves with artwork, fine china and other accessories, and she shows an uncanny ability to earmark what will appeal to her clientele. She carefully trains her seven merchandisers so that her customers receive a consistent level of service and design flair along with the store's signature cheerfulness. Her store has grown from its original 3,500-square-foot space to 13,000 square feet. Look for local artwork, an outstanding jewelry collection and any number of items that bring design into every nook and cranny of your life. Ann also extends her decorating services to several local charity events. For a refreshing shopping experience, visit Casabella. It's more than a store, it's a lifestyle.

4400 Roswell Road, Suite 128A, Marietta GA
(770) 321-1708
www.casabellathestore.com

Black Bear Creek Antiques

Searching for genuine antiques is a passion for Jim Reaves and Carol Cordray, as any visitor to this historic former general store can plainly see. The Rabun County landmark has become a showcase for their love of the old, and it houses the finest collection of top-quality antiques you'll find anywhere. No faux finishes or imports here. The shop boasts rare books (featuring Uncle Remus), classic bamboo fly rods, vintage advertising and sterling and fine estate jewelry, plus antique cameras, radios and Victrolas, military and railroad collectibles, and so much more. All are beautifully displayed, well lighted and beckon shoppers to touch, reminisce and learn about days gone by. Black Bear Creek also proudly offers the works of talented Georgians including a rustic sign painter, knife maker, wood carver, potter, and oil and watercolor artists, to name a few. No visit to the beautiful North Georgia mountains would be complete without experiencing this fascinating shop, which as the slogan says is full of Genuine Antiques & Man Stuff, Too.

6028 Highway 76 W (5 miles west of town), Clayton GA
(706) 782-2829
www.blackbearcreekantiques.com

Parsons

Since 1925, Parsons has sold everything from live chickens and groceries to clothing and shoes and has continually adapted its inventory to meet the needs of the Duluth community. This family-run business is now owned and operated by third generation son Carey Odem and his wife, Patsy, who were handed the reigns by the founder's daughter, Ann Odem Parson. Over the last decade, Parsons has easily bypassed competition with big name one-stop stores by changing its inventory to offer a wide selection of hard-to-find gifts, accessories and home décor pieces, as well as a selection of Ann Odem's original paintings. This colorful shop specializes in personalized customer service reminiscent of a bygone era and is artfully designed to make browsing easy. Parsons is the ideal place to hunt for gifts for many occasions, including bridal showers, housewarmings and birthdays. The shop features a full selection of your favorite collectibles, such as Madam Alexander dolls and Willow Tree angels. The store carries Tyler candles, ladies accessories and its own delicious fudge, which you can sample at the candy counter. Ann, Carey, Patsy and General Manager Kristen dedicate themselves to serving the community and to ensuring that every customer, new or old, receives kindness here. Skip the big name stores and enjoy a truly delightful shopping experience with a visit to Parsons.

2780 Buford Highway, Duluth GA
(770) 476-3327

Eclectic Living

Lodged in a historic Kennesaw house, Eclectic Living lives up to its name with a diverse collection of fun and funky items for your home, body and soul. Owner Tammy Parker was an air traffic controller in Chicago when she met and married her husband, a Georgia native. Tammy dreamed of opening her own boutique, and even had the name of the store picked out more than a decade before opening it. When the couple moved to Kennesaw, she found the opportunity to fulfill her dreams. Step onto the ample porch and into the house, and you will likely be greeted by some swinging jazz music. The shop carries original creations by local artists, from expressive jewelry to handmade soaps. Offerings extend outside to the garden area, with cement statues and outdoor décor. Customers have spread the word among their friends about Eclectic Living's affordable pricing and unusual gifts, home décor and jewelry, making the store popular without the need for traditional advertising. Visit Eclectic Living, where you are certain to find Everything You Never Knew You Needed to Have.

2886 Cherokee Street, Kennesaw GA (770) 427-7557

DuPre's Antiques & Interiors

The *Atlanta Journal-Constitution* has named DuPre's Antiques & Interiors one of the top five antique stores in the Atlanta Metro Area, and it's easy to see why. DuPre's lives and breathes history. From the moment you walk into the 1877 building erected by the DuPre family, you are surrounded by treasures of the past. The selection is huge, from antique furnishings, clocks and jewelry, to chandeliers, Depression-era glass and Confederate memorabilia. DuPre's is a treasure trove that will excite even the veteran antiques hunter. The store features a 17,000-square-foot showroom with more than 90 dealer spaces, all filled with quality antiques and collectibles. DuPre's roots go back to 1848, when William P. Anderson, great, great grandfather of the current owner, opened a retail business one block from where DuPre's now stands. Five generations later, still in the same location, DuPre's continues as a 131-year-old family operation. The storefront was modernized in 1960, back when the store sold appliances, groceries, boats, and feed & seed. The store is located in historic Marietta Square. The next time you are in Marietta, make sure to visit this wonderful antiques market and experience a piece of Georgia history.

17 Whitlock Avenue SW, Marietta GA
(770) 428-2667
www.dupresai.com

Olivia Morgan Antiques

With more than 25,000 square feet of inventory, Olivia Morgan Antiques is certain to have just the collectible or home décor item you need. Jerri James purchased the antiques mall in February 2006 and named it for her five-year-old daughter, Olivia Morgan. The thriving mall features more than 100 dealers and consigners, who specialize in everything from military memorabilia to vintage furs. Jerri's husband, Greg James, owns a remodeling business, Advanced Concepts, and he has put his skills to good use enhancing the mall. Each booth features new paint, decorative molding and other improvements that have given new life and vitality to the building. Antique enthusiasts will be delighted with the Persian rug showroom, as well as with the custom framing shop and the illuminating chandelier boutique. Other popular draws include a collection of antique English stained glass, which features more than 1,000 pieces, and fine estate jewelry. You will find potted plants, Case knives, fine China and silver, as well as distinctive wall art, books and pieces for the garden. The mall offers on-site storage and a restoration supply store, along with pickup and delivery service. Indulge your passion for antiques with a visit to Olivia Morgan Antiques.

4936 Lower Roswell Road, Marietta GA
(770) 579-5108

Gift Basket Originals

Whether you are presenting a corporate thank you gift or celebrating Mother's Day, you'll want your gift to make a lasting and appropriate impression. One of the best ways to do that is with a gift basket, and Gift Basket Originals in Suwanee specializes in this innovative form of expression. Cindy Antila, the store's owner and president, has dedicated herself to baskets since she started the business out of her home in 1988. Today, you can visit the store or order from the extensive Gift Basket Originals website with confidence that attention to quality and detail remains as important as ever to Cindy. If you visit the store in person, you can select the items for your basket, which could include gourmet foods and snacks from the South as well as presents for a new baby, or pampering and bath products. You can choose from preassembled baskets, too, and personalize your sentiments with especially themed baskets that express sympathy, get well, birthday or holiday wishes. You can even aim your basket at the tennis player or golfer in your life. The store specializes in corporate gift giving and fully understands how to make a promotional gift or business-related thank-you stand out. Ask about table favors and hotel welcome baskets. In addition to beautiful gift arrangements, the store has a unique array of gourmet food, jewelry, pottery and other gift items available for purchase. Take a few minutes out of your busy day and stop by and see the wonderful selection of great gifts.

3320 Lawrenceville-Suwanee Road, Suite 2D, Suwanee GA
(770) 271-5681 or (800) 240-4210
www.giftbasketoriginals.com

The Perfect Present

If you're scratching your head over what to buy for the person that has everything, chances are you haven't visited The Perfect Present yet. Owner and buyer Mychelle Henyon and manager Donna Stone aim to offer the best shopping experience in all of Suwanee and Sugar Hill by coupling impeccable customer service with a distinctive gift selection. The shop offers a little bit of everything, from handmade chocolates and seasonal gifts to home décor and greeting cards. You may never have to go to the mall again when you begin exploring the treasures here, including inspirational items, jewelry, oil lamps and pet gifts, along with gourmet foods and bath products. Colorful, signature gift bags come complete with tissue and ribbon, offering a quick way to pull a last-minute gift together. Shopping for babies and kids is a snap, thanks to the store's selection of plush toys, dolls and books. Willow Tree collectible angels, Tyler Candles,

and items featuring logos from the University of Georgia and Georgia Tech satisfy diverse tastes. If you can't resist glass and other collectibles, you will have a tough time deciding between Waterford, Peggy Karr, Lamp Berger and Arthur Court. Mychelle and Donna are happy to special order for you. They also stage special events in the store to bring families and the community together. Take the trouble out of gift giving with a trip to The Perfect Present.

1000 Peachtree Industrial Boulevard, Suite 7, Suwanee GA
(770) 831-1313
www.the-perfectpresent.com

The Prissy Pooch

My name is Barking Bella and I'm considered the barkology expert by my four-legged petite pals. I'm a very cute tea cup poodle and some consider me a little spoiled. I figure it's all about the bow-wow and finally persuaded my two-legged mom and dad to get in the market

for waggin' wear that I would agree to sport around town. That's when they decided to open the Prissy Pooch inside Ambiance Interiors in Suwanee. Now I've never been so yappy with the selection of haute couture. It has everything that any self-respecting canine could want. You name it, beautiful beds and bowls, classy collars, luxurious leashes and tasty treats. For my friends that are designer gurus Jimmy Chew and Vera Wag shoes are an option, are are Chewy Vuitton and Drooly & Bark purses, Chewnel #5 cologne, Dog Perionne champagne, and even Sniffany & Co. The Prissy Pooch has all kinds of fancy rhinestones to put in my hair and even a raincoat complete with rain hat so that my precious paws don't get wet and fluff doesn't turn to curl on rainy days. I've been told that I look perfectly adogable but you can judge for yourself. Stop in for yappy hour and pick up something your mutt will thank you for.

580 Buford Highway, Suwanee GA
(770) 932-1380

The Chandlery

Finding the perfect gift for every person on every special occasion can be a challenge, unless you're shopping at the Chandlery, the Roswell gift-giving hub. This beloved store was opened in 1977 by husband and wife team Jim and Mary Anne Johnson and is currently owned and operated equally by the Johnsons and their daughter, Sally. Additionally, the Chandlery maintains a staff of 24. Many are long-term employees and all are dedicated to providing their customers with optimum service and selection. Over nearly three decades, the Chandlery has acquired its share of media attention, including being named Best of Atlanta by *Atlanta Magazine* three different times and featured in articles in several magazines, such as *Southern Living* and *Atlanta Home*. The Chandlery offers an extensive selection of fabulous gifts and home décor, all of which are beautifully displayed in themed sections of the store. Various departments include men's interests, regional foods and infant items. The shop also carries a wealth of collectibles and decorative accessories from the world's top designers, such as Yves Delorme, Vietri, Simon Pearce, Mariposa and Arthur Court. The Chandlery provides complimentary gift wrapping, a gift registry and special orders. Local delivery and nationwide shipping are also available. The Johnsons' cheerful shop acts as the community's unofficial welcome wagon for visitors and as a gathering place for locals, many of whom have shopped at the Chandlery for generations. Take a class, meet new friends and find gifts that will inspire and delight you at the Chandlery.

950 Canton Street, Roswell GA
(770) 993-5962 or (800) 440-4789
www.chandlerygifts.com

The Savannah Bee Company

An expert beekeeper, Ted Dennard has studied honeybees all over the world. He taught beekeeping in Jamaica while in the Peace Corps and has watched them produce honey from rubber in Vietnam, from lavender in France and from heather in Ireland. Five years ago, Ted began producing his own tupelo honey under the label The Savannah Bee Company. What started as a kitchen project now occupies a warehouse in downtown Savannah. At a 2003 San Francisco food show, Williams-Sonoma took an interest in Ted's tupelo honey; other national firms and publications soon followed the lead. Today, Savannah Bee Company products are sold in more than 1,600 stores across the country as well as directly to consumers on the company website. The wheels are already in motion to take the next step of exporting these great products across the globe. According to Ted, tupelo is the gold standard of honeys, but he also produces orange blossom, black sage, raspberry and sourwood honeys. His sourwood honey, a particularly complex product, has won world titles. In addition to honey, the company produces a line of body products using beeswax, royal jelly and honey. These all-natural products have demonstrated skin-softening benefits without harmful side effects. Sweeten your life with products from The Savannah Bee Company.

(912) 234-0688
www.savannahbee.com

Phoenix and Dragon Bookstore

One day as Candace Apple was driving to her steady job, she asked herself what she wanted to do with her life. Right then and there, she envisioned Phoenix and Dragon Bookstore, a spiritual resource center sitting on a hill and filled with light. The bookstore opened in 1987 and as Candace had hoped, it became an Atlanta oasis for people of diverse ethnic and religious backgrounds who seek spiritual enrichment and holistic health. Islands of bookshelves offer a wide range of resources guaranteed to keep any reader enthralled for hours. A glass wall provides display for a stunning array of crystals in their rough and polished forms. Seven jewelry cases nestled in the middle of the store contain handcrafted pieces created by artisans from all over the world. An entire wall of candles creates a colorful display for the meditation and chakra room. Customers looking for aromatherapy will find oils, incense, candles and herbs from vendors committed to quality. On every shelf, hand-selected gifts and statuary delight the eyes. Phoenix and Dragon also hosts special events including free book signings from major authors in the metaphysical field. Cutting-edge speakers offer the latest ideas and processes for personal growth. Eight staff practitioners in the intuitive arts are available daily for private consultation. As founding board member of the Sandy Springs Business Association, Candace keeps Phoenix and Dragon involved in the community with book donations and volunteer lecturers. In 2002, she was named Retailer of the Year by the Coalition of Visionary Resources. Candace personally invites you to take a serenity break at Phoenix and Dragon Bookstore.

5531 Roswell Road, Atlanta GA
(404) 255-5207 or (800) 957-6800
www.phoenixanddragon.com

Yarn Garden Knit Shop

Have you ever reminisced about your grandmother's knitting needles clacking together? Are you a knitter yourself? If so, make time for a visit to the Yarn Garden Knit Shop. Owner Carol Sigrist and her daughter Joan Horton prove that the art of knitting is back in fashion. Between them, Carol and Joan have more than 70 years of knitting experience. They take great pride in offering personalized service and an extensive inventory of quality yarns, knitting supplies and accessories. Thanks to their broad knowledge and attention to detail, the two can provide customized or adapted patterns. They are also happy to knit an item for you. Just bring in a picture or discuss your concept with them and they will develop it for you. They also finish partially completed projects. The Yarn Garden offers a full range of knitting and crocheting classes for students at all skill levels and supports a variety of knit clubs. The shop's Knitting for Others group meets monthly to create goods for those in need. Past projects have included baby blankets, chemo caps for cancer patients and stuffed animals for area police and firefighters to give to children after traumatic events. The shop schedules open knitting hours each week during which customers can visit and relax, work on their projects and chat with other knitters until closing time. Indulge your inner knitter at the Yarn Garden Knit Shop.

159 W Pike Street, Lawrenceville GA
(678) 225-0920
www.yarngardenknitshop.com

Laughing Moon and In High Cotton

When two individuals are as creative as the husband and wife team of Rhonda and Ron Erwin, it takes two stores to hold their ideas. Rhonda owns Laughing Moon, a gift store, and Ron owns In High Cotton, a home décor gallery. Leave plenty of time to tour both stores, because once you've visited one, you will want to see the other, too. Rhonda's Laughing Moon is on the square in historic downtown Madison, in an 1880s hotel. Laughing Moon's manager, Melissa Noe, and the staff divide the store into themed rooms filled with items for men, women, pets, cooking and outdoor activities. A man who is clueless about what to buy his wife will appreciate the handbags, clothing and jewelry. At In High Cotton, Ron puts together an international mix of new reproductions and antique furnishings, and he also offers his own custom designs. His ideas and accessories, along with a great sales and display staff, attract many designers to the store. You'll find tables, hutches, vases and statuary. Both stores are open every day of the year except Christmas and Thanksgiving. The couple shares a love of pets, demonstrated in Laughing Moon's realistic holiday window displays and in joint fundraisers that benefit a number of regional animal rescue groups and humane societies. Explore the bounty of Laughing Moon and In High Cotton.

183 S Main Street, Madison GA (Laughing Moon)
(706) 342-8008
158 W Jefferson Street, Madison GA (In High Cotton)
(706) 342-7777

Canton Street Antique Market

After two years in business, the Canton Street Antique Market in historic Roswell is already a destination for shoppers near and far. After meeting with success at a space in an antique mall in Dahlonega, owners Royce Haley and Byron Hamilton decided to open their own antique market in a former grocery store in the 1960s. Hamilton had the flower shop, Hamilton Flowers, directly across the street for 20 years and knew the store's potential based on location. The 15,000-square-foot market, with aisles named after early Roswell plantations, holds a mixed bag of merchandise, including American and European antique furniture, jewelry and old books. Look for lighting, vintage linens, architectural artifacts and a wide assortment of decorations for the home, garden and you. The antique market holds outdoor shows each spring and fall. It also participates in Alive After 5, a festival of entertainment, food, drink and casual shopping held on the third Thursday of every month from April to November throughout the historic district. Royce and Byron donate booth space to three non-profit organizations: Friends of the Roswell Library, Roswell United Methodist Church Missions and Aiding & A-Petting. The booths help raise money for these charities. Additionally, Aiding & A-Petting, a pet rescue group, conducts adoptions in the parking lot every Saturday. Visit Canton Street Antique Market for a fresh look at old (and new) merchandise from a business that cares about the community. Visit the website for a current list of events and activities.

970 Canton Street, Roswell GA
(770) 518-7860
www.cantonstreetantiquemarket.com

Weddings
& Events

European Floral Design

Step into European Floral Design and experience an overwhelming visual delight, followed by a host of romantic scents. Owner Magdalena Williams is delighted to hear the comments of those entering her shop for the first time. "I don't feel as though I am in a store" she says. "It's just an extension of my enjoyment of design." Indeed, Magdalena's sense of design is appreciated more with every arrangement that leaves her boutique. She was most recently recognized by her peers with a blue ribbon in the Southeastern Flower Show in Atlanta. European Floral Design is distinct because of Magdalena's talent for creating glorious arrangements with unusual choices of flowers, textures and a variety of containers. Having grown up in Poland, her shop is steeped in European influence and elegant, classic style. Magdalena has experience creating displays and event designs across the United States, and owning European Floral Design is long held dream. Today, the shop has everything for the floral enthusiast, indoor and out, but the heart of this business is Magdalena's wedding and event creations that receive rave reviews long after the celebrations have ended. From presidential banquets to beach weddings, all events get her special attention to design details. She has a warehouse full of beautiful accessories such as elegant candelabras or handmade vine pedestals, and her events are always stunning. For memorable floral arrangements, visit European Floral Design.

2045 W Broad Street, Athens GA
(706) 227-9937 *www.europeanfloraldesign.com*

The Flower & Gift Basket

You'll feel like a treasured member of the family when you make floral plans with Donna Cochran and her mother Joan Dotson, owners of The Flower & Gift Basket. These helpful florists have been creating stunning floral designs for weddings, funerals, birthdays and special occasions in the Athens area since 1984. You will receive all the time and attention you need from these caring florists. For example, a free wedding consultation up to two hours long is not uncommon. It can take that long to tease out the hopes and dreams of a bride, and determine how the bouquets, alter, rehearsal dinner tables and cake flowers should be done. Brides and family can look through albums filled with 23 years of floral artistry. Donna and her experienced staff know how to make all your wedding dreams come true while honoring your pocketbook. The shop is also a great source for custom gift baskets for every occasion, personally designed by Donna's sister Kathy Stewart. The shop stocks more than 100 delicious gourmet food choices for baskets and can add plants, flowers or balloons for more impact. Fruit, chocolate, bath products or gifts for a newborn or graduate are just a few of the possibilities. Name the occasion and Kathy will custom-design a basket with your gift recipient in mind. Place your order online or come in and see for yourself why the lovely ladies at The Flower & Gift Basket have been delivering the most beautiful flowers, goodies and smiles since 1984.

1310 Baxter Street, Athens GA
(706) 549-5526 or (800) 942-4029
www.flowerandgift.com

Photo by Yeakle Photography

Photo by John Campbell Photography

Photo by Liana Lehman Photography

Photo by John Campbell Photography

BB Webb, Carl House owner, pondering her next project.
Photo courtesy of Gwinnett Magazine

Carl House

This magnificent building on a four-acre estate, built in 1903, was originally a private residence. Today, Carl House is a top location for any event that creates life-long memories. Owners BB and Tom Webb have created a fairy tale environment with a full renovation of the historic antebellum-style home, including the addition of a 4,000-square-foot ballroom and a new third floor, along with stunning gardens. *Gwinnett Magazine* lauded Carl House as the best place to get married and the best place to have a business meeting or retreat in both 2005 and 2006. Atlantabridal.com selected Carl House as Best Reception Site. Carl House was lauded in the Best of Weddings issue of *The Knot Magazine*. This is an establishment dedicated to perfection, with a staff that attends to every single detail of your special event and is ready to spoil and please you. The Bride and Groom's Suites are statements in luxury, with stylish appointments and every amenity to make your event a success. Executive Chef John Carter, affectionately known as Cheffie, is innovative and versatile. He handles special requests—including kosher, vegan and children's menus—with ease. Every menu is designed with your taste and budget in mind. BB is an energetic businesswoman who received the Results Count award from Atlanta Women in Business in 2006. She hosts a weekly television show, *Living Life with Style*, and has a second program in the works, *Southern Journeys*. Tom, a former mayor of Carl, owns an import company. He's the behind-the-scenes design mind at Carl House, while BB and the staff greet the guests. Whatever type of special event you're planning, Carl House can make it a runaway success.

1176 Atlanta Highway, Auburn GA
(770) 586-0095
www.carlhouse.com

Botany Bay Tropical Plants & Flowers

Botany Bay Tropical Plants & Flowers is one of Atlanta's favorite florists. Family owned for 32 successful years, Botany Bay has earned the reputation for providing fresh, quality flowers at affordable prices. Buying in quantity directly from growers of several continents, then shipping overnight, ensures a competitive advantage to the freshest product available. Word of mouth has helped to establish Botany Bay in the area and has been its best advertising. The full service floral artistry of Botany Bay's designers can create anything from the simplest thank you gift to the most extravagant cascading wedding bouquet. The huge selection of unusual flowers is available for customers to choose individual stems or to have a custom European vase made to their exact specifications. Customer service and satisfaction is always guaranteed. Botany Bay's large greenhouse has lush, green plants, and the English garden area provides colorful blooming plants. Same day delivery is available throughout the metro Atlanta area if orders are placed by noon. Botany Bay cordially invites you to visit and make a personal selection so you can say it with flowers. Botany Bay Tropical Plants & Flowers is truly a treasured find.

6074 Roswell Road, Atlanta GA
(404) 255-3340 or (800) 344-9315
www.botanybayflorist.com

Payne-Corley House

The Payne-Corley House, built in 1873, was a private dwelling until 1998, when five childhood friends from Duluth turned it into an events center. Margie Ross and Annette Summerour had cooked for church events and catered privately for many years, and it was Margie's dream to open a center where events could come to them. They joined forces with Jane Wilson, Emma Deavours and Judy Burel to accomplish this feat, preserving a family's name and the charm of Duluth's second oldest house along the way. The main house and the more intimate Magnolia Cottage are in demand for weddings, business

meetings and retreats and have been voted the best places to hold any of those functions by readers of *Gwinnett Magazine*. Wedding couples find a setting that promises a lifetime of memories with original stained glass, fine carpentry details and well-kept gardens. An events coordinator helps with all aspects of the day, including menu choices, which feature such favorites as salmon, chicken, shrimp or beef tenderloin. The wedding party enjoys an upstairs bridal suite and a nearby groom's house. The five owners managed events themselves until 2004, when they hired the Sage House Group of professional hospitality planners, trained by the Ritz Carlton. Let the traditional Southern setting of the Payne-Corley House set the stage for your next event.

2987 Main Street, Duluth GA
(770) 476-5366 *www.paynecorleyhouse.com*

Foxgloves & Ivy Floral Design Studio

Foxgloves & Ivy Floral Design Studio offers more than just flowers. It promises European artistry as part of its fresh, inspired floral arrangements. The co-owners—Greg Brown, AIFD (American Institute of Floral Designers) and Larry Hammack—each have their own story about life in the green industry. Greg's grandmother, Ruth, was a florist, and Larry's grandmother, Frankie, grew prizewinning flowers. Since 1997, Atlanta residents have put their trust in Greg and Larry for chemical and pesticide-free floral and plant selections. The vast majority are imported from the Netherlands, Australia and New Zealand. Foxgloves & Ivy is an AIFD-accredited studio, and discriminating customers are assured of quality product and prompt customer service. You'll find a warm welcome whether you're looking for a single stem of your favorite flower, blooming orchid plants or seasonal blooms for the home or office. Floral designs and European plant compositions are custom designed for all clients, whether they phone in or walk in. The European influence is evident in the design of the store as well. Greg and Larry's goal is to have fresh flowers in homes throughout the Atlanta area. You will find gardening gifts, botanical candles, gourmet gift baskets, home fragrances, plants and of course, fresh flowers. As a full-service floral design studio, daily deliveries are the core business; however, weddings, receptions, special events and corporate designs are a specialty. Greg and Larry are also available for speaking engagements and design demonstrations on the latest techniques, donating any proceeds to their favorite charities. Treat yourself or someone special to the gift of flowers from Foxgloves & Ivy.

1058 St. Charles Avenue, Atlanta GA
(404) 892-7272 or (888) 892-7279
www.foxgloves.biz

Turner Field

Turner Field, the home of the Atlanta Braves, is one of the greatest baseball stadiums in the country, but it is also much more than that. With places to hold meetings and events of every variety, a first-rate museum and other chances for recreation and fun, this is one of Atlanta's prime entertainment and business resources. The stadium was first built for the opening and closing ceremonies and track and field events for the 1996 Olympics. Later, it was retrofitted to serve as the home of the Braves. The Ivan Allen Jr. Braves Museum & Hall of Fame covers the history of both the stadium and the team. The museum contains more than 600 Braves photos and artifacts that trace the team's history from its Boston beginnings to the current day. Want to see how the team operates? Take a tour of the stadium, including a visit to the Braves Clubhouse and dugout. Want to hold a memorable event? Check out the 30,000 square feet Lexus Level. This luxury facility can accommodate more than 3,000 guests or between 75 and 100 trade show booths. If you're holding a smaller gathering, the Braves Chophouse overlooks right field and offers indoor and outdoor space. The Top of the Chop is the newest addition, hosting up to 300 people and featuring a cabana bar. You and your guests can test your batting and pitching skills at Scouts Alley. These are just some of the attractions at Turner Field—and of course you can see the Braves. Visit Turner Field for great functions, great baseball and a great tradition.

755 Hank Aaron Drive, Atlanta GA
(404) 522-7630
www.braves.com

The 755 Club

The 755 Club has what it takes to make your next event a home run hit, whether it's a wedding or a corporate function. The club opened in 1996 at Turner Field, the home of the world-famous Atlanta Braves. Guests thrill to the panoramic view of the field and of the majestic Atlanta skyline. The 755 Club has five meeting spaces that total more than 24,000 square feet. Whether you're putting on an event for 75 people or 500, you'll find the space both luxurious and comfortable. Indeed, an event at the 755 Club provides you and your guests access to the entire Turner Field Stadium, including the Interactive Scouts Alley, the Braves Museum, and even tours of the Braves Clubhouse and dugout. Indoor wedding parties can enjoy the amenities of the club and the sense of history that permeates the Braves Museum. Baseball lovers will enjoy the many pictures of the Braves that line the walls, depicting the team's history. Head out to the terrace to enjoy the best view. The 755 Club, renowned for its steak and seafood, also offers an extensive catering menu. Whether you're looking for brunch with eggs, ham and filet of salmon, sandwiches and other finger food, or an extensive dinner, you'll find it here. For a truly unusual experience, you can actually hold your wedding ceremony outdoors at home plate on Turner Field. Let the 755 Club help you make your next event a grand slam.

755 Hank Aaron Drive, Atlanta GA
(404) 614-2177
www.755club.com

Villa Christina

Surrounded by a flowing brook with bridges, winding walkways and waterfalls, Villa Christina brings the sights and flavors of Italy to Atlanta. The three-story, stacked-stone Tuscan villa includes a gourmet Italian restaurant, elegant ballrooms, private dining rooms and a smaller, to-go restaurant, as well as an outdoor pavilion. Executive Chef Andreas Georgakopoulos uses the freshest ingredients in favorites such as corn and spinach chowder and ravioli with ricotta cheese, walnuts and sage. Save room for desserts such as the renowned fried cheesecake. The full bar provides an extensive list of wines that you can enjoy with your meal or as you stroll through the gardens. Feast in the main dining room, which features colorful oil paintings and chic modern furniture, or in one of two comfortable private dining rooms. For a quick bite, check out Caffè Christina, which offers favorites such as brick-oven pizza. The private dining rooms, ballrooms and meeting rooms—20,000 square feet of flexible function space—make Villa Christina an ideal place to hold corporate or social events. The grand ballroom holds 400 people and can be set up for banquets or conferences. Villa Christina also has four meeting rooms that seat between 10 and 120 and provide state-of-the-art audiovisual equipment and high-speed Internet. The villa's beauty makes it an ideal spot for weddings, which can take place in the ballroom or the gardens. Let Villa Christina bring Italian taste, charm and beauty to your next meal or special event.

4000 Summit Boulevard, Atlanta GA
(404) 303-0133
www.villachristina.com

Petals & Pearls

At Petals & Pearls, the staff knows a wedding can be greatly enhanced by the right details. Since most brides wear the traditional white dress and most grooms sport a black tuxedo, the shop's expertise in floral arrangements and color-coordinating can make your wedding a more picture-perfect day. Owners LaShondria Haynie and Wanda Shelley enjoy creating unique,

exotic bridal bouquets and arrangements you won't see anywhere else, with names like Safari Sunset, Bells of Ireland and Curly Willow. They provide free bridal consultations and take into consideration not only your color scheme, but that of the location where you'll be sharing your vows. Then they put together a well-thought-out, original combination that will add both pizzazz and class to your special event. From bouquets to centerpieces, gazebo accents to matching tiaras, LaShondria and Wanda can invent a design to please your needs. With a vast inventory of flowers and foliage to work with, there's no project too big or too small. The shop also carries a large selection of gift ideas that are perfect for baby showers or bridal parties. Consult with the experts at Petals & Pearls, and take the worry out of at least one major detail of your wedding.

3070 Windward Plaza, Suite G, Alpharetta GA
(770) 740-9696 or (866) 743-9696

Dunwoody Flowers

Henry Atkins and Beverly Dougherty, owners of Dunwoody Flowers, have provided floral services to the Atlanta area for more than 30 years. The care they give each customer is at the foundation of their business. A customer is treated as if he or she is the only one to walk in the door that day, with utmost consideration, concern and attention to detail. In contrast to modern services that Beverly refers to as robomechanics, which do not even replace damaged flowers, the personal touch is alive and well with this caring florist. Dunwoody provides flowers for all of life's occasions, from birth through weddings, parties, funerals and wakes. The folks at Dunwoody Flowers share their customers' joys and sorrows. "We say what people cannot say in words," says Henry. Dunwoody Flowers also handles corporate accounts, which have included department stores and country clubs, among others. Henry began his career as a graphic artist working in commercial design for advertising agencies. He saw floral design as a way to stay in an artistic field and has developed his talents over many years. After two years working for Dunwoody Flowers (then called House of Flowers), Henry was able to purchase the shop with Beverly in 1976. Now that many years have passed, Henry and Beverly hope to sell the shop to someone who will maintain their long-standing tradition of outstanding customer support. Dunwoody Flowers is located across from the Georgetown Shopping Center. Be sure to pay a visit.

4511 Chamblee Dunwoody Road, Dunwoody GA
(770) 394-4111 or (888) 777-8222
www.florists.ftd.com/dunwoodyflowers

Gertie Mae's

What was a Pure Oil gas station in the 1930s is now a striking floral and gift shop with fresh flowers, fancies and fineries. At Gertie Mae's, the odd shape of the building, the tongue-in-groove ceilings and the original brick embrace history, while the interior elements help define today's floral art. The shop has a European feel; its fragrances and colors quickly capture your attention. Owner and floral designer Sherry Donnelly named the shop after her grandmothers, Gertrude Burt and Mabel Mae Ferguson. Both displayed green thumbs in the garden and a natural talent for arranging flowers. With such a family inheritance and her own ever-growing passion for flowers, Sherry opened Gertie Mae's in 2003. Since then, Sherry's custom arrangements have become her personal signature in the floral industry. Each distinctive bouquet incorporates unusual elements along with amazingly beautiful flowers and foliage. Sherry's wedding and event pieces have been displayed in *Modern Bride Atlanta*, *Brides Atlanta*, *Northeast Georgia Living* and on the cover of *Atlanta Home Resource*. To complement the fresh-cut flowers, bouquets and custom arrangements, you'll find a range of non-floral gifts for your friends and family, along with items you can't live without such as handmade soaps, one-of-a-kind jewelry and gourmet chocolates. Gertie Mae's is a local favorite and well worth the drive up from Atlanta or down from the Carolinas. When you get to town, just look for the Washington Street Quick-Turn and pull directly into Gertie Mae's.

1500 Washington Street, Clarkesville GA
(706) 754-0406 *www.gertiemaes.com*

Wolf Mountain Vineyards & Winery

When Karl Boegner and his family started Wolf Mountain Vineyards & Winery in 1999, their vision was to create a signature retreat that offered the highest-quality pairings of wine and food. They have succeeded. Wolf Mountain Vineyards in Dahlonega, located five miles north of the historic town square, is a 25-acre estate overlooking the pastoral Appalachian foothills. The Boegners grow their own Cabernet Sauvignon, Syrah, Mourvedre and Touriga Nacional grapes. Situated at an elevation of 1,800 feet, the Winery offers a beautiful venue for both business and social events. It specializes in vineyard weddings and receptions for up to 200 people, corporate parties, and intimate wild game and gourmet dinners in the cask room. Handcrafted wines made with Georgia-grown grapes join together with a creative event program designed to broaden both your knowledge and appreciation of the culinary arts and the marriage of wine and food. The stately winery at Wolf Mountain is fashioned after a raised Craftsman-style cottage that sits atop the fieldstone-encased cellar. The winery includes 7,500 square feet of function space and contains a dance floor, antique bar area and artistic fireplace. The winery houses a exhibition of early wine-making artifacts, and the Boegners serve a much heralded Sunday brunch. If you are inspired by hospitality, natural beauty, food and wine, visit Wolf Mountain Vineyards & Winery.

180 Wolf Mountain Trail, Dahlonega GA
(706) 867-9862
www.wolfmountainvineyards.com

Forrest Hills Mountain Resort and Conference Center

Conference Center offers lodging options and services to accommodate any group. Kraft family members opened the 140-acre oasis in 1978 and built the first six cabins themselves, using lumber culled from the property. Today, the resort offers 98 rooms in a variety of configurations. Stay in one of the rustic cabins and relax in an indoor hot tub while looking out into the wilderness, or choose a beautifully appointed Victorian cottage, complete with a candlelit dinner. Forrest Hill's lodges strike a perfect balance between privacy and group activity for large parties. When holding a family reunion in a lodge, everyone can enjoy their own rooms and come together in the large common area to reminisce and catch up with loved ones. The resort offers all-inclusive wedding packages, too. The Secret Garden wedding gazebo makes a picturesque setting for your ceremony, and you can continue the celebrations throughout the weekend with accommodations for all of your guests at the resort. During your stay, enjoy full day spa services, horseback riding or a scenic wagon ride and cookout. Just a few miles away, you'll find golf courses, great shopping and winery tours. Come to Forrest Hills Mountain Resort and Conference Center for a vacation tailored to you.

135 Forrest Hills Road, Dahlonega GA
(706) 864-6456 or (800) 654-6313
www.forresthillsresort.com

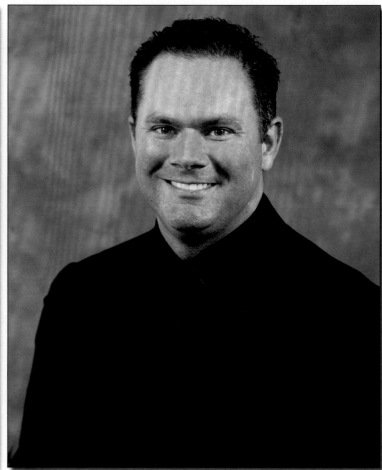

Spectrum Entertainment

Spectrum Entertainment offers a wide variety of music and entertainment options for any event. This includes everything from DJs and bands to ceremony musicians, such as string quartets and classical guitarists. CitySearch recently named Spectrum Entertainment the number-one source for party DJs in the Atlanta area. Spectrum indeed maintains the largest roster of entertainers in the region, which means the company can cover any event, any time. Spectrum specializes in weddings, but they are equipped to handle literally any occasion, be it Bar and Bat Mitzvahs, birthdays, graduation parties or company parties. Customer service is the top priority for Spectrum owners Mat Osborne and Chris Dollar. With each event tailored to exact specifications, customers are able to pick and choose their own personalized music selection. Spectrum uses only the top-of-the-line audio and video equipment for top quality sound and visual experiences. In addition to music and entertainment, the company also provides videography services to professionally capture your event. Spectrum's customers experience courteous, professional service from appropriately attired performers. Let Spectrum Entertainment help plan your next event.

6025 Unity Drive, Suite E, Norcross GA
(770) 441-9806
www.spectrum-ent.com

A White Rolls Royce

In days gone by, a knight in shining armor arrived to collect his lady on a brilliant white steed. A White Rolls Royce provides the modern-day equivalent for today's Prince Charming who is looking for a stylish way to whisk his princess away to the ball. Tim and Susan Lorenz opened their business after deciding that the area could use something beyond the usual stretch limousines. They have three almost identical vintage White Rolls Royce sedans. There's plenty of room to stretch out and enjoy the comfortable ride. Your pleasure trip can begin in true celebrity style with a walk down an actual red carpet into your awaiting limousine. The car itself can be decorated to meet your special needs, perhaps a Just Married sign in the back window and English wedding ribbon on the front of the car. The company also handles the transportation needs of celebrities and executives and can provide that stretch limousine, shuttle bus or motor coach when you need to transport large groups. It serves many cities throughout Georgia, with quotes varying depending on the area. If you're looking for a way to stage a modern-day fairy tale, let A White Rolls Royce be your magic carriage.

(404) 992-4881
www.AWhite-RollsRoyce.com

KaBloom

When you compare spending the day behind a desk with handling fresh-cut flowers and bringing joy to people's lives, it might be easy to see why Don and Lori Bush gave up the corporate lifestyle in 2003 to open KaBloom flower shop. The duo had the American dream—they longed to own their own business, one that would bring smiles to the faces of customers. They found just what they were looking for in KaBloom. This shop encourages you to become involved in the bouquet design process as a way of ensuring that you get exactly the arrangement that fits your needs. Lori explains that a visit to KaBloom offers shoppers an entirely different level of participation than walking into a grocery store and picking up flowers along with the eggs. Lori and Don say they have been fortunate to find talented and artistic designers who can satisfy a wide range of floral needs, from large formal events to someone who stops to pick up a little something for a sweetie. If you prefer, you can create your own bouquet using cut stems from the walk-in cooler, which may include roses, tulips, lilies and other flowers imported directly from the Netherlands and South America. Come to KaBloom and make someone's day with what KaBloom calls the Power of Fresh Flowers.

6555 Sugarloaf Parkway, Suite 305, Duluth GA
(678) 417-9301
www.kabloomofduluthsugarloaf.com

Floristique

Floristique has been providing Gwinnett County residents and businesses with floral excellence for the last 15 years. Owner Delilah Whitesmith is committed to bringing you a level of floral quality that surpasses all others. She is very community minded, which is evidenced by her involvement with the Duluth Merchants Association and the Gwinnett Charter Chapter of the American Business Women's Association. She is also listed in the Biltmore Who's Who and Floristique is a Certified Woman-Owned Business. In 2003, the Gwinnett Chamber of Commerce nominated Floristique as the Small Business of the Year. Teleflora, an international floral wire service, ranked Floristique in their top 2,000 out of 25,000 shops in the United States. Floral designer Vera Gunnels achieves artistic excellence with the hundreds of fresh flowers she

has at her disposal. Floristique will personalize gift baskets, and offers arrangements of silk and dried flowers. It carries an assortment of impressive gift items, including candles, gourmet chocolates and greeting cards. Floristique can handle any of life's special occasions, including weddings and parties. You are limited only by your imagination. Come into Floristique with an idea, let the staff grow with it, and together you will find something that tickles your senses.

3940 Peachtree Industrial Boulevard, Suite A, Duluth GA
(678) 957-8030 or (800) 800-9097
www.floristique.com

173 Carlyle House

The 173 Carlyle House is an ideal location for a wedding reception, a corporate gathering or other gala event. The gracious turn-of-the-century home, located on two acres of old magnolia trees in historic downtown Norcross, features a ballroom and several more intimate rooms all fitted with exquisite chandeliers and other period detail. Mirka and William Janousek opened their special events facility in 1997 and bring a combination of five decades in the hospitality and food service industry to their business. William is the chef, specializing in Continental cuisine. He has been an active member of the Atlanta culinary scene for 30 years, originally training in Paris, then working as Executive Sous Chef for the Hotel Alcron in Prague, Czechoslovakia. A catering specialist will be glad to describe your options for dinner, buffet and hors d'oeuvres along with spectacular cake offerings, all made to your specifications. The ballroom can accommodate up to 300, and your guests will have full use of the entire facility throughout the

event. Preparing for a wedding can be overwhelming. You can make the plans yourself or leave the details to the Perfect Wedding Planner service, knowing that flowers, music and all the rest will be beautifully managed. Call on 173 Carlyle House and let the Janouseks help you arrange a memorable event.

173 S Peachtree Street, Norcross GA
(770) 662-5800
www.173carlylehouse.com

TD Entertainment

Whether you're holding a wedding, corporate function or just a big bash, TD Entertainment is in tune with your music and entertainment needs. The Roswell agency was founded by Tammy Allen, a performing artist with three CDs and more than a decade of touring under her belt, and Terri Harof, a public relations professional who once represented famed boxer Evander Holyfield. The combination of performing pizzazz and PR know-how has let TD Entertainment organize and promote many successful, well-attended events, including the annual Food and Wine Festival at Villa Christina, the local Summer Jazz Series and a $100,000 Wedding Giveaway. The firm has also organized entertainment for events sponsored by Coca-Cola, Korbel Champagne, Delta Airlines and other major corporations. The company can provide musical entertainers for any occasion by drawing from a pool of some of the Atlanta area's most talented musicians. Whether you're looking for the latest R&B and Top 40 styles, jazz, country, blues or reggae, TD Entertainment can provide it. Hip-hop and gospel performers are also on hand, as are DJs. The company can provide salsa and flamenco dancers, mimes and other performance artists. Let TD Entertainment and its staff of entertainers and PR professionals make your next event one to remember.

200 Market Place, Suite 200, Roswell GA
(404) 786-7410
www.tdentertainment.biz

Photos by Tanner Photography

Wineries
& Breweries

Wolf Mountain Vineyards & Winery

When Karl Boegner and his family started Wolf Mountain Vineyards & Winery in 1999, their vision was to create a signature retreat that offered the highest-quality pairings of wine and food. They have succeeded. Wolf Mountain Vineyards in Dahlonega, located five miles north of the historic town square, is a 25-acre estate overlooking the pastoral Appalachian foothills. The Boegners grow their own Cabernet Sauvignon, Syrah, Mourvedre and Touriga Nacional grapes. Situated at an elevation of 1,800 feet, the Winery offers a beautiful venue for both business and social events. It specializes in vineyard weddings and receptions for up to 200 people, corporate parties, and intimate wild game and gourmet dinners in the cask room. Handcrafted wines made with Georgia-grown grapes join together with a creative event program designed to broaden both your knowledge and appreciation of the culinary arts and the marriage of wine and food. The stately winery at Wolf Mountain is fashioned after a raised Craftsman-style cottage that sits atop the fieldstone-encased cellar. The winery includes 7,500 square feet of function space and contains a dance floor, antique bar area and artistic fireplace. The winery houses a exhibition of early wine-making artifacts, and the Boegners serve a much heralded Sunday brunch. If you are inspired by hospitality, natural beauty, food and wine, visit Wolf Mountain Vineyards & Winery.

180 Wolf Mountain Trail, Dahlonega GA
(706) 867-9862
www.wolfmountainvineyards.com

Frogtown Cellars

At the foot of the glorious Appalachian Mountains, equidistant between Dahlonega and Cleveland, sits one of Georgia's most celebrated wineries, Frogtown Cellars. Craig and Cydney Kritzer, along with their daughter and winemaker Jordan Fiorentini, established Frogtown in 1999. Jordan, who holds a masters degree in winemaking from the University of California at Davis, apprenticed in California and Italy before returning home to cultivate the family's 30 acres of vineyards. The 57-acre estate houses a tri-level, gravity flow winery along with a stunning tasting room and special event facility, designed by Craig and constructed from native timbers and hand-carved, stone-encased walls. The Frogtown tasting room features two large decks and a lovely wraparound porch that is ideal for viewing the estate's vineyards and private lake, as well as the picturesque North Georgia mountains. Frogtown produces several fine red and white wines from the 15 varietals grown on the estate. For white wine lovers, the winery offers Chardonnay, Viognier, Marsanne and Seyval Blanc, along with Roussanne, Muscat and both Vidal and Sauvignon Blanc. Connoisseurs of red wines will delight in Frogtown's Cabernet Sauvignon, Merlot and Cabernet Franc, as well as the Touriga, Sangiovese, Norton and the award-winning Tannat. On weekends, Cydney prepares a bistro lunch to accompany your afternoon and Sunday brunch wine tasting. Make a weekend visit to Frogtown Cellars, and enjoy an afternoon getaway unlike any other.

3300 Damascus Church Road, Dahlonega GA
(706) 865-0687
www.frogtownwine.com

Boutier Winery

Boutier Winery makes each bottle of wine into a personal expression. The Acworth winery, owned by Mary Jakupi Boutier and Victor Boutier, can place Your Message on a Bottle. That's right, Boutier will personalize its award-winning wines with your company logo, family crest or a greeting of your choosing and design. Boutier Winery recently won a Concordance Gold award for its 2005 Peach Chardonnay, as well as bronze medals for its 2005 Georgia Chardonnay and its 2005 The Skinny Bitch, a blend of Georgia blueberries and American Syrah. Boutier selects the best grapes from fine vineyards and cultivates 32 of its own acres in the temperate Piedmont region. Daily wine tastings

assure that you pick the right wine for each special occasion. Celebrate a wedding or anniversary in style or keep some special-label bottles in your private wine rack. You can be sure the wine itself and the special labeling will make an impression on anyone who appreciates the good things in life. Come in to Boutier Winery and let the knowledgeable staff help you send the perfect message.

4500 S Main Street, Suite 101, Acworth GA
(770) 529-0490
www.boutierwinery.com

Habersham Vineyards & Winery

When considering the nation's greatest wine producers, California or Washington may come to mind, but Georgia is quickly gaining a reputation for exquisite wines, thanks in part to Habersham Vineyards & Winery. This distinctive winery began growing grapes in 1980 and produced its first wines in 1983, making Habersham one of the oldest wineries in the state. Habersham currently produces 15,000 cases of wine annually, which also makes it one of Georgia's largest producers. Wines are produced under three labels: Creekstone, Habersham and Southern Harvest. These wines use vinifera grapes such as Merlot, Cabernet Sauvignon, Chardonnay, Viognier and Riesling; French-American grapes such as Vidal, Seyval and Chambourcin; and the native Muscadine grape. Most of the grapes for these wines come from the company-owned Mossy Creek and Stonepile Vineyards that yield about 125 tons of grapes annually. Muscadine grapes are purchased from growers in southern Georgia. The winery is located in picturesque Nacoochee Village, one-half mile south of Helen, and is open daily with complimentary tastings. The tasting room has a sensational array of wine, food and gift items, and offers views of the tank and barrel rooms and the bottling line while you sip your way through the winery's extensive wine selections. Explore Georgia's budding wine trade with a visit to Habersham Vineyards & Winery.

7025 S Main Street, Helen GA
(706) 878-9463 or (770) 983-1973
www.habershamwinery.com

SweetWater Brewing Company

What do a couple of college buddies do when they realize they have more of a passion for beer than books? Fredrick Bensch and Kevin McNerney started their own microbrewery in Atlanta—SweetWater Brewing Company. Fredrick and Kevin met when they were in school studying environmental conservation in Boulder, Colorado. The pair worked part-time at a brewery to earn spending money and, they say, for the free beer. After falling in love with the industry, they decided to go into business for themselves. Focusing on aggressive West Coast style beers with careful attention to freshness and quality, SweetWater quickly became popular in what the two men call "the beer desert of the Southeast." The brewery produces six year-round and four seasonal beers, from the popular 420 Extra Pale Ale to the SweetWater Exodus, a classic Porter. The brewery makes beers without preservatives or pasteurization. Both the World Beer Cup and Great American Beer Festival have awarded gold medals to SweetWater beers, proving the popularity of the company's inventive recipes. If it's your first visit to the brewery, you may want to check on the tour schedule so you can discover what it takes to create these microbrews. Some folks bring a lawn chair, a Frisbee and a designated driver for an afternoon of fun. Fredrick and Kevin invite you to come taste some of the finest new beers coming out of the Southeast at SweetWater Brewing Company.

195 Ottley Drive, Atlanta GA (404) 691-2537 *www.sweetwaterbrew.com*

Index by Treasure

Numbers

173 Carlyle House 342
755 Club 78, 333

A

Above the Rest Luxury Cabins 5
Accents 172
Acworth Bookstore and Library 288
Adventure Trail Rides of Cashes Valley 212
Agatha's-A Taste of Mystery 77
Agave Restaurant 276
Air Atlanta Helicopters, Inc. 71
Alvida Art Gallery 133
Ambiance Interiors & Gifts 179
Amici Italian Café 232
Amira's Mediterranean Bistro 228
Andy's BBQ 238
Anne Hathaway 136
Ann Jackson Gallery 141
Anthony's Fine Dining 227
Antiques & Interiors of Sandy Springs 286
Antique Sweets 102
APEX Museum 50
Architectural Accents 186
Armaan—American-Asian Fusion Restaurant
     & Lounge 239
Artrages Gallery 138
Ashford Manor Bed and Breakfast 35
Ashley Park 73
Atlanta Arts and Antiques 287
Atlanta Ballet 55
Atlanta Botanical Garden 54
Atlanta Workshop Players 215
Aurora Theatre 59
Aurum Studios and Aurum Jewelry Art 127
Azalea Inn & Gardens 29

B

Barna Log Homes 193
Barn Inn at Lake Rabun 16
Baron York Tea Room Café & Gift Shop 108
Beach Bed & Breakfast 34
Beechwood Inn 17
Belford's Savannah—Seafood & Steaks 267
Bernie's Nacoochee Valley Guest House 28
Bilt-House 293
Black Bear Creek Antiques 314
Black Forest Bed & Breakfast and Luxury Cabins 22
Blackstone—Steaks, Seafood & Spirits 272
BleuBelle Boutique 119
Blossom Boxes 180
Blue MedSpa 144
Blue Ridge Adventure Wear 284
Blue Ridge Scenic Railway 84
Blue Sky Vacation Rentals 23
Blue Willow Inn 271
Booth Western Art Museum 62
Botany Bay Tropical Plants & Flowers 330
Boutier Winery 348
Bowman & White Gallery 132
Brenda Evans Designs 170, 299
Brighton Collectibles 89
Broad Street Antique Mall 308
Brookwood Grill 272
Busy Bee Café 268

C

c.a.n.o.p.y. 159
Cabin Grille 256
Café Campesino 102
Café Hot Wing 224
Café Intermezzo 101
Café Michel 277
Cagle's Dairy 63
Canton Street Antique Market 323
Carl House 329
Casabella 181, 313

Cast-On Cottage 305
CCBerries 108
Cecilia Villaveces Cakes 107
Certain Something 186
Chandlery 319
Chappelle Gallery 140
Christmas & More 300
City Market 82
City Segway Tours Atlanta 86
Classic Expressions 153, 281
Classics 300
Cobblestone Corner 173
Collins Hill Golf Club 208
Corkscrew Café 232
Cottonwood Village 309
Courtyard Home 93
Creekside Grill 240
Crew Outfitters 290
Crimson Moon Café 105, 274
Crocker Pottery 130
Cynthia Aiken Interiors—Mountain Cottage 157

D

D&B Designs 160
D. Morgan's 237
Dantanna's Surf & Turf 229
Dearing Antiques 298
DE Fine Art 129
Delkwood Grill 255
Designer Antiques 90
Details Design Center 161
Dillard's BBQ & Biscuits 228
Divas and Dames Boutique 116, 292
Dogwood Bar & Grill 220
Dominick's 245
Donna M's Custom Arts 171
Douceur de France 104
Dunwoody Flowers 336
DuPre's Antiques & Interiors 316

E

Eagle Island Lodge 36
Earth Products 183
Eclectic Living 315
Eddy West 162
Elegant Attic 182
El Torero Mexican Restaurant 250
Enchanted Mountain Trout & Gourmet Meats 196
Etowah Indian Mounds State Historic Site 64
Eufloria, Flowers & Little Luxuries 189
European Floral Design 326

F

Family Tradition Restaurant 249
Farmhouse Inn at Hundred Acre Farm 41
Feddeaux 107
Firefly Café 240
First Class Cabin Rentals 15, 192
Fleetwood Dance Center 206
Floristique 342
Flower & Gift Basket 327
Flying Machine 222
Forrest Hills Mountain Resort
    and Conference Center 37, 339
Forum on Peachtree Parkway 87
Four Seasons Pottery 184
Foxgloves & Ivy Floral Design Studio 331
Fräbel Glass Art Studio 74, 291
Fräbel Studio 124
Frogtown Cellars 347
Funk Heritage Center 72

G

G-Art Europe 126
Gado Gado Home Gallery 160
Gallery at Spalding Corners 134
Gems of Africa 130
Georgia Aquarium 53

Georgia Ensemble Theatre & Conservatory 68
Georgia Originals 140
Georgia Shakespeare 58
Gertie Mae's 337
Gift Basket Originals 318
Girasoles 233
Gogo 121
Gold 'n Gem Grubbin 211
Gotta Dance Atlanta 207
Grace 17-20 88
Granny's Cottage 158
Grape 90
Grapes & Hops Bar & Bistro 246
Green Palm Inn 40

H

Habersham Vineyards & Winery 348
Hamilton-Turner Inn 32
Happy Acres Farm 21
Happy Valley Pottery 140
Hastings Entertainment–Newnan 294
Healing Onion 144
Heavenly Touch Wellness Center & Spa 148
Heirloom Iron Bed Company and Fine Linens 185
Helendorf River Inn & Conference Center 40
Henry County Library System 69
Hillcrest Orchards 84
Hillside Orchard Farms Country Store & Farm 67
Hilton Garden Inn Atlanta Perimeter Center 6
Historic Downtown Lawrenceville 51
Historic Glen-Ella Springs Country Inn 30, 253
Historic Green Manor Restaurant 223
Hofer's of Helen 106
Homestead House 310
Home Sweet Georgia 247, 311
Hotel Indigo 11
Hummingbird Embroidery & Gifts 296
Hummingbird Lane 139

I

ImageSpa 148
Inn at Ellis Square 13
Inside Design 175
Iron Wok China Bistro 234
Isabelle's on the Gorge 228

J

James Madison Inn & Conference Center 24
Jere's Antiques 187
Jimmy Carter Library and Museum 57
Juices Wild 98
JWR Jewelers 112

K

K-la Boutique 93
KaBloom 342
Kafe Kelly's 260
Kani House 252
Karen's Gifts 304
Kennesaw Trains 312
Knitch 308

L

Laughing Moon and In High Cotton 322
Laura Leiden Calligraphy 131
Lavender Asian Bistro 222
La Villa 167
Lil' River Grill 251
Limetree 92
Little g's Mountain Garden Center 168
Little Shop 284
Logan Turnpike Mill 200
Love Street Gifts and Gardens 166
Love Street Home 166
Lucille's Mountain Top Inn 26
Lydia's, Something a Little Different 154

M

Madison Chophouse Grille 222

Magnolia Bakery Café 98

Main Street Gallery 126

Maison Bleu 240

Manna to Go 199

Marcus Jewish Community Center 48

Margot's Closet 217

Marietta Wine Market 201

Maritza & Frank's 260

Mark of the Potter 81, 283

Marsh Hen 304

Martha's Mountain Gallery 135

Martin Luther King, Jr. National Historic Site 61

Matilda's Gallery of Folk Art and Whimsy 137

McDonough Hospitality & Tourism Bureau 47

Meg Pie Too 295

Mercier Orchards 198

Michon's Smoked Meats & Seafood Restaurant 260

Miss Scarlet's Chocolat Emporium 100

Misty Mountain Inn & Cottages 8

Misty Mountain Pottery 138

Mittie's Tea Room Café 96

Mittie's Café & Tea Room of Alpharetta 252

Mountain Laurel Creek Inn & Spa 30

Mountain Treasures 152, 294

My Sister's Gifts 302

N

Nature's Own Herb Shop 146

Ninja Steak & Sushi 234

Nirvana Café & Grille 273

Noodle 243

Nora Mill Granary—Grist Mill & Country Store 200

Northern Star Coffeehouse 99

O

O.B.'s Bar BQ 258

Oar House 248

Ocean Lodge 34

Old Clarkesville Mill 86

Old Clayton Inn 26

Old Sautee Store 304

Olivia Morgan Antiques 317

Outdoor Traditions 209

Out of the Blue 285

Outrageous Bargains 172

Outside World 212

OwenLawrence 177

P

Paco's 254

Padriac's 270

Pappy's Fudge & Gifts 104

Parsons 314

Payne-Corley House 330

Pecan 275

Perfect Present 318

Perk Place Coffee Shop 102

Petal Pushers 155

Petals & Pearls 336

Phoenix and Dragon Bookstore 321

Pine Mountain Loft & Gallery 152

Pinetree Country Club 213

Planter's Inn on Reynolds Square 31, 83

Polka Dot Peach 296

Prissy Pooch 318

Prospect Park 70

Pura Vida USA 20, 147

Q

Queen of Hearts Antiques & Interiors 303

R

Rattles & Rhymes 298

Redfern Jewelers 117

Red Hound 163

Red Sky Café & Coffeehouse 244

Redz 259

Repose MedSpa 146

Rib Ranch 264

Rose Cottage Furniture 176

Rust & Dust Antiques 310

S

Sandy Springs Galleries 292

Savannah Bee Company 320

Savannah Bulldog Cigar Company 306

Savannah Day Spa 145

Savannah Fine Linens 172

Savannah Harbor 19

Savannah Wine Shop 203

Scarlett's Retreat Day Spa & Mercantile 149

Scarlet Tassel 165

Seasons Bistro 265

Serendipity House 280

Serene Bean 103

Sevananda Natural Foods Cooperative 197

Shoki Japanese Steak House & Sushi Bar 221

Shucker's Seafood Bar & Grill 244

Sia's 234

Silver Skillet Restaurant 256

Snip-Its 92

Soho South Café 262

Southern Comforts Consignments 188

Southern Expression 288

Southern Museum of Civil War and Locomotive History 66

Southern Sweets Bakery 97

Southern Tree Plantation 75

Spa Sydell 89

Spectrum Entertainment 340

Stained Glass at Sugar Creek 134

Stanton Home Furnishings 188
State of Georgia 45
Stefan's Off the Square Restaurant 264
Step Above Stables 208
Stovall House Country Inn & Restaurant 16
Studio Atlanta Dance 216
Sugar Magnolia Bed & Breakfast 7
Sugar Mill Creek RV Resort 8
Sunburst Stables 215
Sunrise Grocery and Sunrise Cabins 39
Sweet Auburn Curb Market 196
SweetWater Brewing Company 349
Swoozie's 91
Sycamore Grill 261
Sylvan Falls Mill Bed & Breakfast 27

T

Talbots 91
Tanglewood Farm 64
Tara Inn and Suites 25
TD Entertainment 343
Teaching Museum North 76
Teacup Cottage 100
Ted's Montana Grill 88
Tellus: Northwest Georgia Science Museum 49
Thomas Orchards, Greenhouse & Giftshop 202
Tica Cabin Rentals 14
Timpson Creek Gallery 169
Topaz Gallery 113
Trackrock Campground & Cabins 9, 210
Treasure Chest 115
Turner Field 79, 332

U

UMI Japanese Steak House & Sushi Bar 236
Unicoi Outfitters 212
Upscale Fashions Consignment Boutique 120
Up the River Outfitters 214
Uptown Gardening & Hardware 188

V

Van Gogh's 266
Varsity 231
Vic's on the River 263
Villa Christina 335
Village Corner 241
Village Inn and Pub 33
Village Porch Café 244
Vinings Gallery 125
Vinny's New York Pizza & Italian Grill 230
Vintage Tavern 269
Vintage Tea 109
Virginia Highland Bed and Breakfast 10

W

Washington Plantation Bed and Breakfast 38
Whidby Jewelers 116
Whiskey River Entertainment Complex 85
Whistle Stop Café 65, 225
White Rolls Royce 341
Whole Nine Yarns 307
William Word Fine Antiques 289
Willingham's Kitchen 257
Willows Pottery 138
Winchester Woodfire Grill 235
Wolf Mountain Vineyards & Winery 338, 346
Wrapsody in Blue 297

Y

Yarn Garden Knit Shop 322
Yonah Treasures 301

Z

Zanzo Italian Café 242
Zeigler House Inn 26
Zïa Boutique 118
Zucca 269

Index by City

A

Acworth

Bakeries, Treats, Coffee & Tea
Miss Scarlet's Chocolat Emporium 100
Teacup Cottage 100

Fashion & Accessories
Divas and Dames Boutique 116

Health & Beauty
Healing Onion 144

Home & Garden
Lydia's, Something a Little Different 154

Shopping & Antiques
Acworth Bookstore and Library 288
Divas and Dames Boutique 292
Serendipity House 280
Southern Expression 288

Wineries & Breweries
Boutier Winery 348

Adairsville

Shopping & Antiques
Sandy Springs Galleries 292

Alpharetta

Attractions & Culture
Prospect Park 70

Bakeries, Treats, Coffee & Tea
Vintage Tea 109

Galleries & Fine Art
Matilda's Gallery of Folk Art and Whimsy 137

Home & Garden
Classic Expressions 153
Earth Products 183
Eddy West 162
Outrageous Bargains 172
Red Hound 163

Recreation & Fitness
Atlanta Workshop Players 215
Fleetwood Dance Center 206

Restaurants & Cafés
Dogwood Bar & Grill 220
Mittie's Café & Tea Room of Alpharetta 252
Nirvana Café & Grille 273

Shopping & Antiques
Classic Expressions 281
My Sister's Gifts 302
Queen of Hearts Antiques & Interiors 303

Weddings & Events
Petals & Pearls 336

Americus

Bakeries, Treats, Coffee & Tea
Café Campesino 102

Athens

Bakeries, Treats, Coffee & Tea
Cecilia Villaveces Cakes 107

Fashion & Accessories
JWR Jewelers 112

Galleries & Fine Art
Aurum Studios and Aurum Jewelry Art 127

Restaurants & Cafés
Amici Italian Café 232
Shoki Japanese Steak House & Sushi Bar 221

Shopping & Antiques
Rattles & Rhymes 298

Weddings & Events
European Floral Design 326
Flower & Gift Basket 327

Atlanta

Accommodations & Resorts
Hilton Garden Inn Atlanta Perimeter Center 6
Hotel Indigo 11
Sugar Magnolia Bed & Breakfast 7
Virginia Highland Bed and Breakfast 10

Attractions & Culture
755 Club 78
Agatha's-A Taste of Mystery 77
Air Atlanta Helicopters, Inc. 71
APEX Museum 50
Atlanta Ballet 55
Atlanta Botanical Garden 54
City Segway Tours Atlanta 86
Fräbel Glass Art Studio 74
Georgia Aquarium 53
Georgia Shakespeare 58
Jimmy Carter Library and Museum 57
Martin Luther King, Jr. National Historic Site 61
State of Georgia 45
Turner Field 79

Bakeries, Treats, Coffee & Tea
Café Intermezzo 101

Fashion & Accessories
Topaz Gallery 113

Galleries & Fine Art
Anne Hathaway 136
DE Fine Art 129
Fräbel Studio 124
G-Art Europe 126
Gems of Africa 130

Health & Beauty
Blue MedSpa 144
Repose MedSpa 146

Home & Garden
Architectural Accents 186
Four Seasons Pottery 184
Gado Gado Home Gallery 160
Heirloom Iron Bed Company and Fine Linens 185
OwenLawrence 177
Stanton Home Furnishings 188

Markets & Delis
Sevananda Natural Foods Cooperative 197
Sweet Auburn Curb Market 196

Recreation & Fitness
Gotta Dance Atlanta 207
Studio Atlanta Dance 216

Restaurants & Cafés
    Agave Restaurant 276
    Anthony's Fine Dining 227
    Busy Bee Café 268
    Dantanna's Surf & Turf 229
    Noodle 243
    Padriac's 270
    Silver Skillet Restaurant 256
    Varsity 231

Shopping & Antiques
    Atlanta Arts and Antiques 287
    Bilt-House 293
    Dearing Antiques 298
    Fräbel Glass Art Studio 291
    Knitch 308
    Phoenix and Dragon Bookstore 321
    William Word Fine Antiques 289

Weddings & Events
    755 Club 333
    Botany Bay Tropical Plants & Flowers 330
    Foxgloves & Ivy Floral Design Studio 331
    Turner Field 332
    Villa Christina 335

Wineries & Breweries
    SweetWater Brewing Company 349

Auburn

Weddings & Events
    Carl House 329

B

Bishop

Markets & Delis
    Thomas Orchards, Greenhouse & Giftshop 202

Blairsville

Accommodations & Resorts
    Misty Mountain Inn & Cottages 8
    Sunrise Grocery and Sunrise Cabins 39
    Trackrock Campground & Cabins 9

Attractions & Culture
    Southern Tree Plantation 75

Bakeries, Treats, Coffee & Tea
    Pappy's Fudge & Gifts 104

Home & Garden
    Granny's Cottage 158

Markets & Delis
    Logan Turnpike Mill 200

Recreation & Fitness
    Step Above Stables 208
    Trackrock Campground & Cabins 210

Blue Ridge

Accommodations & Resorts
    First Class Cabin Rentals 15
    Tica Cabin Rentals 14

Attractions & Culture
    Blue Ridge Scenic Railway 84

Lifestyle Destinations
    First Class Cabin Rentals 192

Markets & Delis
    Mercier Orchards 198

Recreation & Fitness
    Unicoi Outfitters 212

Restaurants & Cafés
    Cabin Grille 256

Shopping & Antiques
    Blue Ridge Adventure Wear 284
    Little Shop 284
    Out of the Blue 285
    Wrapsody in Blue 297

Buford

Restaurants & Cafés
    Kani House 252
    Red Sky Café & Coffeehouse 244
    Vinny's New York Pizza & Italian Grill 230

Shopping & Antiques
    Queen of Hearts Antiques & Interiors 303

C

Canton

Attractions & Culture
    Cagle's Dairy 63
    Tanglewood Farm 64

Restaurants & Cafés
    Winchester Woodfire Grill 235

Cartersville

Attractions & Culture
    Booth Western Art Museum 62
    Etowah Indian Mounds State Historic Site 64
    Tellus: Northwest Georgia Science Museum 49

Home & Garden
    c.a.n.o.p.y. 159

Restaurants & Cafés
    D. Morgan's 237
    Village Porch Café 244

Shopping & Antiques
    Meg Pie Too 295

Chamblee

Restaurants & Cafés
    El Torero Mexican Restaurant 250

Shopping & Antiques
    Broad Street Antique Mall 308
    Rust & Dust Antiques 310

Cherrylog

Home & Garden
Little g's Mountain Garden Center 168

Recreation & Fitness
Adventure Trail Rides of Cashes Valley 212

Clarkesville

Accommodations & Resorts
Historic Glen-Ella Springs Country Inn 30
Sugar Mill Creek RV Resort 8

Attractions & Culture
Mark of the Potter 81
Old Clarkesville Mill 86

Bakeries, Treats, Coffee & Tea
Baron York Tea Room Café & Gift Shop 108

Home & Garden
Eddy West 162

Markets & Delis
Manna to Go 199

Recreation & Fitness
Sunburst Stables 215

Restaurants & Cafés
Historic Glen-Ella Springs Country Inn 253
Zanzo Italian Café 242

Shopping & Antiques
Homestead House 310
Mark of the Potter 283

Weddings & Events
Gertie Mae's 337

Clayton

Accommodations & Resorts
Beechwood Inn 17
Old Clayton Inn 26

Galleries & Fine Art
Main Street Gallery 126

Home & Garden
Timpson Creek Gallery 169

Shopping & Antiques
Black Bear Creek Antiques 314

Cleveland

Home & Garden
Donna M's Custom Arts 171

Recreation & Fitness
Gold 'n Gem Grubbin 211

Shopping & Antiques
Yonah Treasures 301

College Park

Restaurants & Cafés
Noodle 243
Pecan 275

Covington

Restaurants & Cafés
Amici Italian Café 232

Cumming

Home & Garden
D&B Designs 160

D

Dacula

Bakeries, Treats, Coffee & Tea
Feddeaux 107

Home & Garden
Certain Something 186

Restaurants & Cafés
Iron Wok China Bistro 234
Ninja Steak & Sushi 234

Dahlonega

Accommodations & Resorts
Forrest Hills Mountain Resort
and Conference Center 37
Happy Acres Farm 21
Mountain Laurel Creek Inn & Spa 30
Pura Vida USA 20

Bakeries, Treats, Coffee & Tea
Crimson Moon Café 105

Galleries & Fine Art
Hummingbird Lane 139

Health & Beauty
Pura Vida USA 147

Restaurants & Cafés
Corkscrew Café 232
Crimson Moon Café 274
Oar House 248

Weddings & Events
Forrest Hills Mountain Resort
and Conference Center 339
Wolf Mountain Vineyards & Winery 338

Wineries & Breweries
Frogtown Cellars 347
Wolf Mountain Vineyards & Winery 346

Darien

Accommodations & Resorts
Eagle Island Lodge 36

Dawsonville

Recreation & Fitness
Outdoor Traditions 209
Outside World 212

Decatur

Bakeries, Treats, Coffee & Tea
Southern Sweets Bakery 97

Home & Garden
Gado Gado Home Gallery 160

Restaurants & Cafés
Noodle 243

Duluth

Bakeries, Treats, Coffee & Tea
Magnolia Bakery Café 98

Health & Beauty
Heavenly Touch Wellness Center & Spa 148

Home & Garden
Outrageous Bargains 172

Restaurants & Cafés
Armaan—American-Asian Fusion Restaurant
& Lounge 239
Kani House 252
Sia's 234

Shopping & Antiques
Parsons 314

Weddings & Events
Floristique 342
KaBloom 342
Payne-Corley House 330
White Rolls Royce 341

Dunwoody

Attractions & Culture
Marcus Jewish Community Center 48

Home & Garden
Southern Comforts Consignments 188

Weddings & Events
Dunwoody Flowers 336

E

Eatonton

Restaurants & Cafés
Andy's BBQ 238
Shucker's Seafood Bar & Grill 244

Ellijay

Attractions & Culture
Hillcrest Orchards 84

Home & Garden
Brenda Evans Designs 170
Mountain Treasures 152

Shopping & Antiques
Brenda Evans Designs 299
Hummingbird Embroidery & Gifts 296
Mountain Treasures 294

F

Flowery Branch

Restaurants & Cafés
Grapes & Hops Bar & Bistro 246

G

Gainesville

Restaurants & Cafés
Home Sweet Georgia 247

Shopping & Antiques
Cottonwood Village 309
Home Sweet Georgia 311

Greensboro

Galleries & Fine Art
Aurum Studios and Aurum Jewelry Art 127

H

Hapeville

Bakeries, Treats, Coffee & Tea
Perk Place Coffee Shop 102

Health & Beauty
Nature's Own Herb Shop 146

Restaurants & Cafés
Kafe Kelly's 260
Maritza & Frank's 260
Michon's Smoked Meats & Seafood Restaurant 260

Shopping & Antiques
Crew Outfitters 290

Helen

Accommodations & Resorts
Black Forest Bed & Breakfast and Luxury Cabins 22
Blue Sky Vacation Rentals 23
Helendorf River Inn & Conference Center 40

Bakeries, Treats, Coffee & Tea
Hofer's of Helen 106

Galleries & Fine Art
Martha's Mountain Gallery 135
Willows Pottery 138

Markets & Delis
Nora Mill Granary—Grist Mill & Country Store 200

Recreation & Fitness
Unicoi Outfitters 212

Shopping & Antiques
Christmas & More 300
Classics 300

Wineries & Breweries
Habersham Vineyards & Winery 348

Heritage Village

Health & Beauty
ImageSpa 148

Hoschton

Restaurants & Cafés
Vinny's New York Pizza & Italian Grill 230

Howell

Home & Garden
OwenLawrence 177

J

Jonesboro

Accommodations & Resorts
Tara Inn and Suites 25

Restaurants & Cafés
Café Hot Wing 224

Juliette

Attractions & Culture
Whistle Stop Café 65

Restaurants & Cafés
Whistle Stop Café 225

K

Kennesaw

Attractions & Culture
Southern Museum of Civil War
and Locomotive History 66

Home & Garden
Cobblestone Corner 173
Outrageous Bargains 172
Rose Cottage Furniture 176

Recreation & Fitness
Pinetree Country Club 213

Shopping & Antiques
Eclectic Living 315
Kennesaw Trains 312

L

Lakemont

Accommodations & Resorts
Barn Inn at Lake Rabun 16

Lawrenceville

Attractions & Culture
Aurora Theatre 59
Historic Downtown Lawrenceville 51

Recreation & Fitness
Collins Hill Golf Club 208

Restaurants & Cafés
Dominick's 245
Flying Machine 222
Lavender Asian Bistro 222
Lil' River Grill 251

Shopping & Antiques
Yarn Garden Knit Shop 322

Lula

Galleries & Fine Art
Crocker Pottery 130

M

Mableton

Restaurants & Cafés
Paco's 254

Macon

Attractions & Culture
Whiskey River Entertainment Complex 85

Madison

Accommodations & Resorts
Farmhouse Inn at Hundred Acre Farm 41
James Madison Inn & Conference Center 24

Bakeries, Treats, Coffee & Tea
Antique Sweets 102

Fashion & Accessories
Whidby Jewelers 116

Galleries & Fine Art
Misty Mountain Pottery 138

Home & Garden
Inside Design 175

Restaurants & Cafés
Amici Italian Café 232
Madison Chophouse Grille 222

Shopping & Antiques
Laughing Moon and In High Cotton 322

Marble Hill

Home & Garden
Cynthia Aiken Interiors—Mountain Cottage 157

Marietta

Bakeries, Treats, Coffee & Tea
CCBerries 108
Douceur de France 104

Home & Garden
Blossom Boxes 180
Casabella 181
Earth Products 183

Markets & Delis
Marietta Wine Market 201

Restaurants & Cafés
Delkwood Grill 255
Rib Ranch 264
Stefan's Off the Square Restaurant 264

Shopping & Antiques
Casabella 313
DuPre's Antiques & Interiors 316
Olivia Morgan Antiques 317
Queen of Hearts Antiques & Interiors 303

McDonough

Attractions & Culture
Henry County Library System 69
McDonough Hospitality & Tourism Bureau 47

Health & Beauty
Scarlett's Retreat Day Spa & Mercantile 149

Restaurants & Cafés
O.B.'s Bar BQ 258
Redz 259
Seasons Bistro 265
Willingham's Kitchen 257

Milledgeville

Restaurants & Cafés
Amici Italian Café 232

Morganton

Accommodations & Resorts
Above the Rest Luxury Cabins 5

Markets & Delis
Enchanted Mountain Trout & Gourmet Meats 196

N

Newnan

Attractions & Culture
Ashley Park 73

Shopping & Antiques
Hastings Entertainment–Newnan 294

Norcross

Attractions & Culture
Brighton Collectibles 89
Courtyard Home 93
Designer Antiques 90
Forum on Peachtree Parkway 87
Grace 17-20 88
Grape 90
K-la Boutique 93
Limetree 92
Snip-Its 92
Spa Sydell 89
Swoozie's 91
Talbots 91
Ted's Montana Grill 88

Bakeries, Treats, Coffee & Tea
Magnolia Bakery Café 98
Northern Star Coffeehouse 99

Galleries & Fine Art
Bowman & White Gallery 132
Gallery at Spalding Corners 134

Restaurants & Cafés
Dominick's 245

Weddings & Events
173 Carlyle House 342
Spectrum Entertainment 340

P

Pine Mountain

Home & Garden
Pine Mountain Loft & Gallery 152

Lifestyle Destinations
Barna Log Homes 193

R

Rabun Gap

Accommodations & Resorts
Sylvan Falls Mill Bed & Breakfast 27

Roswell

Attractions & Culture
Georgia Ensemble Theatre & Conservatory 68
Teaching Museum North 76

Bakeries, Treats, Coffee & Tea
Mittie's Tea Room Café 96

Galleries & Fine Art
Ann Jackson Gallery 141

Home & Garden
Elegant Attic 182
Heirloom Iron Bed Company and Fine Linens 185

Restaurants & Cafés
Brookwood Grill 272
Nirvana Café & Grille 273
Van Gogh's 266

Shopping & Antiques
Bilt-House 293
Canton Street Antique Market 323
Cast-On Cottage 305
Chandlery 319

Weddings & Events
TD Entertainment 343

S

Sandy Springs

Galleries & Fine Art
Artrages Gallery 138

Home & Garden
Scarlet Tassel 165

Shopping & Antiques
Antiques & Interiors of Sandy Springs 286

Sautee

Accommodations & Resorts
Bernie's Nacoochee Valley Guest House 28
Lucille's Mountain Top Inn 26
Stovall House Country Inn & Restaurant 16

Shopping & Antiques
Old Sautee Store 304

Savannah

Accommodations & Resorts
Azalea Inn & Gardens 29
Green Palm Inn 40
Hamilton-Turner Inn 32
Inn at Ellis Square 13
Planter's Inn on Reynolds Square 31
Savannah Harbor 19
Zeigler House Inn 26

Attractions & Culture
City Market 82
Planter's Inn on Reynolds Square 83

Fashion & Accessories
BleuBelle Boutique 119
Treasure Chest 115
Zïa Boutique 118

Galleries & Fine Art
Alvida Art Gallery 133

Health & Beauty
Savannah Day Spa 145

Home & Garden
Eufloria, Flowers & Little Luxuries 189
Jere's Antiques 187
La Villa 167
Savannah Fine Linens 172
Uptown Gardening & Hardware 188

Markets & Delis
Savannah Wine Shop 203

Restaurants & Cafés
Belford's Savannah—Seafood & Steaks 267
Creekside Grill 240
Firefly Café 240
Soho South Café 262
Vic's on the River 263

Shopping & Antiques
Savannah Bee Company 320
Savannah Bulldog Cigar Company 306

Smyrna

Bakeries, Treats, Coffee & Tea
Café Michel 277

Galleries & Fine Art
Vinings Gallery 125

Home & Garden
Love Street Gifts and Gardens 166
Love Street Home 166

Recreation & Fitness
Studio Atlanta Dance 216

Restaurants & Cafés
Vintage Tavern 269
Zucca 269

Shopping & Antiques
Karen's Gifts 304

Social Circle

Restaurants & Cafés
Blue Willow Inn 271

St. Simons Island

Accommodations & Resorts
Beach Bed & Breakfast 34
Ocean Lodge 34
Village Inn and Pub 33

Fashion & Accessories
Gogo 121
Redfern Jewelers 117

Home & Garden
Accents 172

Shopping & Antiques
Marsh Hen 304

Stockbridge

Fashion & Accessories
Upscale Fashions Consignment Boutique 120

Restaurants & Cafés
UMI Japanese Steak House & Sushi Bar 236

Stone Mountain

Restaurants & Cafés
Sycamore Grill 261
Village Corner 241

Sugar Creek

Galleries & Fine Art
Stained Glass at Sugar Creek 134

Sugar Hill

Bakeries, Treats, Coffee & Tea
Juices Wild 98

Recreation & Fitness
Up the River Outfitters 214

Restaurants & Cafés
Amira's Mediterranean Bistro 228

Suwanee

Home & Garden
Ambiance Interiors & Gifts 179

Restaurants & Cafés
Dillard's BBQ & Biscuits 228

Shopping & Antiques
Gift Basket Originals 318
Perfect Present 318
Prissy Pooch 318

T

Tallulah Falls

Restaurants & Cafés
Isabelle's on the Gorge 228

Tiger

Attractions & Culture
Hillside Orchard Farms Country Store & Farm 67

U

Union City

Restaurants & Cafés
Historic Green Manor Restaurant 223

V

Vinings

Restaurants & Cafés
Blackstone—Steaks, Seafood & Spirits 272

W

Waleska

Attractions & Culture
Funk Heritage Center 72

Washington

Accommodations & Resorts
Washington Plantation Bed and Breakfast 38

Home & Garden
Petal Pushers 155

Watkinsville

Accommodations & Resorts
Ashford Manor Bed and Breakfast 35

Galleries & Fine Art
Chappelle Gallery 140
Georgia Originals 140
Happy Valley Pottery 140
Laura Leiden Calligraphy 131

Home & Garden
Details Design Center 161

Restaurants & Cafés
Girasoles 233
Maison Bleu 240

Shopping & Antiques
Polka Dot Peach 296

Woodstock

Bakeries, Treats, Coffee & Tea
Serene Bean 103

Recreation & Fitness
Margot's Closet 217

Restaurants & Cafés
Family Tradition Restaurant 249
Kani House 252

Shopping & Antiques
Whole Nine Yarns 307